DATA ANALYTICS

About the Author

Anil K. Maheshwari, Ph.D. is a Professor of Management and Information Systems at Maharishi International University (MIU), in Fairfield, Iowa, USA. He teaches courses in data analytics, among others. He has published 16 books, 40 research papers and book chapters, and has made 40 conference presentations. His book *Data Analytics Made Accessible* has been consistently #1 recommended book globally. He is a listed member of Who's Who in America.

He has 20 years of IT industry experience, including 9 years in leadership roles at IBM. He also has 20 years of academic experience as a Professor at MIU, the University of Cincinnati, City University of New York, University of Illinois, and others. He earned a B.Tech. in Electrical Engineering from Indian Institute of Technology in Delhi, an MBA from Indian Institute of Management in Ahmedabad, and a Ph.D. in Management from Case Western Reserve University, Cleveland, Ohio. He can be contacted at akm2030@gmail.com.

DATA ANALYTICS

Second Edition

Anil Maheshwari

Professor of Management Information Systems and
Director of Center for Data Analytics
Maharishi University of Management,
Fairfield, Iowa, USA.

McGraw Hill Education (India) Private Limited

Published by McGraw Hill Education (India) Private Limited
Registered Office: Anjana Complex No: 5/90 A, Butt Road, St. Thomas Mount, Chennai – 600016

Data Analytics, 2e

First reprint 2025

Print Edition
ISBN-13: 978-93-5532-455-9
ISBN-10: 93-5532-455-3

EBook Edition
ISBN-13: 978-93-5532-458-0
ISBN-10: 93-5532-458-8

02 03 04 05 06 MAG 29 28 27 26 25

Typeset at Chandra Creative and Contents Solutions Pvt Ltd, B-130, Sector 65, Noida and printed and bound in India at Magic International Pvt. Ltd., Plot No. 26E, Sector 31, Industrial), Site – IV, Greater Noida – 201306.

Cover Designer: Anita Kanojia
Cover Image Source: Shutterstock

Visit us at: www.mheducation.co.in
Write to us at: support.india@mheducation.com
CIN: U80302TN2010PTC111532
Toll Free Number: 1800 103 5875

Dedication

This book is dedicated to all the youth of the world

Go forth boldly and confidently to explore new frontiers!
Dissolve old problems and devise new solutions,
Using Compassion, Creativity, and all the tools at hand!
Most importantly, Have Fun!

Advance Praise for this Book

Dr. Maheshwari's book is a very nice introduction to analytics. He explains concepts very clear and to the point. I like particularly his chapter on decision trees and the process to obtain them. His explanation is very clear.

– Ramon A. Mata Toledo, Professor of Computer Science, Rollins College, Florida.

This book is a splendid and valuable addition to this subject. The whole book is well-written and I have no hesitation in recommending that this can be adapted as a textbook for graduate courses in Business Intelligence and Data Mining.

– Edi Shivaji, St. Louis, Missouri.

Bottom line is that for anyone interested in learning about Data Analytics, this is THE book to start your learning path with and hope it will spur your interest in the field and enable you to grasp more in-depth topics and further your skills.

– Keith S Safford, Maryland.

Really well written and timely as the world gets in the Big Data mode! I think this can be a good bridge and primer for the uninitiated manager who knows Big Data is the future but doesn't know where to begin!

Alok Mishra, Singapore.

This book has done a great job of taking a complex, highly important subject area and making it accessible to everyone. It begins by simply connecting to what you know, and then bang – you've suddenly found out about Decision Trees, Regression Models and Artificial Neural Networks, not to mention cluster analysis, web mining and Big Data.

– Charmaine Oak, United Kingdom

I took a course in data mining from Professor Maheshwari as part of a business masters. I had never heard of data mining nor had any idea what it was about. By using this book, I now have a firm understanding and can even work out a few data mining techniques myself. The logic is easy to follow and the concepts are presented very clearly. It's fun to read because Dr. Maheshwari relates the knowledge to real-life cases and also discusses some of the deeper issues we face in terms of privacy and influence. I highly recommend this book to students or anyone interested in finding out about data mining.

– Susi Halley, Ohio, USA.

This book is particularly of value for all business executives and managers, especially those in human resources, marketing, operations, finance, accounting, and then too for IT professionals to be up to date with their clients!

– Dan Saint, USA.

Preface

Data is the new oil, and Artificial Intelligence is the new electricity. Data Analytics continues to be the hottest discipline, along with Artificial Intelligence, in this decade. The second edition has added many new hot topics such as Data Privacy, Artificial Intelligence, and Data Wrangling. It has also added an additional tutorial in Python language for data analytics. For the busy readers, it has added a summary chapter that encapsulates all the knowledge in just 50 main points in a few pages. Finally, this edition includes a sample data analytics student project, which uses all the data mining techniques to solve a real socially relevant problem.

I have been teaching courses in Data Analytics and Big Data for almost a decade. My students found other textbooks seem too long, too technical, too complex, or too focused on specific tools. My goal was to write a conversational book that feels easy and informative. This is an accessible book that covers everything important, with concrete examples, and invites the reader to join this field. Many people have entered this field upon reading this book. This second edition is updated to address some of the situations arising from the coronavirus pandemic, and new technological developments like data lakes.

This book can be easily read in a short period by anyone who wants to understand data-based decision-making for their business or other organizations, without any expertise with software tools. The text is almost entirely devoid of complex jargon or programming code. This edition continues to include a primer on Statistics, Databases, and Big Data, for those interested in these topics. A simple yet extensive tutorial on R, a popular, free, open-source, high-level programming language that is very popular with data scientists, is included at the end of the book. As stated earlier, this edition also includes a short tutorial on Python, another very popular high-level general-purpose programming language.

This book reflects my four decades of global IT experience in academia and industry. The chapters are organized for a typical one-semester graduate course. There are caselets from real-world stories at the beginning of every chapter. There is a running case study across the chapters as exercises. There are review questions at the end of each chapter. Many universities around the world have adopted this as a textbook for their courses. The book has continued to evolve in response to the thoughts and suggestions expressed by the reviewers and students. Thanks to many reviewers for sharing many ideas for improvement. I am delighted to offer this edition to inspire students as well as practitioners.

The book is designed to unfold like the petals of a flower.

- Chapter 1 is designed to provide the wholeness of business intelligence and data mining, to provide the reader with an intuition over this area of knowledge. The rest of the book is divided into four sections.
- Section 1 unfolds the data processing chain described in Chapter 1. Chapter 2 covers the field of business intelligence and its applications across industries and functions. Chapter 3 explains Data Warehousing and how does it help with data mining. Chapter 4 then describes data mining with an overview of its major tools and techniques. Chapter 5 shows insights from data that can be visualized for better communication and consumption.
- Section 2 expands chapter 4 on core data mining techniques. Every technique is shown through solved examples in detail. Chapter 6 shows the power and ease of decision trees, which are the most popular data mining technique. Chapter 7 describes statistical regression modeling techniques. Chapter 8 provides an overview of Artificial Neural Networks. Chapter 9 describes how Cluster Analysis can help with market segmentation. Finally, Chapter 10 describes the Association Rule Mining technique, also called Market Basket Analysis, which helps find shopping patterns.
- Section 3 covers more advanced data mining techniques beyond the core techniques covered in Section 2. Chapter 11 introduces the concepts and techniques of Text Mining that helps discover insights from text data including social media data. Chapter 12 covers Naïve-Bayes, a classification technique used for text mining such as spam filtering. Chapter 13 covers Support Vector Machines, a mathematically rigorous classification technique, also used for spam and other applications with high dimensional data. Chapter 14 provides an overview of the growing field of web mining, which includes mining the structure, content, and usage of web sites. Chapter 15 introduces the concept of Social Network Analysis, which helps analyze both text communication and web structure. This section mostly completes the Data Mining techniques.
- Section 4 further covers on-ramps to advanced topics such as Big Data, Data Privacy, and Artificial Intelligence, and Data Wrangling. Chapter 16 provides an overview of the field of Big Data. Chapter 17 provides an overview of the field of Artificial Intelligence, including the latest Transformer Models. Chapter 18 describes the Data Ownership and Privacy regimes around the world. Chapter 19 discusses data science careers and some additional case studies. Finally, Chapter 20 provides a primer to Data Wrangling, or data preparation.
- There are seven appendices to the book. Appendix A is a primer on Data Modeling, for those who do not have any background in databases, and should be used if necessary. Appendix B is a tutorial on Statistics. Appendix C covers the entire

book in 50 main points. Appendix D presents a sample data analytics project. Appendix P is a tutorial on the use of Python language to solve the data analytics problems discussed in the book. Appendix R is a tutorial on the use of R language to solve the data analytics problems discussed in the book. Another tutorial is to do the same with Python language. Finally, Appendix W is a tutorial on the use of Weka tool to solve the data analytics problems discussed in the book.

WEB SUPPLEMENTS

To enhance the utility of the book for students and instructors, the following web supplements are available online:

For Instructors:

Available through https://connect.mheducation.com (See the inside front cover for more details)

- PowerPoint charts
- Solutions Manual

For Students:

Available through https://www.mheducation.co.in (See the inside back cover for more details)

- Datasets

We also wish you, the reader, a happy and healthy life. Please take all precautions to stay safe and maintain a healthy routine.

Anil Maheshwari
Fairfield, IA
May 2023

Preface to the First Edition

Data Science is a new discipline and this book on data analytics fills a need for an accessible book on this topic. Other textbooks seem too technical and complex for use by the students. The goal behind the making was to write a conversational book that feels easy and informative. This is a comprehensible book that covers everything important, with concrete examples, and invites the reader to join this field.

The book has been developed from author's own class notes. It reflects his two decades of global IT industry experience, as well as more than a decade of academic experience. The chapters are organized for a typical one-semester graduate course. The book contains caselets from real world stories at the beginning of each chapter. There is a running case study across the chapter exercises. There are also review questions at the end of each chapter.

The book can be easily read in a short period by anyone who wants to understand data based decision-making for their business or other organizations, but has no expertise with software tools. The text is almost entirely devoid of complex jargon or programming code.

ORGANIZATION OF THE BOOK

Chapter 1 is designed to provide the wholeness of business intelligence and data mining, to provide the reader with an intuition over this area of knowledge. The rest of the book is divided into four sections as follows

- Section 1 covers the data processing chain. Chapter 2 covers the field of business intelligence and its applications across industries and functions. Chapter 3 explains Data Warehousing and how does it help with data mining. Chapter 4 then describes data mining with an overview of its major tools and techniques. Chapter 5 shows insights from data that can be visualized for better communication and consumption.
- Section 2 is focused on core data mining techniques. Every technique is shown through solved examples in detail. Chapter 6 shows the power and ease of decision trees, which are the most popular data mining technique. Chapter 7 describes statistical regression modeling techniques. Chapter 8 provides an overview of Artificial Neural Networks. Chapter 9 describes how Cluster Analysis can help

with market segmentation. Finally, Chapter 10 describes the Association Rule Mining technique, also called Market Basket Analysis that helps find shopping patterns.

- Section 3 covers more advanced topics. Chapter 11 introduces the concepts and techniques of Text Mining that helps discover insights from text data including social media data. Chapter 12 covers Naïve-Bayes, a classification technique used for text mining such as spam filtering. Chapter 13 covers Support Vector Machines, a mathematically rigorous classification technique, also used for spam and other applications with high dimensional data. Chapter 14 provides an overview of the growing field of web mining, which includes mining the structure, content and usage of web sites. Chapter 15 introduces the concept of Social Network Analysis, which helps analyze both text communication and web structure.
- Section 4 further covers more advanced topics. Chapter 16 provides an overview of the field of Big Data. Chapter 17 has been added as a primer on Data Modeling, for those who do not have any background in databases, and should be used if necessary. Chapter 18 discusses data science careers and some additional case studies.
- The book ends with an extensive R tutorial to help with many of the techniques explained in the book. No prior experience with R is needed for using this tutorial. Also few pages have been dedicated for Weka tutorial for data mining for further subject knowledge.

Anil Maheshwari

Acknowledgments

My family encouraged and supported me in writing and improving this book. I would like to express my gratitude to my father Mr. R. L. Maheshwari, brother Dr. Sunil Maheshwari, wife Neerja, and daughters Ankita and Nupur, for their continuous encouragement and support while writing this book. I am also grateful to my students and others who read this book and provide feedback and suggestions. Finally, thanks to Maharishi Mahesh Yogi for providing a wonderful environment of consciousness-based education that provided the inspiration for writing this book from wholeness. This book is a 'guru-dakshina', or homage, to Maharishi.

I wish to thank the McGraw Hill team for being diligent and patient in gaining feedback from the universities, and systematically working through the various aspects of the revision process. The entire MHE team specially Aditee Agrawal, Sanjeev Jha and Suhaib Ali who worked hard on bringing this out in a short time; sincere thanks to all of them.

I am grateful to the following reviewers who took out time and gave their valuable suggestions on various chapters of the book:

Sandeep Kumar, Associate Professor, IIT Roorkee

Debanga Raj Neog , Assistant Professor, IIT Guwahati

Dharavath Ramesh, Assistant Professor, IIT Dhanbad

Regi Mathew, Professor, NMIMS, Bangalore

C. Vijayakumaran , Associate Professor, SRM Institute of Science and Technology, Chennai

Mamta Mittal, Head and Associate Professor, Bhai Parmanand DSEU, Delhi

Sanjay Kumar Vij, Dean, Academics, ITM Universe, Vadodra

Sohail D. Pandya, Assistant Professor, SVIT, Anand, Gujarat

Pratosh Bansal, Professor, DAVV, Indore, Madhya Pradesh

Kirti Wanjale, Associate Professor, Vishwakarma Institute of Information Technology, Pune

Any suggestions for improving the book will be gratefully acknowledged.

Anil Maheshwari

Contents

SECTION 2

POPULAR DATA MINING TECHNIQUES

SECTION 3

ADVANCED DATA MINING

SECTION 4

RELATED TOPICS

CHAPTER 1

Wholeness of Data Analytics

Learning Objectives

LO 1 Understand Business Intelligence and Data Mining Cycle

LO 2 Learn about the tools and purpose of Business Intelligence

LO 3 Discover what are patterns, their types, and the process of discovering patterns

LO 4 Understand the data processing chain

LO 5 Learn in brief about the components of the data processing chain

LO 6 Process a simple example dataset through complete data processing chain

LO 7 Learn about datafication and various types of data

LO 8 Learn in brief about key terms and Data Science careers

Business is the act of doing something productive to serve someone's needs, and thus earn a living and make the world a better place. Business activities are recorded on paper or using electronic media, and then, these records become data. There is more data from customers' responses and on the industry as a whole. All this data can be analyzed and mined using special tools and techniques to generate patterns and intelligence, which reflect how the business is functioning. These patterns can then be fed back into the business as new ideas so that it can evolve to become more effective and efficient in serving the needs of all stakeholders. And the cycle continues on leading to an exponential growth in data, intelligence, and business effectiveness (Figure 1.1).

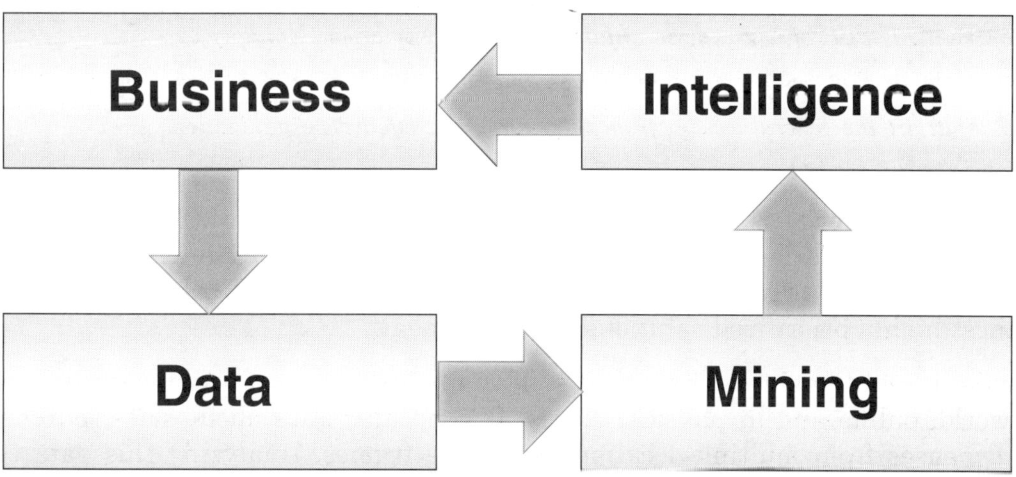

Figure 1.1 Business Intelligence and Data Mining (BIDM) Cycle

BUSINESS INTELLIGENCE

Any organization needs to continually monitor its business and technological environment and its own performance, and then rapidly adjust its future plans. This includes monitoring the industry, the competitors, the suppliers, and the customers. The organization also needs to develop a balanced scorecard to track its own health and vitality. Executives typically determine what they want to track based on their key performance indexes (KPIs) or key result areas (KRAs). Customized reports need to be designed to deliver the required information to every executive. These reports can be converted into customized dashboards that deliver the information rapidly and in easy-to-grasp formats.

CASELET

MoneyBall – Data Mining in Sports

Analytics in sports was made popular by the book and movie, Moneyball. Statistician Bill James and Oakland A's general manager, Billy Bean, placed an emphasis on crunching numbers and data instead of watching an athlete's style and looks. Their goal was to make a team better while using fewer resources. The key action plan was to pick important role players at a lower cost while avoiding the famous players who demand higher salaries but may provide a low return on a team's investment. Rather than relying on the scouts' experience and intuition, Bean selected players based almost exclusively on their on-base percentage (OBP). By finding players with a high OBP, but with characteristics that lead scouts to dismiss them, Bean assembled a team of undervalued players with far more potential than the A's hamstrung finances would otherwise allow.

Using this strategy, they proved that even small market teams can be competitive—a case in point, the Oakland A's. In 2004, two years after adopting the same sabermetric model, the Boston Red Sox won their first World Series since 1918. (To know more see Lewis, M. (2004). *Moneyball: The art of winning an unfair game. WW Norton & Company.).*

Q1: *Could similar techniques apply to the games of football, or cricket? If so, how?*

Q2: *What are the general lessons from this story for a business organization?*

Business intelligence is a broad set of information technology (IT) solutions that includes tools for gathering, analyzing, and reporting information to the users about performance of the organization and its environment. These IT solutions are among the most highly prioritized solutions for investment.

Consider a retail business chain that sells many kinds of goods and services around the world, online and in physical stores. It generates data about sales, purchases, and expenses from multiple locations and time frames. Analyzing this data could help identify fast-selling items, regional-selling items, seasonal items, fast-growing customer segments, and so on. It might also help generate ideas about what products sell together, which people tend to buy which products, and so on. These insights and intelligence can help design better promotion plans, product bundles, and store layouts, which in turn lead to a better-performing business.

The vice president of sales of a retail company would want to track the sales to date against monthly targets, the performance of each store and product category, and the top store managers of that month. The vice president of finance would be interested in tracking daily revenue, expense, and cash flows by store; comparing them against plans; measuring cost of capital; and so on. The patterns and intelligence needed by everyone of these functional heads will be different, and they will need uniquely customized sets of information.

PATTERN RECOGNITION

A pattern is a design or a model that helps grasp something. Patterns help connect things that may not appear to be connected. Patterns help cut through complexity and reveal simpler understandable trends. A lot of human learning is about becoming aware of appropriate patterns about the reality of their existence. Patterns can be as definitive as hard scientific rules, like the rule that the Sun always rises in the East. They can also be simple and softer generalizations, such as the Pareto principle, which states that 80 percent of effects come from 20 percent of the causes.

A perfect pattern or model is one that (a) accurately describes a situation, (b) is broadly applicable, and (c) can be described in a simple manner. $E = MC^2$ would be such a general, accurate, and simple (GAS) model. Very often, all three qualities are not achievable in a single model, especially in human and social environments, and one has to settle for two of three qualities in the model.

Types of Patterns

Patterns are essentially about what hangs together and what is separate. Patterns can be temporal, which is something that regularly occurs over time. Patterns can also be spatial, such as things being organized in a certain way. Patterns can be functional, in that doing certain things leads to certain effects. Good patterns are often symmetric. They are echo basic structures and patterns that we are already aware of.

A temporal rule would be that "some people are always late," no matter what the occasion or time is. Some people may be aware of this pattern and some may not be. Understanding a pattern like this would help dissipate a lot of unnecessary frustration and anger. One can just joke that some people are born "10 minutes late," and laugh it away. Similarly, Parkinson's law states that work expands to fill up all the time available to do it.

A spatial pattern would involve the context of our three-dimensional spatial reality. The layout of cities often follows the hub-and-spoke model of a city center or downtown, surrounded by residential population areas. Even whole countries are organized around national capital cities surrounded by layers of smaller cities that are capitals of smaller units such as states. The layout of desks in an office may follow certain patterns such as pods of four cubicles facing each other, or all desks may face east.

A functional pattern, following the 80–20 rule, could be that the top 20 percent of customers lead to 80 percent of the business. Or 20 percent of products generate 80 percent of the business. Or 80 percent of incoming customer service calls are related to just 20 percent of the products. This last pattern may simply reveal a discrepancy between a product's features and what the customers believe about the product. The business can then decide to invest in educating the customers better so that the customer service calls can be significantly reduced.

An interesting functional pattern may involve test-taking skills. Some students perform well on essay-type questions. Others do well in multiple-choice questions. Yet, other students enjoy hands-on projects, or oral presentations. An awareness of such a pattern in a class of students can help the teacher design a balanced testing mechanism that is fair to all.

However, long-established patterns can also be broken. The past cannot always predict the future. A pattern like "all swans are white" does not mean that there may not be a black swan. Once enough anomalies are discovered, the underlying pattern itself can shift. The economic meltdown in 2008–2009 was because of the collapse of an accepted pattern, that is, "housing prices always go up." A deregulated financial environment made markets more volatile and led to greater swings in markets, leading to the eventual collapse of the entire financial system. More recent patterns in the spread of Covid virus have shown the idea of waves, and that any declaration of victory by any country and community against the virus may be premature.

Finding a Pattern

Diamond mining is the act of digging into large amounts of unrefined ore to discover precious gems or nuggets. Similarly, data mining is the act of digging into large amounts of raw data to discover unique nontrivial useful patterns. Data should be cleaned up, and then, special tools and techniques can be applied to search for patterns. Diving into clean and nicely organized data from the right perspectives can increase the chances of making the right discoveries.

A skilled diamond miner knows what a diamond looks like. Similarly, a skilled data miner should know what a good pattern looks like. Therefore, knowing the business domain well is very important. It takes knowledge and skill to discover the patterns.

It is like finding a needle in a haystack. Sometimes, the pattern may be hiding in plain sight. At other times, it may take a lot of work, and looking far and wide, to find surprising useful patterns. Thus, a systematic approach to mining data is necessary to efficiently reveal valuable insights.

Uses of Patterns

When used in clever ways, data mining can lead to interesting insights and be a source of new ideas and initiatives.

Retaining students is an ongoing challenge for universities. Recent data-based research shows that students leave school for social reasons more than they do for academic reasons. This pattern/insight can instigate schools to pay closer attention to students engaging in extracurricular activities and developing stronger bonds at school. The school can invest in entertainment activities, sports activities, camping trips, and other activities. The school can also begin to actively gather data about every student's participation in those activities, to predict at-risk students and take corrective action.

As another instance, the attitude of employees toward their employer may be hypothesized to be determined by many factors, such as level of education, income, tenure in the company, and gender. It may be surprising if the data reveals that the attitudes are determined first and foremost by their age bracket. Such a simple insight could be powerful in designing organizations effectively. The data miner must be open to any and all possibilities.

As another instance, the traffic pattern on highways can be surmised from the movement of cell phone (in the car) locations on the highway. If the locations of cell phones on a highway or roadway are not moving fast enough, it may be a sign of traffic congestion. Google and other companies can thus provide real-time traffic information to the drivers on their cell phones, or on their GPS devices, without the need of any video cameras or traffic reporters.

Yet another instance, organizations can find out an employee's arrival time at the office when their cell phone shows up in the parking lot. Similarly, observing the log of the swipe of the parking permit card in the company's parking garage can inform the organization whether an employee is in the office building or out of the office at any moment in time, or how long were they in the office.

Some patterns may be so sparse that a very large amount of diverse data has to be seen together to notice any connections. For instance, locating the debris of a flight that may have vanished midcourse would require bringing together data from many sources, such as satellites, ships, and navigation systems. The raw data may come with different degrees of quality, and may even be conflicting. The data at hand may or may not be adequate for finding good patterns. Additional dimensions of data may need to be added to help solve the problem.

DATA PROCESSING CHAIN

Data is the new natural resource. Some call it the new oil. Implicit in this statement is the recognition of the value in data in delivering value to business. Data lies at the heart of business intelligence and artificial intelligence. There is a sequence of steps to be followed to benefit from the data in a systematic way. Data needs to be gathered, modeled, and stored in a database. Relevant data can then be extracted from the operational data stores according to certain reporting and analyzing purposes and stored in a data warehouse or data lakes. The data from these stores can be combined with other sources of data, to provide richer data sets. These data sets can be mined using data mining techniques to generate new insights. The insights need to be represented and communicated to the right audience to help them visualize the situation. These insights need to be delivered in real time for competitive advantage. Figure 1.2 explains the progression of data processing activities. The rest of this chapter will cover these five elements in the data processing chain.

Figure 1.2 Data Processing Chain

Data – What is it?

Anything that is recorded is data. Observations and facts are data. Anecdotes and opinions are also data, of a different kind. Employment numbers, business transactions, stock prices, bank statements, etc., are one kind of data. Published schedules for classes, games, holidays, flights, etc., are another kind of data. Search terms used in google and web traffic are another kind of data. Social conversations on phone, social media, email, etc., are another kind of data.

Datafication is a term that is often used to mean that almost every phenomenon is now being observed and information about it is being recorded. As more devices are connected to the Internet, and more people are constantly connected to "the grid," by their phone network or the Internet, more data is being generated. Every click on the web, and every movement of the mobile devices, is being recorded. Machines such as an electric motor or a refrigerator are also generating data about their health status and other parameters. This "Internet of things" is growing faster than the Internet of people. All of this is generating an exponentially growing volume of data, at a high velocity. Kryder's law predicts that the density and capability of hard drive storage media will double every 18 months. As storage costs keep coming down at a rapid rate, there is a greater incentive to record and store more events and activities at a higher resolution. Data is getting stored in more detailed resolution, and many more variables of their metadata are being captured and stored.

Sources of Data

Data can come from different types of sources. It can impact the volume and analyzability of data.

1. Data could come from any number of sources. It could come from operational records inside an organization, and it can come from records compiled by the industry bodies and government agencies. Data could come from individuals telling stories from memory and from people's interaction in social contexts. Data could come from machines reporting their own status or from logs of web usage.
2. Data can be represented in many ways. It may come as paper reports. It may come as a file stored on a computer. It may be words spoken over the phone. It may be an e-mail or a chat on the Internet. It may come as movies and songs in legacy stores such as CDs and DVDs, and so on.
3. There is also data about data. It is called *metadata.* For example, people regularly upload videos on YouTube. Metadata would include the format of the video file (whether it is high or lower resolution), the time of uploading, the account from which it was uploaded, the record of downloads of the video, the ad revenue generated, and so on. Google provides many such analytics for free for your videos.

Data Types

Data can be of different types. Data can be numbers, like the record of daily weather, or daily sales. Data can be alphanumeric, such as the names of employees and customers.

1. Data could be an unordered collection of values. For example, a retailer sells shirts in red, blue, and green colors. There is no intrinsic ordering among these color values. One can hardly argue that any one color is higher or lower than the other. This is called nominal (means names) data.
2. Data could be in ordered values like small, medium, and large. For example, the sizes of shirts could be extra-small, small, medium, and large. There is a clear sequence that medium is bigger than small, and large is bigger than medium. But the differences between the gradations may or may not be equal. This is called ordinal (ordered) data.

3. Data could also be discrete numeric values defined in a certain range, with the assumption of equal distance between the values. Customer satisfaction score may be ranked on a 10-point scale with 1 being lowest and 10 being highest. This requires the respondent to carefully calibrate the entire range as objectively as possible and place his own measurement in that scale. This is called interval (equal intervals) data.
4. Data could be fully numeric, or what is called ratio data, as it can take on any numeric value including decimal values. The weights, heights and ages of all employees would be numeric values. The price of a shirt will also take any numeric value. It is called ratio (any fraction) data.
5. There is another kind of data that does not lend itself to much mathematical analysis, at least not directly. This includes data like audio, video, images, and graphs files, often called BLOBs (Binary Large Objects). Such data needs to be first structured and then analyzed. These kinds of data lend themselves to different forms of analysis through mining of their metadata. Songs may be tagged as happy or sad, fast-paced or slow, and so on. They may contain sentiment and intention, but these are not quantitatively precise. Facial recognition software is able to tag the content of images, so that the tags can be used for search.

Data Usability

The precision of analysis of the data increases as data becomes more numeric. Ratio data could be subjected to rigorous mathematical analysis. For example, precise weather data about temperature, pressure, and humidity can be used to create rigorous mathematical differential equation (calculus) models that can accurately predict future weather.

Data privacy is an increasingly important concern. Data may be publicly available and sharable, or it may be marked private. Traditionally, national laws allow the right to *privacy* concerning the storage and usage of one's personal data. There is a big ongoing ethical debate on whether the personal data shared on social media conversations is private or it can be used for commercial purposes. Data.gov is the official repository of the U.S. Government's open data. One can find federal, state, and local data, for education, health, economics, environment, census, and more kinds of domains.

Data Quality is another area of concern. The data should be accurate and relevant for the task at hand. Timeliness of data is thus an important aspect to feed insights quickly back into business. Data should also be comprehensive enough to cover all major aspects of the task under consideration. Finally, the data should be internally consistent and not lead to incorrect or unfeasible values. This leads to the need for formal data management systems called databases.

Database

A database is a modeled collection of data that is accessible in many ways. A data model can be designed to integrate the operational data of the organization. The data model abstracts the key entities involved in an action and their relationships. Most databases today follow the relational data model and its variants. Each data modeling technique imposes and enforces rigorous rules and constraints to ensure the integrity and consistency of data over time.

Take the example of a database for a sales organization. A data model for managing customer orders will involve data about customers, orders, products, and their interrelationships. The relationship between the customers and orders would be such that one customer can place many orders, but one order will be placed by one and only one customer. It is called a one-to-many relationship. The relationship between orders and products is a little more complex. One order may contain many products. And one product may be contained in many different orders. This is called a many-to-many relationship. Different types of relationships can be modeled in a database.

Databases have grown tremendously over time. They have grown in complexity in terms of the number of objects and their properties being recorded. They have also grown in the quantity of data being stored. A decade ago, a terabyte-sized database was considered big. Now databases are in petabytes and exabytes. Video and other media files have greatly contributed to the growth of databases. E-commerce and other web-based activities also generate huge amounts of data. Data generated through social media has also generated large databases. The e-mail archives, including attached documents of organizations, are in similar large sizes. This is called big data.

Many database management software systems (DBMSs) are available to help store and manage this data. These include commercial systems, such as Oracle and IBM's DB2 system. There are also open-source, free DBMS, such as MySQL and Postgres. These DBMSs help process and store millions of transactions worth of data every second.

Table 1.1 shows a small and simple database of the sales of movies for a retail organization. It shows sales transactions of movies over a period of time. Using such a file, data can be appended, accessed, and updated, or deleted as needed.

Table 1.1 Movies Transactions Database

Order #	Date sold	Product name	Location	Amount
1	April 2022	Yaarana	US	$9
2	May 2022	Deewar	US	$15
3	June 2022	Yaarana	India	$9
4	June 2022	Deewar	UK	$15

Order #	Date sold	Product name	Location	Amount
5	July 2022	Sholay	US	$12
6	July 2022	Yaarana	India	$9
7	July 2022	Deewar	US	$15
8	Aug 2022	Sholay	US	$12
9	Sept 2022	Sholay	India	$12
10	Sept 2022	Yaarana	India	$9
11	Sept 2022	Deewar	US	$15
12	Oct 2022	Yaarana	India	$9
13	Nov 2022	Deewar	US	$15
14	Dec 2022	Yaarana	India	$9
15	Dec 2022	Yaarana	India	$9

Data Warehouse

A data warehouse is an organized store of data from all over the organization, specially designed to help make management decisions. Data can be extracted from operational databases to answer a particular set of queries. This data, combined with other data, can be rolled up to a consistent granularity and uploaded to a separate data store called the data warehouse. Therefore, the data warehouse is a simplified version of the operational database, with the purpose of addressing reporting and decision-making needs only. The data in the data warehouse cumulatively grows as more operational data becomes available and is extracted and appended to the data warehouse. Unlike in the operational database, the data values in the warehouse are not updated.

As the flows of data increase, the concept of data streams and lakes has become more prevalent. A data lake is a system or a repository of large and diverse types of data, typically in their raw or native format. These data lakes can be tapped and structured to provide data for specific types of analyses.

To create a simple data warehouse for the movies sales data, assume a simple objective of tracking sales of movies and making decisions about managing inventory. In creating this data warehouse, all the sales transaction data will be extracted from the operational data files. The data will be rolled up for all combinations of time period and product number. Thus, there will be one row for every combination of time period and product. The resulting data warehouse will look as Table 1.2.

Table 1.2 Movies Sales Data Warehouse

Row#	Quarter sold	Product name	Amount
1	Q2	Yaarana	$18
2	Q2	Deewar	$30
3	Q3	Yaarana	$18
4	Q3	Sholay	$36
5	Q3	Deewar	$30
6	Q4	Yaarana	$27
7	Q4	Deewar	$15

The data in the data warehouse is of much less granularity (detail) than the transaction database. The data warehouse could have been designed at a lower or higher level of granularity. If the data warehouse were designed on a monthly level, instead of a quarterly level, there would be many more rows of data. When the number of transactions approaches millions and higher, with dozens of attributes for each transaction, the data warehouse created from such data can be large and rich with potential insights. One can then mine (slice and dice) the data in many ways and discover unique meaningful patterns. Aggregating the data helps improve the speed of mining. A separate data warehouse allows analysis to go on separately in parallel, without burdening the operational database systems (Table 1.3).

Table 1.3 Comparing Database Systems with Data Warehousing Systems

Dimension	Database	Data Warehouse
Purpose	Data stored in databases can be used for many purposes including day-to-day operations.	Data stored in data warehouse is cleansed data useful for reporting and analysis.
Granularity	Highly granular data including all activity and transaction details.	Lower granularity data; rolled up to certain key dimensions of interest.
Complexity	Highly complex with dozens or hundreds of data files, linked through common data fields.	Typically organized around a large fact table and many lookup tables.
Size	Database grows with growing volumes of activity and transactions. Old completed transactions are deleted to reduce size.	Grows as data from operational databases is rolled-up and appended every day. Data is retained for long-term trend analyses.
Architectural choices	Relational, and object-oriented, databases	Star schema, or Snowflake schema
Data Access mechanisms	Primarily through high-level languages such as SQL. Traditional programming access DB through Open DataBase Connectivity (ODBC) interfaces.	Accessed through SQL; SQL output is forwarded to reporting tools and data visualization tools.

Data Mining

Data Mining is the art and science of discovering useful and novel patterns from data. The definition of creativity is also to create something novel and useful. Thus, data mining can be a very creative and engrossing activity. There is a wide variety of patterns that can be discovered in the data. There are many techniques, simple or complex, that help with finding patterns. One can continue to play with the data to discover new patterns.

In this example, a simple data analysis technique can be applied to the data in the data warehouse above. A simple cross-tabulation of results by quarter and products will reveal some easily visible patterns (see Table 1.4).

Table 1.4 Movies Sales by Quarters – Cross-tabulation

Quarter/Product	Yaarana	Sholay	Deewar	Total Sales Amount
Q2	$18	**0**	$30	$48
Q3	$18	**$36**	$30	**$84**
Q4	$27	**0**	$15	$42
Total Revenue	$63	$36	**$75**	$174

Based on the cross-tabulation above, one can readily answer some product sales questions, like:

1. What is the best-selling movie by revenue? – ***Deewar.***
2. What is the best quarter by revenue this year? – ***Q3***
3. Any other patterns? – ***Sholay movie sells only in Q3 (seasonal item).***

The first two questions are Management Reporting questions. Such information is routinely compiled and delivered using traditional management information systems. Only the third question above is a data mining question, as it provides exception reporting. Data mining projects may also be useful in comparing non-adjacent concepts, such as exploring the relationship between Education and Divorce. These insights from data mining can help plan marketing promotions and manage inventory of various items.

If a cross tabulation was designed to include customer location data, one could answer other questions, such as

1. What is the best-selling geography? – India
2. What is the worst selling geography? – UK
3. Any other patterns? – Yaarana sells mostly in India, while Deewar sells only outside India.

Notice that when the data was seen at the individual transaction level, or even at a monthly level, it would be easy to miss the seasonality of the sales. However, one could have observed that September is the highest selling month.

The previous example shows that many unique patterns can be noticed by analyzing data in different ways. However, some insights are more important than others. The value of an insight depends upon the problem being solved. The insight that there are more sales of a product in a certain quarter helps a manager plan what products to focus on. In this case, the store manager should stock up on the movie Sholay in the third quarter (Q3). Similarly, knowing which quarter has the highest overall sales allows for different resource decisions in that quarter. In this case, if Q3 is bringing almost half of total revenue, this requires greater attention on the e-commerce website in the third quarter.

Selecting Data Mining Projects

Data mining should be done to solve high-priority, high-value problems. Much effort is required to gather data, clean it, organize it, mine it with many techniques, interpret the results, and find the right insight. It is important to understand the expected pay-offs from finding the insights for making the business case for a data mining project. One should select the right subset of data, organize it into a nice and imaginative framework that brings relevant data together, and then apply the right data mining techniques to deduce the right insight to answer the right questions.

A retail company may initiate many different types of data mining projects. For example, the use of data mining can help determine which new product categories to add to which of their stores; how to increase sales of existing products; which new locations to open stores in; how to segment the customers for more effective communication; and so on. Organizations will need to prioritize those ideas to choose the project with the highest expected payoff.

Data can be analyzed at multiple levels of granularity and could lead to many interesting combinations of interesting patterns. Some of the patterns may be more meaningful than the others. Highly granular data is often used, especially in finance and high-tech areas, so that one can gain even the finest patterns and gain a slight edge over the competition.

Data Mining Techniques

Here are brief descriptions of some of the most important data mining techniques used to generate insights from data.

Decision Trees: They help classify populations into classes and help make decisions in a simple-to-understand hierarchical way. Examples of classes are high-risk patients or low-risk patients, of high-value customer or low-value customer. It is said that 70% of all data mining work is about classification solutions,and that 70% of all classification work uses decision trees. Thus, decision trees are the most popular and important data mining technique. There are many popular algorithms to make decision trees. They differ in terms of their mechanisms, and different techniques work well for different situations. It is possible to use multiple decision-tree algorithms on a data set and compare the classification accuracy of each type of tree.

Regression: This is a statistical technique to find the best fitting curve through the many data points in a multi-dimensional space. This is a mature and well-understood technique from the field of statistics, with many variants. The output of regression is a best fitting curve which minimizes the (error) distance between the actual data points and the values predicted by the curve. Regression models can be used for projecting into the future for prediction and forecasting purposes.

Artificial Neural Networks: ANNs are multi-layer, non-linear information processing models that learn from past data and predict future values. Originating in the field of artificial intelligence and machine learning, these models predict well, leading to their extreme popularity. The model's parameters may however not be very intuitive. Thus, neural networks are opaque like a black box. ANN systems require a large amount of past data to adequately train the system. If data is the new oil, then Artificial Intelligence systems such as ANN are considered the new electricity. There are many types of neural networks, based on the kinds of data they work on. Many AI systems have been launched recently. These will completely change the way data is analyzed and communicated.

Cluster Analysis: This is an algorithmic technique that helps understand, or conquer, large data sets by dividing them into smaller meaningful datasets. Using this technique, a data set can be divided into a certain number of clusters, based on certain similarities and dissimilarities within the data. There is no one right answer for the number of clusters in the data. The analyst needs to decide the number of clusters by examining how well the number of clusters serves their purpose. Cluster analysis is most commonly used for market segmentation and is also used for exploring the complexity of phenomena in many domains. Unlike decision trees and regression, there is no one right answer for cluster analysis. Different techniques may produce different cluster structures.

Association Rule Mining: This algorithmic technique identifies causal or correlational associations between data values. It is also called Market Basket Analysis in retail industry. An analysis of items frequently found together in a market basket can help cross-sell products and create attractive product bundles. A version of this technique is called the Recommendation engine. It compares coexistence of certain activities or elements at higher frequencies. This is used, for example, when Netflix recommends the next movie to watch, or Amazon recommends the next product to purchase.

Data Visualization

As data and insights grow in number, an important new requirement is the ability of the executives and decision makers to absorb this information and insights in real time. There is a limit to human cognition and comprehension capacity. There is also a limit to human courage to accept and act on new information. That is a good reason to prioritize and communicate fewer but key insights that relate directly to the KRAs of a role.

Here are few considerations when making presentations using data:

1. Present the conclusions and not just report the data.
2. Choose wisely from a palette of graphs to suit the data.
3. Organize the results to make the central point(s) stand out.
4. Ensure that the visuals accurately reflect the numbers. Inappropriate visuals can create misinterpretations and misunderstandings.
5. Make the presentation unique, imaginative, and memorable.

Executive dashboard is a generic term to describe an attractive way to present relevant information on a select few variables for every executive based on their KPIs. Dashboards use graphs, dials, and lists to show the status of important parameters. These dashboards also have a drill-down capability to enable a root-cause analysis of exception situations (Figure 1.3).

Data visualization has been an interesting problem across disciplines, including in military history and geographical explorations. Magna Carta was the first major visualization of the world, and Google Maps is the currently most popular visualization tool. Many dimensions of data can be effectively displayed on a two-dimensional surface to give a rich and more insightful description of the totality of the situation. Dynamic visualizations can make a situation come alive for the decision maker. Tableau is a popular tool for data visualization.

DATA SCIENCE TERMINOLOGY AND CAREERS

Many overlapping terms are used in the marketplace. Here is a brief look at the most popular terms used.

Business Intelligence (BI) is a business-oriented term, and so is Decision science. BI is the field of using data-driven insights to make superior business decisions. This is a broad category which includes data analytics or data mining as a provider of the insights to present to decision makers in an easy-to-consume way.

Data Analytics is a technology-oriented term, and so is Data Mining. Both involve the use of techniques and tools to find novel and useful patterns from data. They involve organizing and modeling the data to test particular hypotheses to answer a question. Knowledge of machine learning algorithms and statistics can be useful in this role.

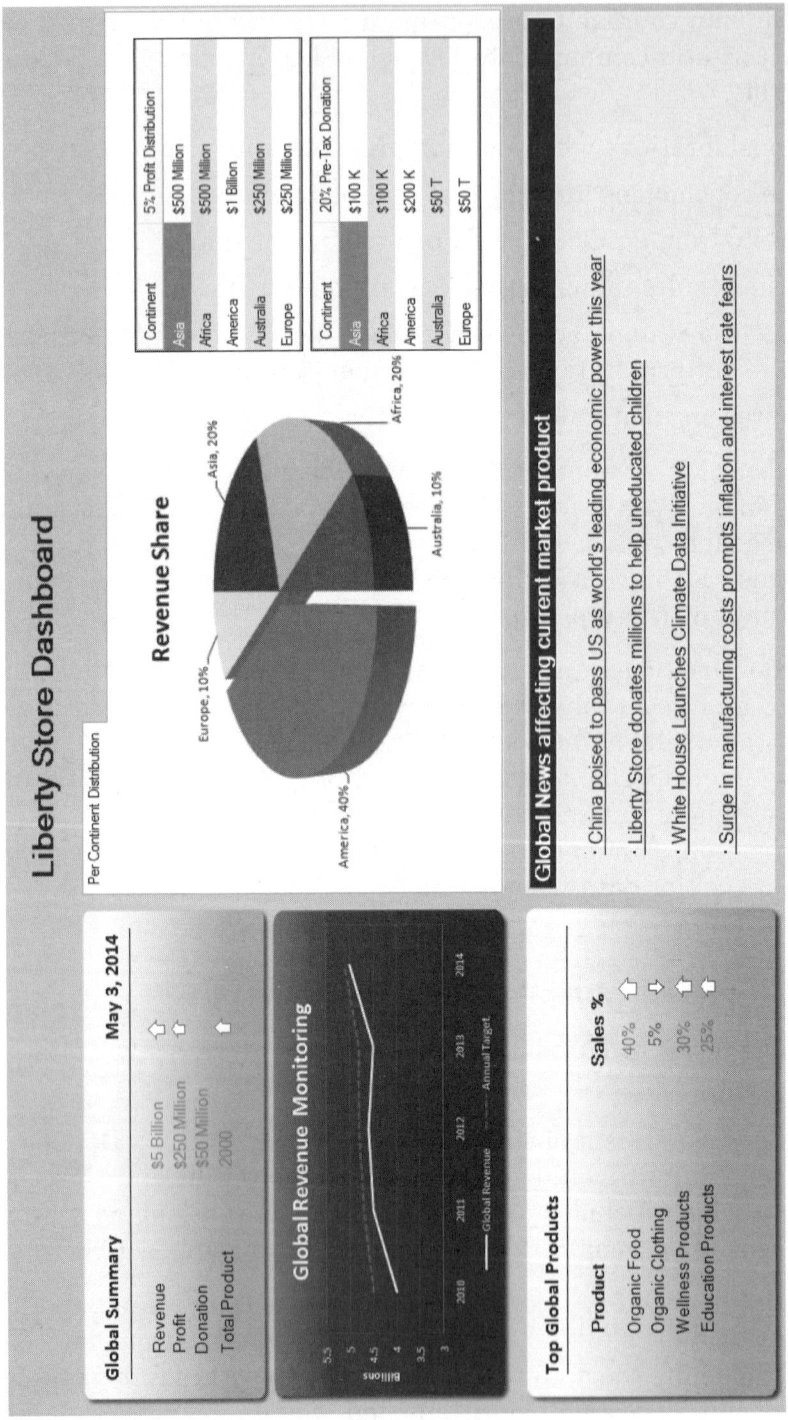

Figure 1.3 Sample Executive Dashboard

Big data is a special type of data ... large, fast, and complex. Gathering, storing, and managing all this data to generate a data pipeline and a data lake are more technical tasks and it requires the use of more technical tools. This field is more attractive to the more technical computer scientists. Cloud computing is an attractive solution to store and process big data. These topics are beyond the scope of this book and may be seen in my associated book Big Data Made Accessible.

Data Science is a new discipline born in the early 2000s. The scope includes the entire data processing chain. A data scientist would ideally be familiar with all aspects of the discipline while specializing in a part of the area. This field was seeded by companies who needed many data scientists in the coming years, for themselves as well as for their clients. Data Science is now taught at practically all universities. This helps increase the supply of data scientists, which has been called the "sexiest" or hottest job of the decade.

Data Engineering is a relatively new discipline related to preparing data for analytics. About 80–90 percent of the effort involved in a data science project involves data preparation. This includes gathering and cleaning up data and making it compatible for use by data analytics platforms.

ORGANIZATION OF THE BOOK

This first chapter is designed to provide the wholeness of business intelligence and data mining, to provide the reader with an intuition for this area of knowledge. The rest of the book can be considered in four sections.

Section 1 covers the data processing chain. Chapter 2 covers the field of business intelligence and its applications across industries and functions. Chapter 3 explains data warehousing and how it helps with management reporting. Chapter 4 describes the wholeness of data mining with an overview of its major tools and techniques. Chapter 5 shows how insights from data can be visualized for better communication and consumption.

Section 2 focuses on core data mining techniques. Every technique is shown through solving an example in detail. Chapter 6 shows the power and ease of decision trees, which are the most popular data mining techniques. Chapter 7 describes statistical regression modeling techniques. Chapter 8 provides an overview of artificial neural networks, a versatile machine learning technique that is so much in the news lately. Chapter 9 describes cluster analysis and how it can help with market segmentation. Finally, Chapter 10 describes association rule mining technique, also called market-basket analysis, that helps find shopping patterns and make purchase recommendations.

Section 3 covers advanced data mining topics. Chapter 11 introduces the concepts and techniques of text mining, which help discover insights from text data including social media data. Chapter 12 covers Naïve-Bayes, a probability-based classification technique used for text mining applications such as spam filtering. Chapter 13 covers support vector machines, a mathematically rigorous classification technique, that is also often used for spam filtering and other applications with high dimensional data. Chapter 14 provides an overview of the growing field of web mining, which includes mining the structure, content, and usage of websites. Chapter 15 covers social network analysis, which helps analyze both text communication and web structure.

Section 4 provides primers of related topics. Chapter 16 provides an overview of the field of big data. Chapter 17 is a primer on Artificial Intelligence and machine intelligence, the hottest and most controversial topics of the current times. Chapter 18 covers data privacy and ethics issues related to gathering, analyzing, and using data. Chapter 19 covers Data Science careers and the skills needed. It also includes some additional data analytics case studies. Chapter 20 covers data collection and preparation, and dimensionality reduction using PCA.

There are additional appendices in the book. One contains an extensive tutorial on R, a statistical language, to help with many of the techniques shown in the book. No prior experience with R is needed for using this tutorial. The other appendix covers an extensive tutorial on Python, a machine learning language. Once again, no prior knowledge of Python is assumed. The third appendix describes a nice Data Mining project to examine relationships between non-adjacent variables such as education and marriage.

REVIEW QUESTIONS

1. Describe the Business Intelligence and Data Mining (BIDM) cycle.
2. Describe the data processing chain.
3. What is data? What is datafication? What are the different data types? What are the different types of sources of data?
4. What is a pattern? What are the different types of patterns? What is a GAS model?
5. What are the similarities between diamond mining and data mining?
6. What are the main data mining techniques? Which of these would be relevant in your current work-related projects?
7. What is an executive dashboard? Why do they need to be customized?

8. Create a visual to show the current weather pattern in your city. Could you show together on one sheet the temperature, humidity, wind, and rain/snow over a period of one week?

TRUE/FALSE

1. Business intelligence is a measure of the intelligence of business people.
2. 'Datafication' means that without data one cannot do data mining.
3. A pattern helps to grasp something abstract.
4. In the context of pattern description, GAS stands for Good, Accurate and Simple.
5. There is a sequence of steps to be followed to benefit from data in a systematic way.
6. Selecting a good research question is an important part of doing a data mining project.
7. Data warehouse is a method to archive the data for later use.
8. Data for mining comes only from sources within the organization.
9. The names and addresses of customers and employees is an example of ordinal data.
10. Interval scale data is more amenable to analysis than the ratio data.
11. Density of data storage in disk drives doubles every 5 years.
12. A data warehouse is a more complex version of the operational database.
13. Data should be analyzed at only the most detailed levels of granularity.
14. Regression is the most popular and important data mining technique.
15. Cluster analysis is a data mining technique for dividing and conquering large datasets.
16. A good data visualization should present the conclusions and not just report the data.
17. Big data is a special type of data – very large, fast and complex.
18. Social media interactions are a form of big data.
19. A data analyst must have a computer science background.
20. Data Science is a growing and multidisciplinary field.

CASELET

Introductory Exercise on Data Analytics

Use the following transaction set to create a Data Warehouse (using a Pivot Table in Excel) to show the total revenue by Salesperson and Month. Do a cross-tabulation to identify about three to five interesting analytical observations from the data warehouse.

Salesperson	Month	Sale
1	January	600
1	January	300
2	January	700
2	January	400
3	January	700
1	February	400
2	February	800
3	February	200
4	February	800
4	February	750
3	February	450
1	February	200
1	March	500
2	March	800
4	March	300
3	March	400
1	March	250
1	March	350
4	March	600
2	March	550

Section 1

This section covers four important high-level topics.

- Chapter 2 will cover business intelligence concepts, and its applications in many industries.
- Chapter 3 will describe data warehousing systems, and ways of creating and managing them. It will also provide an overview of data lakes.
- Chapter 4 will describe data mining as a whole, its many techniques, and many do's and don'ts of effective data mining.
- Chapter 5 will describe data visualization, with techniques and examples, and many thumb rules of effective data visualizations.

CHAPTER 2

Business Intelligence Concepts and Applications

Learning Objectives

LO 1	Understand the concept of Business Intelligence and its role in decision-making
LO 2	Understand the two major types of decisions
LO 3	Know about the type and range of tools for Business Intelligence
LO 4	Outline the wide range of applications of Business Intelligence across industry domains

Business intelligence (BI) is an umbrella term that includes a variety of IT applications that are used to analyze an organization's data and communicate the information to relevant users (Figure 2.1). This is the same picture from Chapter 1 and shows that BI is the upper half of the BIDM cycle.

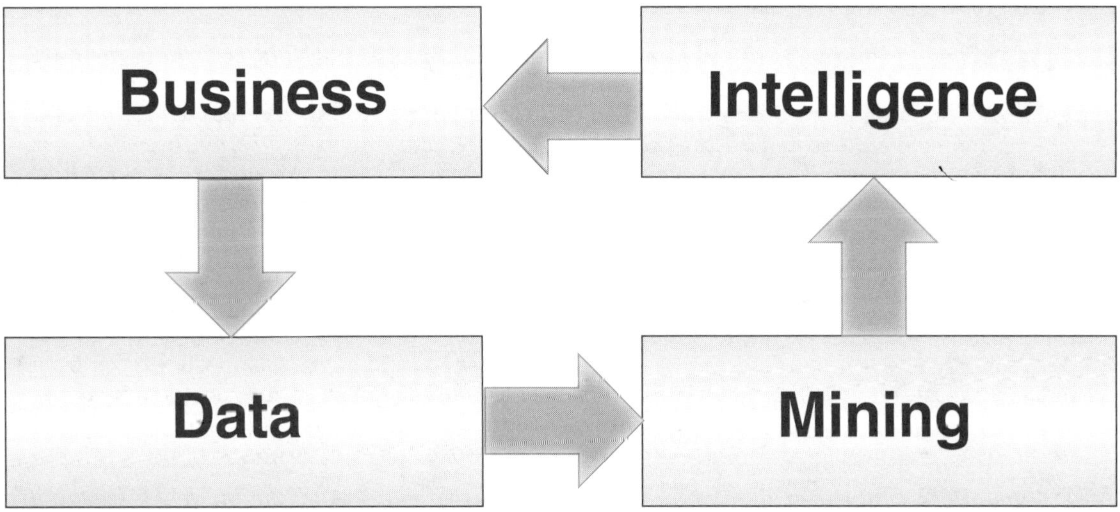

Figure 2.1 BIDM Cycle

The nature of life and businesses is to grow. Information is the lifeblood of business. Businesses use many techniques for understanding their environment and predicting the future for their own benefit and growth. Decisions are made from facts and feelings. However, there is a limit to how much data can one person know, remember, recall, and use. Data analytics systems can routinely compute insights from billions of data elements. Data-based decisions are thus considered more effective than those based on feelings alone. Actions based on accurate data, information, knowledge, experimentation, and testing, using fresh insights, can more likely succeed and lead to sustained growth.

One's own data is generally the more trustworthy, and thus can be the most effective teacher. Therefore, organizations should gather data, sift through it, analyze and mine it, find insights, and then embed those insights into their operating procedures.

There is a new sense of importance and urgency around data, as it is being viewed as a new natural resource. It can be mined for value, insights, and competitive advantage. In a hyperconnected world, where everything seems to be connected to everything else, with potentially infinite correlations, data represents the impulses of nature in the form of certain events and attributes. A skilled executive is motivated to use this cache of data to harness nature, and to find new niches of unserved opportunities that could become profitable ventures.

CASELET

Khan Academy – BI in Education

Khan Academy is an innovative non-profit educational organization that is turning the K-12 education system upside down. It provides short YouTube-based video lessons on thousands of topics for free. It shot into prominence when Bill Gates promoted it as a resource that he used to teach his own children. With this kind of a resource, classrooms are being flipped ... i.e., students do their basic lecture-type learning at home using those videos, while the class time is used for more one-on-one problem solving and coaching. Students can access the lessons at any time to learn at their own pace. The students' progress is recorded, including what videos they watched how many times, which problems they stumbled on, and what scores they got on online tests.

Khan Academy has developed tools to help teachers get a pulse on what's happening in the classroom. Teachers are provided a set of real-time dashboards to give them information from the macro level ("How is my class doing on geometry?") to the micro level ("How is Jane doing on mastering polygons?"). Armed with this information, teachers can place selective focus on the students that need certain help. (To know more visit KhanAcademy.org)

Q1: *How does a dashboard improve the teaching experience? And the student's learning experience?*

Q1: *Design a dashboard for tracking the KPIs of your own job.*

BI FOR BETTER AND FASTER DECISIONS

The future is inherently uncertain. VUCA world means volatile, uncertain, complex, and ambiguous world. Risk is the result of a probabilistic world where there are no certainties but there are high complexities. People use crystal balls, astrology, palmistry, ground hogs, and mathematics and numbers to mitigate risk in decision-making.

The goal of business executives is to make effective decisions, while reducing risk. Businesses calculate risks and make decisions based on a broad set of facts and insights. Reliable knowledge about the future can help managers make the right decisions with lower levels of risk.

The speed of action has risen exponentially with the growth of the Internet, the web, and artificial intelligence. In a hypercompetitive and exponentially changing world, the speed of a decision and the consequent action is a crucial advantage. The Internet and mobile technologies allow decisions to be made anytime, anywhere. Ignoring fast-moving changes can threaten the organization's future. Research has shown that unfavorable comment about the company and its products on social media should not go unaddressed for long. On the other hand, a positive sentiment expressed on social media should also be utilized as a potential sales and promotion opportunity, while the opportunity lasts.

DECISION TYPES

There are two main kinds of business decisions: strategic decisions and operational decisions. BI can help make both better. Strategic decisions are those that impact the direction of the company over a long period of time. The decision to reach out to a new customer set or to expand into a new geographical region would be a strategic decision. Operational decisions are more routine and tactical decisions, focused on developing greater efficiency. Updating an old website with new features would be an operational decision.

In strategic decision-making, the overall mission and vision may be clear, but the specific goal itself may or may not be clear, and the path to reach the goal would not be clear. The consequences of such a decision would become visible a long time later in the future. Thus, businesses are constantly scanning for new possibilities and new targets to reach, and new paths to achieve their goals. BI can help with what-if analysis of many possible scenarios. BI can also help create new ideas based on new patterns found from data mining.

Operational decisions can be made more efficiently using an analysis of past data. A classification system can be created and modeled using the data of past instances to develop a good model of the domain. This model can help improve operational decision-making in the future. BI can help automate operations-level decision-making and improve efficiency by making millions of microlevel operational decisions in a model-driven way. For example, a bank might want to make decisions about making financial loans in a more scientific way using data-based models. A decision tree based model implemented using a neural network could provide consistently accurate loan-making decisions. Developing such decision models is one of the main applications of data mining techniques.

Effective BI has an evolutionary component, as business models evolve. When people and organizations act, new facts (data) are generated. Current business models can be tested against the new data, and it is possible that those models will not hold up well. In such a case, decision models should be revised and new insights should be incorporated. An unending process of generating fresh new insights in real time can help make better decisions, and thus can be a significant competitive advantage.

BI TOOLS

BI includes a variety of software tools and techniques to provide the managers with the information and insights needed to run the business. Information can be provided about the current state with the capability to drill down into details, as needed. BI tools can provide insights about emerging patterns, which lead to projections into the future. BI tools include the entire gamut of the data processing chain, including data warehousing, online analytical processing, social media analytics, dashboards, and querying.

BI tools can range from simple tools that could be considered end-user tools, to very sophisticated tools that offer a very broad and complex set of functionalities. Thus, even executives can become their own BI experts, or they can rely on BI specialists to set up the elaborate dashboard mechanisms for them. Thus, large organizations invest in expensive sophisticated BI solutions that provide good information and insights to their executives in real time.

A spreadsheet tool, such as Microsoft Excel, can act as an easy and effective BI tool by itself or by using many add-on tools available in the market. Data can be downloaded and stored in the spreadsheet, then analyzed to produce insights, and then presented in the form of graphs. This system offers limited automation using macros and other features. The analytical features include basic statistical and financial functions. Pivot tables help to do sophisticated what-if analysis. Add-on modules can be installed to enable moderately sophisticated statistical analysis.

A dashboarding system, such as Tableau, can offer a sophisticated set of tools for gathering, analyzing, and presenting data. At the user end, modular dashboards can be designed and redesigned easily with a graphical user interface. The back-end data analytical capabilities include many statistical functions. The dashboards are linked to data warehouses at the back end to ensure that the tables and graphs and other elements of the dashboard are updated in real time.

There are also commercial industrial strength systems that provide capabilities to apply a wide range of analytical models on large data sets. Open-source systems, such as Weka, Python, and R, are popular platforms designed to help mine large amounts of data to discover patterns.

BI SKILLS

As data grows and exceeds the human capacity to make sense of it, the tools to manage need to evolve, and so should the imagination of the BI specialist. "Data Scientist" has been called the hottest job for many years.

A skilled and experienced BI specialist should be open enough to go outside the box, open the aperture, and take a wider perspective that includes more dimensions and variables, to find important patterns and insights. The objective of the project needs to be looked at from a wider perspective to consider many more angles that may not be immediately obvious. An imaginative solution should be proposed for the problem so that interesting and useful results can emerge. BI goals need careful consideration.

Data mining goes hand in hand with BI. A good data mining project begins with an interesting problem to solve. Selecting the right data mining problem is an important skill. As Einstein famously said, given an hour to solve a problem, he would spend 55 minutes defining the problem and alternatives and 5 minutes in solving it. The problem should be valuable enough that solving it would be worth the time and expense. It takes a lot of time and energy to gather, organize, cleanse, and prepare the data for mining and other analysis. The data mining specialist needs to persist with the exploration of patterns in the data. The skill level must be deep enough to persistently engage with the data and make it yield new useful insights.

BI APPLICATION TYPES

BI tools are required in almost all industries and functions. The nature of the information and the speed of action may be different across businesses, but every manager today needs access to BI tools to have up to date metrics about business performance. Businesses need to embed new insights into their operating processes to ensure that their activities continue to evolve with more efficient practices.

There are several types of applications in terms of their benefit to the organization:

Descriptive Analytics works on data from the past to provide insight into what happened. For example, visualizing the product-wise sales for the last four quarters would be descriptive of the past performance.

Diagnostic Analytics enables drilling down to do root cause analysis of what happened. For example, drilling down from the aggregate sales numbers, to identifying the underlying performing products or salespersons could help understand the cause of any anomalies.

Predictive Analytics identifies exceptional insights that may form the basis of effective future action. For example, identifying sudden spurts in sales of specific products in certain territories might suggest a weak market signal, which can be acted upon to gain market advantage.

Prescriptive Analytics recommends a specific course of action using a robust set of algorithms that continually learn from data. These systems would typically use sophisticated artificial intelligence and machine learning algorithms to model the market phenomenon and continue to learn about its changing state and predict future values. For example, the Einstein AI from Salesforce.com enables an organization to predict future sales from the current opportunity pipeline.

BI APPLICATIONS BY INDUSTRY

The following are some areas of applications of BI and data mining.

Customer Relationship Management

A business exists to serve a customer. A happy customer becomes a repeat customer. A business should understand the needs and sentiments of the customer, sell more of its offerings to the existing customers, and expand the pool of customers it serves. BI applications can impact many aspects of marketing.

1. *Maximize the return on marketing campaigns*: Understanding the customer's key pain points from data-based analysis can ensure that the marketing messages are fine-tuned to better resonate with customers.
2. *Improve customer retention (churn analysis)*: It is more difficult and expensive to win new customers than it is to retain existing customers. Scoring each customer on their likelihood to quit can help the business design effective interventions, such as discounts or free services, to retain profitable customers in a cost-effective manner.
3. *Maximize customer value (cross-, up-selling)*: Every contact with the customer should be seen as an opportunity to gauge and meet their current needs. Offering a customer new products and solutions based on those imputed needs can help increase revenue per customer. Even a customer complaint can be seen as an opportunity to wow the customer. Using the knowledge of the customer's history and value, the business can choose to sell a premium service to the customer.
4. *Identify and delight highly valued customers*. By segmenting the customers, the best customers can be identified. They can be proactively contacted, and delighted, with greater attention and better service. Loyalty programs can be managed more effectively.
5. *Manage brand image*. A business can create a listening post to listen to social media chatter about itself. It can then do sentiment analysis of the data to

understand the nature of comments and respond appropriately to the prospects and customers.

HealthCare and Wellness

Healthcare is one of the biggest sectors in advanced economies. Evidence-based medicine is the newest trend in data-based healthcare management. BI applications can help apply the most effective diagnoses and prescriptions for various ailments. They can also help manage public health issues and reduce waste and fraud.

1. *Diagnose disease in patients*: Diagnosing the cause of a medical condition is the first critical step in medical engagement. Accurately diagnosing cases of cancer or diabetes can be a matter of life and death for the patients. In addition to the patient's current situation, many other factors can be considered, including the patient's health history, medication history, family history, and other environmental factors. This makes diagnosis as much of an art form as it is science. Modern AI systems, for example, absorb all the medical research to date and make probabilistic diagnoses in the form of a decision tree, along with a full explanation for their recommendations. Such systems take away most of the guess work done by doctors in diagnosing ailments.
2. *Treatment effectiveness*: Prescription of medication and treatment is often a difficult choice out of many possibilities. For example, there are more than 100 medications for hypertension (high blood pressure) alone. There are also interactions in terms of which drugs work well with others and which drugs do not. Decision trees can help doctors learn about and prescribe more effective treatments. Thus, the patients could recover their health faster with a lower risk of complications and cost.
3. *Wellness management*: This includes keeping track of patient health records, analyzing customer health trends, and proactively advising them to take any needed precautions. Some companies can check the biome with a person's saliva and create custom nutrition supplements for the customer.
4. *Manage fraud and abuse*: Some medical practitioners have unfortunately been found to conduct unnecessary tests, and/or overbill the government and health insurance companies. Exception reporting systems can identify such providers and action can be taken against them.
5. *Public health management*: The management of public health is one of the important responsibilities of any government. By using effective forecasting tools and techniques, governments can better predict the onset of diseases and pandemics in certain areas in real time. They can thus be better prepared to fight the diseases. Google has been known to predict the movement of certain diseases by tracking the search terms (like flu, vaccine) used in different parts of the world.

6. *Drug discovery and development*: BI applications can help manage the portfolio of potential drugs and their effectiveness in curing certain diseases. They can also help with managing clinical trials. Artificial intelligence systems discover matching molecules for specific customers, leading perhaps to custom medication in the near future.

Education

As higher education becomes more expensive and competitive, it becomes a great user of data-based decision-making. There is a strong need for efficiency, increasing revenue, and improving the quality of student experience at all levels of education.

1. *Student enrollment (recruitment and retention)*: Marketing to new potential students requires schools to develop profiles of the students that are most likely to attend. Schools can develop models of what kinds of students are attracted to the school, and then reach out to those students. The students who are at risk of not returning can be flagged and corrective measures can be taken in time.
2. *Attractive course offerings*: Schools can use class enrolment data to develop models of which new courses are likely to be more popular with students. This can help increase class size, reduce costs, and improve student satisfaction. This can also help recruit the right sets of teachers with the skills needed to offer the popular courses.
3. *Fund-raising from Alumni and other donors*: Schools can develop predictive models of which alumni are most likely to pledge financial support to the school. Schools can create a profile for alumni who are more likely to pledge donations to the school. This could lead to a reduction in the cost of mailings and other forms of outreach to alumni.
4. *Customized learning*: As the Khan Academy case shows, BI systems can help track the progress of every single student, or every course or for every teacher. This can help with more effective teaching and learning.

Retail

Retail organizations grow by meeting customer needs with quality products, in a convenient, timely, and cost-effective manner. Understanding emerging customer shopping patterns can help retailers organize their products, inventory, store layout, and web presence to delight their customers, which in turn would help increase revenue and profits. Retailers generate a lot of transaction and logistics data that can be mined to diagnose and solve problems.

1. *Optimize inventory levels at different locations*: Retailers need to manage their inventories carefully. Carrying too much inventory imposes carrying costs, while carrying too little inventory can cause stock-outs and lost sales opportunities.

Predicting sales trends dynamically can help retailers move inventory to where it is most in demand. Retail organizations can provide their suppliers with real-time information about sales of their items, so the suppliers can deliver their product to the right locations and minimize stock-outs.

2. *Improve store layout and sales promotions*: A market basket analysis can develop predictive models of which products sell together often. This knowledge of affinities between products can help retailers co-locate those products. Alternatively, those affinity products could be located farther apart to make the customer walk the length and breadth of the store, and thus be exposed to other products. Promotional discounted product bundles can be created to push a less-selling item along with a set of products that sell well together.
3. *Optimize logistics for seasonal effects*: Seasonal products offer tremendously profitable short-term sales opportunities, yet they also offer the risk of unsold inventories at the end of the season. Understanding which products are in season in which market can help retailers dynamically manage prices to ensure their inventory is sold during the season. If it is raining in a certain area, then the inventory of umbrellas and ponchos could be rapidly moved there from non-rainy areas to help increase sales.
4. *Minimize losses due to limited shelf life*: Perishable goods offer challenges in terms of disposing off the inventory in time. By tracking sales trends, the perishable products at risk of not selling before the sell-by date can be suitably discounted and promoted.

Banking

Banks make loans and offer credit cards to millions of customers. They are most interested in improving the quality of loans and reducing bad debts. They also want to retain more of the good customers and sell more services to them.

1. *Automate the loan application process*: Decision models can be generated from past data that predict the likelihood of a loan proving successful. These models can be inserted in business processes to automate the financial loan approval process.
2. *Detect fraudulent transactions*: Billions of financial transactions happen around the world every day. Exception-seeking models can identify patterns of fraudulent transactions. For example, if money is being transferred to an unrelated account for the first time, it could be a fraudulent transaction.
3. *Maximize customer value (cross-, up-selling).* Selling more products and services to existing customers is often the easiest way to increase revenue. A checking account customer in good standing could be offered a home, auto, or educational

loan on more favorable terms than other customers, and thus, the value generated from that customer could be increased.

4. *Optimize cash reserves with forecasting.* Banks must maintain certain liquidity to meet the needs of depositors who may like to withdraw money. Using past data and trend analysis, banks can forecast how much to keep and invest the rest to earn interest.

Financial Services

Stock brokerages are an intensive user of BI and data mining systems. Fortunes can be made or lost based on access to accurate and timely information. Past data can be utilized to develop mathematical models to predict market situations just a few seconds before the competition can

1. *Predict changes in bond and stock prices*: Forecasting the price of stocks and bonds is a favorite pastime of financial experts as well as lay people. Stock transaction data from the past, along with other variables, can be used to predict future price patterns. This can help traders develop long-term trading strategies.
2. *Assess the effect of events on market movements.* Decision models using decision trees can be created to assess the impact of events on changes in market volume and prices. Monetary policy changes (such as Federal Reserve interest rate changes) or geopolitical changes (such as war in a part of the world) can be factored into the predictive model to help act with greater confidence and less risk.
3. *Identify and prevent fraudulent activities in trading*: There have unfortunately been many cases of insider trading, leading to many prominent financial industry stalwarts going to jail. Fraud detection models seek out-of-the-ordinary activities and help identify and flag fraudulent activity patterns.
4. *Attracting and retaining customers.* Understanding the needs of high-net-worth customers can help create unique portfolios from a wide variety of options. This can create a deeper relationship with clients, and thus help with retention.

Insurance

This industry is a prolific user of prediction models in pricing insurance proposals and managing losses from claims against insured assets.

1. *Forecast claim costs for better business planning*: When natural disasters, such as hurricanes and earthquakes strike, loss of life and property occurs. By using the best available data to model the likelihood (or risk) of such events happening, the insurer can plan for losses and manage resources and profits effectively.
2. *Determine optimal rate plans*: Pricing an insurance rate plan requires covering the potential losses and making a profit. Insurers use actuary tables to project

life spans and disease tables to project mortality rates, and thus price themselves competitively yet profitably.

3. *Optimize marketing to specific customers*: By micro-segmenting potential customers, a data-savvy insurer can cherry pick the best customers and leave the less profitable customers to its competitors. Progressive Insurance is a US-based company that is known to actively use data mining to cherry pick customers and increase its profitability.
4. *Identify and prevent fraudulent claim activities.* Patterns can be identified as to where and what kinds of fraud are more likely to occur. Decision tree based models can be used to identify and flag fraudulent claims.

Manufacturing and Supply Chain Management

Manufacturing operations are complex systems with inter-related sub-systems. From machines working right, to workers having the right skills, to the right components arriving with the right quality at the right time, to money to source the components, many things have to go right. Toyota's famous lean manufacturing company works on just-in-time inventory systems to optimize investments in inventory and to improve flexibility in their product-mix.

1. *Discover novel patterns to improve product quality*: The quality of a product can also be tracked, and this data can be used to create a predictive model of product quality deteriorating. Many companies, such as automobile companies, must recall their products if they have found defects that have a public safety implications. Data mining can help with a root cause analysis that can be used to identify sources of errors and help improve product quality in the future.
2. *Predict/prevent machinery failures*: Statistically, all equipment is likely to break down at some point in time. Predicting which machine is likely to shut down is a complex process. Decision models to forecast machinery failures could be constructed using past data. Preventive maintenance can be planned, and manufacturing capacity can be adjusted, to account for such maintenance activities.
3. *Managing the supply chain*: Supply chains have become global and subject to disruption because of environmental, commercial, political, and logistical considerations. BI systems are being used to track every shipment so that it can be rerouted, as needed, to improve customer delivery and satisfaction.

Telecommmunications

BI in telecom can help with the customer side as well as the network side of the operations. Key BI applications include churn management, marketing/customer profiling, network failure, and fraud detection.

1. *Churn management*: Telecom customers have shown a tendency to switch their providers in search of better deals. Telecom companies tend to respond with many incentives and discounts to hold on to customers. However, they need to determine which customers are at a real risk of switching and which others are just negotiating for a better deal. The level of risk should be factored into the kind of deals and discounts that should be given. Millions of such customer calls happen every month. Telecom companies need to provide a consistent and data-based way to predict the risk of customer switching, and then make an operational decision in real time while the customer call is taking place. A decisiontree or a neural network-based system can be used to guide the customer-service call operator to make the right decisions for the company, in a consistent manner.
2. *Marketing and product creation*. In addition to customer data, telecom companies also store call detail records (CDRs), which can be analyzed to precisely describe the calling behavior of each customer. This unique data can be used to profile customers and then can be used for creating new products/services bundles for marketing purposes. Telecom companies create bundled programs, such as TV and internet and phone, to effectively lock many customers into their network.
3. *Network failure management*: Failure of telecom networks for technical failures or malicious attacks can have devastating impacts on people, businesses, and society. In telecom infrastructure, some equipment will likely fail with a certain mean time between failures. Modeling the failure pattern of various components of the network can help with preventive maintenance and capacity planning.
4. *Fraud Management*: There are many kinds of fraud in consumer transactions. Subscription fraud occurs when a customer opens an account with the intention of never paying for the services. Superimposition fraud involves illegitimate activity by a person other than the legitimate account holder. Decision rules can be developed to analyze each CDR in real time to identify chances of fraud and take effective action.

Public Sector

The government gathers a large amount of data by virtue of its regulatory function. That data could be analyzed for developing models of effective functioning. There are innumerable applications that can benefit from mining that data. A couple of sample applications are shown here.

1. *Law enforcement*: Social behavior is a lot more patterned and predictable than one would imagine. For example, Los Angeles Police Department (LAPD) mined the data from its 13 million crime records over 80 years and developed models of what kind of crime is going to happen when and where. By increasing patrolling in those areas, LAPD was able to reduce property crime by 27 percent. Internet chatter can be analyzed to learn of and prevent any evil designs.

2. *Scientific research*: Any large collection of research data is amenable to being mined for patterns and insights. Protein folding (microbiology), nuclear reaction analysis (sub-atomic physics), disease control (public health) are some examples where data mining can yield powerful new insights.
3. *Public health management*: The coronavirus pandemic has brought great attention to the need to bring accurate and relevant information to the notice of the public at large, without creating panic. Setting medical standards and tracking outbreaks of pandemic activity can help contain the spread of the disease and use appropriate policy choices.

CONCLUSION

Business Intelligence is a comprehensive framework along with a set of technological tools to support decision-making with imaginative solutions for a variety of problems. BI can help improve the performance in nearly all industries and applications.

REVIEW QUESTIONS

1. Businesses need timely information to succeed. What does that mean to you?
2. Why should organizations invest in BI solutions? How would you compare investment in BI tools and IT security solutions?
3. Customer service management is one of the key applications across industries. Fraud management is another. Describe how these would apply in your favorite industry and in your own organization.
4. Describe two BI tools used in your organization.

TRUE/FALSE

1. Business intelligence is a measure of intelligence of the business people.
2. There are four major types of decisions that are supported by BI.
3. It requires a great deal of expertise to use any BI tool.
4. A dashboard is a tool to display useful information for the decision-maker.
5. BI tools are useful mainly for tracking financial success.
6. Customer relationship management is a form of BI.
7. BI tools are applicable across almost all the industries.
8. A customer invoice is a valid output of a BI tool.

9. A video-surveillance system is a form of a BI tool.
10. Only large organizations can afford BI systems.

CASELET

MAALA STORES Case Exercise: Step 1

Maala Stores Inc is a specialized global retail chain that sells organic food, organic clothing, wellness products, and education products to enlighten LOHAS (Lifestyles of the Healthy and Sustainable) citizens worldwide. The company is 30 years old, and is growing rapidly. It now operates in 5 continents, 70 countries, 200 cities, and has 800 stores. It sells 30,000 products and has 15,000 employees. The company has revenues of over $10 billion and has a profit of about 7% of revenue. The company pays special attention to the conditions under which the products are grown and produced. It donates about one-fifth (20%) of its pre-tax profits from global local charitable causes.

1: *Create a comprehensive dashboard for the CEO of the company.*

2: *What kind of BI applications would be useful for this company?*

CHAPTER 3

Data Warehousing

Learning Objectives

LO 1 Understand the concept of Data Warehouse (DW) and its role in data analytics

LO 2 Appreciate the design choices in developing a DW

LO 3 Understand the top-down and bottom approaches of developing a DW and their various advantages

LO 4 Discuss the architecture of a DW

LO 5 Understand the type and range of data sources

LO 6 Understand the Extract-Transform-Load (ETL) processes

LO 7 Explain the star schema for organizing a DW

LO 8 Appreciate the key best practices for designing an effective DW

A data warehouse (DW) is an organized collection of integrated, subject-oriented databases designed to aid decision support functions. DW is organized at the right level of granularity to provide clean enterprise-wide data in a standardized format for reports, queries, and analysis. DW is physically and functionally separate from an operational and transactional database. Creating a DW for analysis and queries represents a significant investment in time and effort. It has to be constantly kept up to date for it to be useful. DW offers many business and technical benefits.

DW supports business reporting activities. It can facilitate distributed access to up-to-date business knowledge for departments and functions, thus improving business efficiency and customer service. DW can present a competitive advantage by facilitating decision-making and helping reform business processes.

DW enables a consolidated view of corporate data, all cleaned and organized. Thus, the entire organization can see an integrated view of itself. DW thus provides better and more timely information. It simplifies data access and allows end users to perform extensive analysis, and thus also supports data mining. It enhances overall IT performance by not burdening the operational databases used by Enterprise Resource Planning (ERP) and other systems.

CASELET

Innovative Universal Health System - BI in Healthcare

Innovative Universal Health (IUH), a fictional healthcare system, decided to build an enterprise data warehouse (EDW) to foster a genuinely data-driven management culture. IUH hired a data warehousing vendor to develop an EDW that also integrates with their Electronic Health Records (EHR) system. They loaded 20 billion rows of data into the EDW—fully 10 years of clinical data from across IUH's network. Clinical events, patient encounters, lab and radiology, and other patient data were included, as were IUH's performance management, revenue cycle, and patient satisfaction data. They soon put in a new interactive dashboard using the EDW that provided IUH's leadership with the daily operational insights they need to solve the quality/cost equation. It offers visibility into key operational metrics and trends to easily track the performance measures critical to controlling costs and maintaining quality. The EDW can easily be used across IUH's departments to analyze, track, and measure clinical, financial, and patient experience outcomes. (To know more visit healthcatalyst.com)

Q1: *What are the benefits of a single large comprehensive EDW?*

Q2: *What kinds of data would be needed for an EDW for an airline company?*

DESIGN CONSIDERATIONS FOR DATA WAREHOUSE

The objective of DW is to provide business knowledge to support decision-making. For DW to serve its objective, it should be aligned around supporting those business decisions. It should be relevant, organized, easy to access, and up to date. Here are some requirements for a good DW:

1. *Subject oriented*: To be effective, a DW should be designed around a subject domain, that is, to help solve a certain category of problems, such as sales management.
2. *Integrated*: The DW should include data from all the functions that can shed light on a particular subject area. Thus, the organization can benefit from a comprehensive view of the subject area, such as including sales targets and sales performance.
3. *Time-variant (time series):* The data in DW should grow at daily or other chosen intervals. That allows for making the latest comparisons over time. No data from the past can be changed or deleted.
4. *Nonvolatile*: DW should be persistent, that is, it should not be created on the fly from the operations databases. Thus, DW should be consistently available for analysis across the organization and over time.
5. *Summarized*: DW contains data at the right level for queries and analysis. The process of rolling up the data helps create consistent granularity for effective comparisons. It also helps reduce the number of meaningful variables or dimensions of the data to make it easier for decision makers.

6. *Not normalized*: DW often uses a star schema, which is a rectangular central table, surrounded by some look-up tables. The single table view significantly enhances the speed of responding to queries.
7. *Metadata*: Many of the variables in the database are computed from other variables in the operational database. For example, total daily sales may be a computed field. The method of calculation for each variable should be effectively documented. Every element in the DW should be sufficiently well-defined. Any change in the computation formula can affect comparability over time.
8. *Near real-time and/or right-time (active)*: DWs should be updated in near real-time in many high transaction volume industries, such as airlines. The cost of implementing and updating DW in real time could be discouraging though. Another downside of real-time DW is the possibility of inconsistencies in reports drawn just a few minutes apart.

DATA WAREHOUSE DEVELOPMENT APPROACHES

There are two fundamentally different approaches to developing DW: top-down and bottom-up. The top-down approach is to make a comprehensive DW that covers all the information needs of the whole enterprise. The bottom-up approach is to produce small data marts for the reporting needs of specific departments or functions, as needed. The smaller data marts may eventually align to deliver comprehensive EDW capabilities. The top-down approach provides consistency but takes more time and resources. The bottom-up approach leads to healthy local ownership and maintainability of data but can create a fractured and inconsistent view of the organization (Table 3.1).

Table 3.1 Comparing Data Mart and Data Warehouse

	Functional Data Mart	Enterprise Data Warehouse
Scope	One subject or functional area	Complete enterprise data needs
Value	Functional area reporting and insights	Deeper insights connecting multiple functional areas
Target organization	Decentralized management	Centralized management
Time	Low to medium	High
Cost	Low	High
Size	Small to medium	Medium to large
Approach	Bottom-up	Top-down
Complexity	Low (fewer data transformations)	High (data standardization)
Technology	Smaller scale servers and databases	Industrial strength

DATA WAREHOUSE ARCHITECTURE

The process of producing a DW has four key steps (Figure 3.1). The first step is identifying the data sources that provide the raw data. The second step is the process of transforming that data to meet the decision needs. The third step is the method of regularly and accurately loading that data into EDW or data marts. The fourth step is data access and analysis part, where devices and applications use the data from DW to deliver insights and other benefits to users.

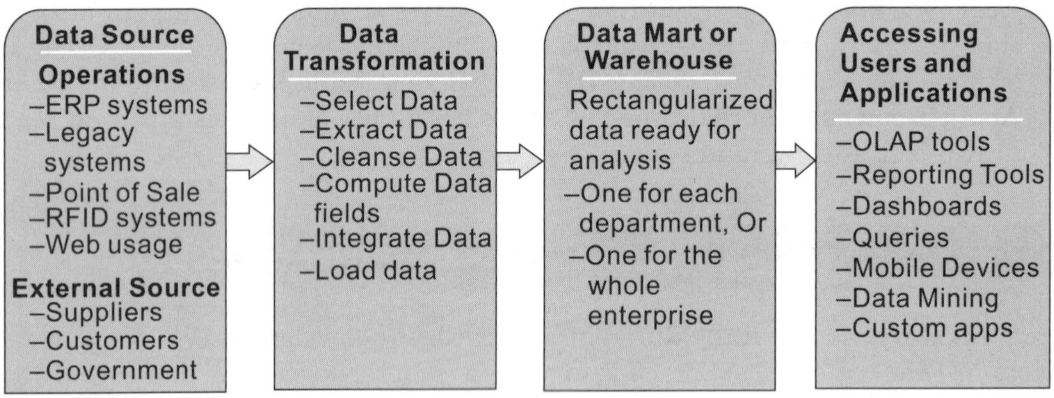

Figure 3.1 Data Warehousing Architecture

DATA SOURCES

Data Warehouses are created from structured data sources. Unstructured data such as text data would need to be structured before being inserted into the DW.

1. *Operations data:* This includes data from all business applications, including from ERPs systems that form the backbone of an organization's IT systems. The data to be extracted will depend upon the subject matter of the data warehouse. For example, for a sales/marketing data mart, only the data about customers, orders, customer service, and so on would be extracted.
2. *Specialized applications*: This includes applications such as Point of Sale (POS) terminals, and e-commerce applications, which also provide customer-facing data. Supplier data could come from Supply Chain Management systems. Planning and budget data should also be added as needed for making comparisons against targets.
3. *External syndicated data*: This includes publicly available data such as weather or economic activity data. It could also be added to the DW, as needed, to provide good contextual information to decision makers.

EXTRACT-TRANSFORM-LOAD CYCLE

The heart of a useful DW is the process to populate the DW with good quality data. This is called the Extract-Transform-Load (ETL) cycle.

1. Data should be extracted from the operational (transactional) database sources, as well as from other applications, on a regular basis.
2. The extracted data should be aligned and joined together by key fields and integrated into a single data set. It should be cleansed of any irregularities or missing values. It should be rolled-up together to the same level of granularity. Desired fields, such as daily sales totals, should be computed. The entire data should then be brought to the same format as the central table of DW.
3. This transformed data should then be uploaded into the DW. This data is appended to the existing data in the DW.

This ETL process should be run at a regular frequency. For example, daily transaction data can be extracted from ERPs, transformed, and uploaded to the database the same night. Thus, the DW is up to date every morning. If a DW is needed for near-real-time information access, then the ETL processes would need to be executed more frequently. ETL work is usually done using automated programming scripts that are written, tested, and then deployed for periodically updating the DW.

DATA WAREHOUSE DESIGN

Star schema is the preferred data architecture for most DWs. There is a central fact table that provides most of the information of interest. There are lookup tables that provide detailed values for codes used in the central table. For example, the central table may use numeric digits to represent a salesperson. The lookup table will help provide the name for that salesperson's numeric code. Here is an example of a star schema for a data mart for monitoring sales performance (Figure 3.2).

Other schemas include the snowflake architecture, which is a fractally expanded version of the star model. The difference between a star and a snowflake is that in the latter, the look-up tables can have dimensions, which will have their own further look-up tables.

There are many technology choices for developing DW. This includes selecting the right database management system and the right set of data management tools. There are a few big and reliable providers of DW systems. The provider of the operational DBMS may be chosen for DW also. Alternatively, a best-of-breed DW vendor could be used. There are also a variety of tools out there for data migration, data upload, data retrieval, and data analysis.

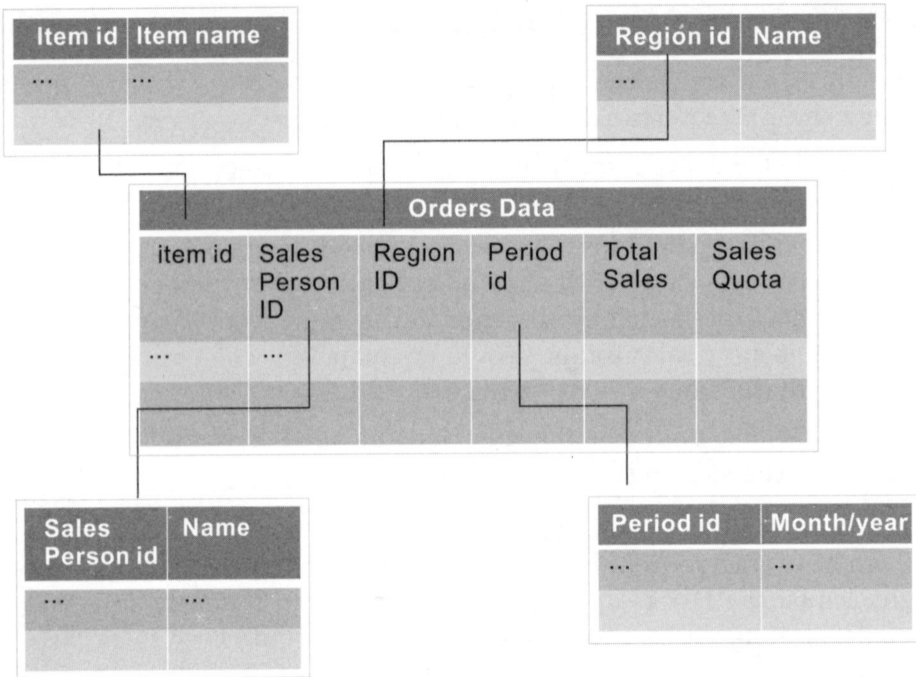

Figure 3.2 Star Schema Architecture for Data Warehouse

DATA WAREHOUSE ACCESS

Data from the DW could be accessed for many purposes, by many users, through many devices, and many kinds of systems. The primary use of DW is to produce routine management and monitoring reports.

1. OLAP (online analytical processing) systems are query and reporting tools that help to slice the multi-dimensional data in the DW and produce desired reports. For example, a sales performance report would show sales by many dimensions as compared with sales targets. One could request a list of all products sold in a region in a certain price range during a certain time period, and have them displayed in a report format.
2. A dashboarding system will use data from the warehouse and present analysis to users. The data from DW can be used to populate customized performance dashboards for executives. The dashboard could include drill-down capabilities to analyze the performance data for root cause analysis.
3. The data from DW could be used for ad-hoc queries and any other applications that make use of the internal data.

4. Data from DW is used to provide data for mining purposes. Parts of the data would be extracted, and then combined with other relevant data, for data mining.

DATA LAKES

Data lake is a more recent and expanded concept to represent highly voluminous and fast data called big data. It addresses the limitations of the concept of data warehouse that was invented in the 1990s. DWs were expensive and proprietary, and are often not flexible enough to handle the evolving needs of companies. A data lake is conceived to be a centralized repository where all structured and unstructured data can flow in, speedily, at any scale, and typically dammed on a cloud storage platform. A data lake uses a flat architecture and object storage to store the data "as is," without imposing a fixed schema or structure on it. Thus, big data from all sources and in all stages of processing can be ingested and stored alongside an organization's structured, tabular data sources, in a data lake. By leveraging inexpensive object storage and open formats, data lakes enable many applications to store exponentially large amounts of data. The open format of the data lakes also helps avoid being locked into a proprietary system, while providing high durability, interoperability, and low cost. Additionally, almost all advanced analytics and machine learning tools for unstructured data are now available for use in data lakes. Thus, the openness of architecture and the availability of low-cost, secure, and scalable cloud platforms make data lakes the way for the future. Creating a Data Lake system requires greater technical knowledge for gathering and organizing data at scale and speed. It is often described as the work of Data Engineers.

DATA WAREHOUSE BEST PRACTICES

A DW project reflects a significant investment in information technology (IT) to serve business needs. All best practices in implementing any IT project should be followed.

1. *Align with the corporate strategy.* Top management should be consulted about setting objectives. Financial viability (ROI) should be established. The project must be managed by both IT and business professionals. The DW design should be carefully tested before beginning development work. It is often much more expensive to redesign after development work has begun.

2. *Manage user expectations.* The DW should be built incrementally. Users should be trained in using the system so that they can absorb the many features of the system. Setting the right expectations will avoid underuse or disuse of the system.

3. *Quality and adaptability:* Flexibility is the key to continued relevance. Only relevant, cleansed, and high-quality data should be loaded. The system should be able to adapt to new tools for access. As business needs change, new data lakes may need to be created for meeting new needs.

CONCLUSION

Data Warehouses are special data management facilities intended for creating reports and analysis to support managerial decision-making. They are designed to make reporting and querying simple and efficient. The sources of data are operational systems, and external data sources. The DW needs to be updated with new data regularly to keep it useful. Data from DW provides a useful input for data mining activities. Data lakes are the new incarnation of DW, including vast unstructured data.

REVIEW QUESTIONS

1. What is the purpose of a data warehouse?
2. What are the key steps in creating a data warehouse? Describe each one.
3. What are the sources and types of data for a data warehouse?
4. How is a data lake better suited to serve an organization in the age of social media?

TRUE/FALSE

1. A data warehouse can help the entire organization to see an integrated view of itself.
2. There are three approaches to build a data warehouse – top-down, bottom-up, and global.
3. ETL stands for Extract, Transfer and Label the data into the DW.
4. A star schema consists of a central fact table and smaller lookup tables.
5. A data warehouse is an expensive project and should align with corporate strategy.
6. Once created, the data warehouse should be protected from adding data into it.
7. Social media data such as customer comments should be directly transferred into the data warehouse to allow for quick insights.

8. A data warehouse contains metadata about how data is organized and how to use it effectively.
9. POS is not a data source to a data warehouse.
10. Data warehouse is a valuable source of data for data mining.

CASELET

MAALA STORES Case Exercise: Step 2

The Maala Stores company wants to be fully informed about its sales of products and take advantage of growth opportunities as they arise. It wants to analyze sales of all its products by all store locations. The newly hired Chief Knowledge Officer has decided to build a Data Warehouse.

1: *Design a DW structure for the company to monitor its sales performance. (Hint: Design the central table and look-up tables).*

2: *Design another DW for the company's sustainability and charitable activities.*

CHAPTER 4

Data Mining

Learning Objectives

LO 1	Outline the concept of Data Mining
LO 2	Understand the process of gathering, selecting, cleansing, and otherwise preparing the data for mining
LO 3	Identify the outputs of data mining
LO 4	Learn to evaluate the effectiveness of various data mining models
LO 5	Understand the CRISP-DM data mining process
LO 6	Summarize the range of data mining techniques
LO 7	Appreciate the wide range of toolsets available for data mining and their respective strengths

Data mining is the art and science of discovering knowledge, insights, and patterns in data. It is the act of extracting useful patterns from an organized collection of data. Patterns should be valid, novel, potentially useful, and understandable. The implicit assumption is that data about the past can reveal patterns of activity that can be projected into the future.

Data mining is a multidisciplinary field that borrows techniques from a variety of fields. It utilizes the knowledge of data quality and data organization from the databases area. It draws modeling and analytical techniques from statistics and computer science (artificial intelligence) areas. It also draws the knowledge of decision-making from the field of business management.

The field of data mining emerged in the context of pattern recognition in defense, such as identifying a friend-or-foe on a battlefield. Like many other defense-inspired technologies, it has evolved to help gain a competitive advantage in business.

For example, "customers who buy cheese and milk also buy bread 90 percent of the time" would be a useful pattern for a grocery store, which can then stock the products appropriately. Similarly, "people with blood pressure greater than 160 and an age greater than 65 were at a high risk of dying from a heart stroke" is of great diagnostic value for doctors, who can then focus on treating such patients with urgent care and great sensitivity.

Past data can be of predictive value in many complex situations, especially where the pattern may not be so easily visible without the modeling technique. Here is a dramatic case of a data-driven decision-making system that beats the best of human experts. Using past data, a decision tree model was developed to predict votes for a particular Justice of the US Supreme Court, who had a swing vote in a 5–4 divided US Supreme Court. All her previous decisions were coded on a few variables. What emerged from data mining was a simple four-step decision tree that was able to accurately predict her votes 71 percent of the time. In contrast, legal analysts could at best correctly predict 59 percent of the time. (To know more see Martin, A. D., Quinn, K. M., & Epstein, L. (2004). The median justice on the united states supreme court. *NCL rev., 83, 1275.*)

CASELET

Target Corp – Data Mining in Retail

Target is a large retail chain that crunches data to develop insights that help target marketing and advertising campaigns. Target analysts managed to develop a pregnancy prediction score based on a customer's purchasing history of 25 products. In a widely publicized story, they figured out that a teenage girl was pregnant before her father did. The targeting can be quite successful and dramatic as this example published in the New York Times illustrates.

About a year after Target created its pregnancy-prediction model, a man walked into a Target store and demanded to see the manager. He was clutching coupons that had been sent to his daughter and he was angry, according to an employee who participated in the conversation. "My daughter got this in the mail!" he said. "She's still in high school, and you're sending her coupons for baby clothes and cribs? Are you trying to encourage her to get pregnant?"

The manager didn't have any idea what the man was talking about. He looked at the mailer. Sure enough, it was addressed to the man's daughter and contained advertisements for maternity clothing, nursery furniture, and pictures of smiling infants. The manager apologized and then called a few days later to apologize again.

On the phone, though, the father was somewhat subdued. "I had a talk with my daughter," he said. "It turns out there have been some activities in my house I haven't been completely aware of. I owe you an apology." (To know more see https://www.nytimes.com/2012/02/19/magazine/shopping-habits.html).

Q1: *Do Target and other retailers have full rights to use their acquired data as it sees fit, and to contact desired consumers with all legally admissible means and messages? What are the issues involved here?*

Q2: *Facebook and Google provide many services for free. In return, they mine our email and blogs and send us targeted ads. Is that a fair bargain?*

GATHERING AND SELECTING INPUT DATA

The total amount of data in the world is doubling every 18 months. There is an avalanche of data coming with higher velocity, volume, and variety. This is called big data. One has to quickly use the data or it quickly loses value. Smart data mining requires choosing where to mine. One must make judicious decisions about what to gather and what to ignore, based on the purpose of the data mining projects. It is like deciding where to fish, as not all streams of data will be equally rich in potential insights.

To learn from data, high-quality data needs to be available. Data should be effectively gathered, cleaned, organized, and then efficiently mined. One requires the skills and technologies for consolidation and integration of data elements from many sources. Most organizations develop an enterprise data model (EDM) to organize their data. An EDM is a unified, high-level model of all the data stored in an organization's databases. The EDM is usually inclusive of the data generated from all internal systems. The EDM provides the basic menu of data to create a data warehouse for a particular decision-making purpose. DWs help organize all this data in an easy and usable manner so that it can be selected and deployed for mining. The EDM can also help imagine what relevant external data should be gathered to provide context and develop good predictive relationships with the internal data. In the United States, the various federal and local governments and their regulatory agencies make a vast variety and quantity of data available at data.gov.

Gathering and curating data takes time and effort, particularly when it is unstructured or semi-structured. Unstructured data can come in many forms like databases, blogs, images, videos, audio, and chats. There are streams of unstructured social media data from blogs, chats, and tweets. There are streams of machine-generated data from connected machines, RFID tags, the Internet of Things, and so on. Eventually, the data should be tabulated, that is, put in rectangular data shapes with clear columns and rows, before submitting it for data mining.

Knowledge of the business domain helps select the right streams of data for pursuing new insights. Only the data that suits the nature of the problem being solved should be gathered. The data elements should be relevant, and suitably address the problem being solved. They could directly impact the problem, or they could be a suitable proxy for the effect being measured. Select data could also be gathered from the data warehouse. Every industry and function will have its own requirements and constraints. The healthcare industry will provide different type of data with different data names. The HR function would provide different kinds of data. There would be different issues of quality and privacy for these data.

DATA CLEANSING AND PREPARATION

The quality of data is critical to the success and value of the data mining project. Otherwise, the situation will represent *garbage in and garbage out (GIGO)*. The quality of incoming data varies depending on the source and nature of data. Data from internal operations is likely to be of higher quality, as it will be accurate and consistent. Unstructured data from social media and other public sources is less under the control of businesses and is less likely to be reliable.

Data should be cleansed and transformed before it can be used for data mining. There are many ways in which data may need to be cleansed – filling missing values, reigning in the effects of outliers, transforming fields, binning continuous variables, and much more – before it can be ready for analysis. Data cleansing and preparation is a labor-intensive or semi-automated activity that can take up to 80-90% of the time needed for a data mining project.

1. *Duplicate data needs to be removed.* The same data may be received multiple times, and from multiple sources. When merging the data sets, data must be de-duped.
2. *Missing values need to be filled in*, or those rows should be removed from the analysis. Missing values can be filled in with average or modal or default values.
3. *Data elements should be in common units.* They may need to be transformed from one unit to another. For example, total costs of healthcare and the total number of patients may need to be reduced to cost/patient to allow comparability of that value across health systems. Similarly, financial numbers may need to be converted to a common currency.
4. *Comparability over time.* Data elements may need to be adjusted to make them comparable over time. For example, currency values may need to be adjusted for inflation; they would need to be converted to the same base year for comparability.
5. *Same granularity.* Data should be brought to the same level of granularity to ensure comparability. For example, sales data may be available daily, but the salesperson compensation data may only be available monthly. To relate these variables, the data must be brought to the lowest common denominator, in this case, monthly.
6. *Continuous values may need to be binned* into a few buckets to help with some analyses. For instance, work experience could be binned as low, medium, and high.
7. *Outlier data elements need to be removed* after careful review, to avoid the skewing of results. For example, one big donor could skew the analysis of alumni donors in an educational setting.
8. *Ensure that the data is representative of the phenomena* under analysis by correcting for any biases in the selection of data. For example, if the data includes many more members of one gender than is typical of the population of interest, then adjustments need to be applied to the data.

9. Data may need to be selected to *increase information density*. Some data may not show much variability, because it was not properly recorded or for other reasons. This data may dull the effects of other differences in the data and should be removed to improve the information density of the data.

DATA MINING TECHNIQUES

There are two primary kinds of data mining techniques: supervised learning and unsupervised learning. In supervised learning, a decision model can be created using past data, and the model can then be used to predict the correct answer for future data instances. Classification is the main category of supervised learning activity. Classification models may help make more efficient decisions in the future. Unsupervised learning may be used to explore the data to find interesting associative patterns. The right technique depends upon the kind of problem being solved (Figure 4.1).

Supervised Learning (Predictive ability based on past data)	Classification – Machine Learning	Decision Trees
		Neural Network
	Classification – Statistics	Regression
Unsupervised Learning (Exploratory analysis to discover patterns)	Clustering Analysis	
	Association Rules	

Figure 4.1 Important Data Mining Techniques

The most important class of problems solved using data mining are classification problems. Classification techniques are called supervised learning, as there is a way to supervise whether the model is providing the right or wrong answers. These are problems where data from past decisions is mined to extract a few rules and patterns that would improve the accuracy of the decision-making process in the future. The data of past decisions is organized and mined for decision rules or equations, which are then codified to produce more accurate decisions.

Decision trees are the most popular data mining technique, for many reasons.

1. Decision trees are easy to understand and easy to use, for analysts as well as executives. They also show a high predictive accuracy.
2. Decision trees select the most relevant variables automatically out of all the available variables for decision-making.
3. Decision trees are tolerant of data quality issues and do not require much data preparation from the users.
4. Even non-linear relationships can be handled well by decision trees.

There are many algorithms to implement decision trees. Some of the popular ones are C5, CART, and CHAID.

Regression is the most popular statistical data mining technique. The goal of regression is to derive a smooth well-defined curve to best fit the data. Regression analysis techniques, for example, can be used to model and predict the energy consumption as a function of daily temperature. Simply plotting the data may show a non-linear curve. Applying a non-linear regression equation will fit the data very well with high accuracy. Once such a regression model has been developed, the energy consumption on any future day can be predicted using this equation. The accuracy of the regression model depends entirely upon the dataset used and not at all on the algorithm or tools used.

Artificial Neural Networks (ANN) is a sophisticated data mining technique from the Artificial Intelligence stream in Computer Science. It mimics the behavior of human neural structure: Neurons receive stimuli, process them, and communicate their results to other neurons successively, and eventually a neuron outputs a decision. A decision task may be processed by just one neuron and the result may be communicated soon. Alternatively, there could be many layers of neurons involved in a decision task, depending upon the complexity of the domain. The neural network can be trained into making a good decision repeatedly using many data points. It will continue to learn by adjusting its internal computation and communication parameters based on feedback received on its previous decisions. The intermediate values passed within the layers of neurons may not make any intuitive sense to an observer. Thus, neural networks are considered a black-box system.

For many applications, the predictions of some ANNs that have been trained over a long period of time with a large amount of data have become decisively more accurate than human experts. At that point, the ANNs can begin to be seriously considered for deployment, in real situations in real time. ANNs are popular because they are eventually able to reach high predictive accuracy. ANNs are also relatively simple to implement and do not have any issues with data quality. However, ANNs require a lot of data to train them to develop good predictive ability.

Cluster Analysis is an unsupervised or exploratory learning technique that helps in identifying sets of similar groups in the data. It is a computational technique used for automatic identification of natural groupings of things. Data instances that are similar to (or near) each other are categorized into one cluster, while data instances that are different (or far away) from each other are categorized into separate clusters. There can be any number of clusters that could be produced by the data. The K-means technique is a popular technique and allows the user guidance in selecting the right number (K) of clusters from the data.

Cluster analysis is also known as the segmentation technique. It helps divide and conquer large data sets. The technique shows the clusters of things from past data. The output is the centroids for each cluster and the allocation of data points to their cluster. The centroid definition is used to assign new data instances that can be assigned to their cluster homes. Clustering is also a part of the artificial intelligence family of techniques.

Association rules are a popular data mining method in business, especially where selling is involved. Also known as market basket analysis, it helps in answering questions about cross-selling opportunities. The technique helps find interesting relationships (affinities) between variables (items or events). These are represented as rules of the form *X* ®*Y*, where *X* and *Y* are sets of data items. A form of unsupervised learning, it has no dependent variable; and there are no right or wrong answers. There are just stronger and weaker associations or affinities. Thus, each rule has a confidence level assigned to it. A part of the machine learning family, this technique achieved legendary status when a fascinating relationship was found in the sales of diapers and beers. A variant of this technique is called a Recommendation Engine, which is the heart of the personalization engine used by e-commerce sites like Amazon.com and streaming sites like Netflix.com.

OUTPUTS OF DATA MINING

Data mining techniques can serve different types of objectives. The outputs of data mining will reflect the objective being served. There are many ways of representing the outputs of data mining.

One popular form of data mining output is a decision tree. It is a hierarchically branched structure that helps visually follow the steps to make a model-based decision. The tree may have certain attributes, such as probabilities assigned to each branch. Decision trees can be directly translated into a set of business rules, which are if-then statements that show causality. If the objective function is a prediction, then a decision tree or business rules are the most appropriate mode of representing the output.

Another popular form of output is a regression equation. It is a mathematical function that represents the best fitting curve to represent the data. This equation may include linear and non-linear terms. Regression equations are a good way of representing the output of classification exercises. These are also a good representation of forecasting formulae.

Population "centroid" is a statistical measure for describing central tendencies of a collection of data points. These might be defined in a multidimensional space. For example, a centroid could be "middle-aged, highly educated, high-net worth professionals, married with two children, living in the coastal areas." Or a population of "20-something, ivy-league-educated, tech entrepreneurs based in Silicon Valley." Or it could be a collection of "vehicles more than 20 years old, giving low mileage per gallon, which failed environmental inspection." These are typical representations of the output of a cluster analysis exercise.

Association rules are an appropriate representation of the output of a market basket analysis exercise. These rules are if-then statements with some probability parameters associated with each rule. For example, those that buy milk and bread will also buy butter (with 80 percent probability). Business rules can be converted into decision trees and vice versa.

EVALUATING DATA MINING RESULTS

A common metric for all classification techniques is predictive accuracy.

Predictive Accuracy = (Correct Predictions) / Total Predictions

Suppose a data mining project has been initiated to develop a predictive model for cancer patients using a decision tree. Using a relevant set of variables and data instances, a decision tree model has been created. The model is then used to predict other data instances. When a true positive data point is judged by the model as positive, that is a correct prediction, called a true positive (TP). Similarly, when a true negative data point is classified as negative by the model, that is a true negative (TN). On the other hand, when a true positive data point is classified by the model as negative, that is an incorrect prediction, called a false negative (FN). Similarly, when a true negative data point is classified as positive, that is classified as a false positive (FP). This is represented using the confusion matrix (Figure 4.2).

Confusion Matrix		True Class	
		Positive	**Negative**
Predicted Class	**Positive**	True Positive (TP)	False Positive (FP)
	Negative	False Negative (FN)	True Negative (TN)

Figure 4.2 Confusion Matrix

Thus, the predictive accuracy can be specified by the following formula:

$$\text{Predictive Accuracy} = \frac{(\text{TP}+\text{TN})}{(\text{TP}+\text{TN}+\text{FP}+\text{FN})}.$$

All classification techniques have a predictive accuracy associated with a predictive model. The highest value can be 100%. In practice, predictive models with more than 70% accuracy can be considered usable in business domains, depending upon the nature of the business. Neural networks have achieved very high predictive accuracy reaching 90% and above in some domains.

There are no good objective measures to judge the accuracy of unsupervised learning techniques such as Cluster Analysis. There is no single right answer for the results of these techniques. For example, the value of the segmentation model depends upon the value the decision-maker sees in those results. Similarly, a recommendation engine or an association rule is associated with a certain probability of accuracy, and the user can decide which rules to use.

TOOLS AND PLATFORMS FOR DATA MINING

Data Mining tools have existed for many decades. However, they have recently become more important, as the values of data have grown and the field of big data analytics has come into prominence. There are a wide range of data mining platforms available in the market today.

1. *Stand-alone or Embedded*: There are standalone tools and there are tools embedded in an existing transaction processing or data warehousing or ERP system.

2. *Sophistication of features*: There are simple end-user data mining tools such as MS Excel, and there are more sophisticated tools such as IBM SPSS Modeler.
3. *Open source or Commercial*: There are open source and freely available tools such as Weka, and there are commercial products.
4. *User interface*: There are text-based tools such as R and Python that require some programming skills, and there are also GUI based drag-and-drop format tools available.
5. *Data formats*: There are tools that work only on proprietary data formats and there are those that directly accept data from a host of popular data management tools formats.

Table 4.1 compares four platforms that we have used extensively and effectively for many data mining projects.

Table 4.1 Comparison of Some Popular Data Mining Platforms

Feature	Excel	Weka	R	IBM SPSS Modeler
Ownership	Commercial	Open-source, free	Open-source, free	Commercial, expensive
Data Mining Features	Limited; extensible with add-on modules	Extensive features, issues with large data sets	Extensive features	Extensive features, unlimited data sizes
Stand-alone	Stand-alone	Stand-alone	Embeddable in other systems	Embedded in BI software suites
User skills needed	End-users	Skilled BI analysts	Programming skills	For skilled BI analysts
User interface	Text and click, Easy	GUI, mostly b&w text output	Integrated Development Environment	Drag & Drop use, colorful, beautiful GUI
Data formats	Industry-standard	Proprietary, CSV	CSV	Variety of data formats

MS Excel is a relatively simple and easy data mining tool. It can get quite versatile once Analyst Pack and some other add-on products are installed on it.

Weka is an open-source GUI based tool that offers a large number of data mining algorithms.

R is an extensive and extensible, versatile open-source statistical programming language with 600+ libraries and 120,000 functions. It is very popular with startup companies, and increasingly so in large organizations. Python is similarly an extensible open-source language.

IBM's SPSS Modeler is an industry-leading data mining platform. It offers a powerful set of tools and algorithms for the most popular data mining capabilities. It has a colorful GUI format with drag-and-drop capabilities. It can accept data in multiple formats including reading Excel files directly.

SAP has its Business Objects (BO) software. BO is considered one of the leading BI suites in the industry and is often used by organizations that use SAP.

DATA MINING BEST PRACTICES

Effective and successful use of data mining activity requires both business and technology skills. The business aspects help understand the domain and the key questions. It also helps one imagine possible relationships in the data and create hypotheses to test them. The IT aspects help fetch the data from many sources, clean up the data, assemble it to meet the needs of the business problem, and then run the data mining techniques on the platform.

An important element in data mining is to create an effective process to go after the problem iteratively. It may be better to pilot the project with smaller amounts of representative data and get closer to the heart of the solution in an iterative sequence of steps. There are several best practices learned from the use of data mining techniques over a long period of time. The Data Mining industry has proposed a Cross-Industry Standard Process for Data Mining (CRISP-DM). It has six essential steps (Figure 4.3):

Figure 4.3 CRISP-DM Data Mining Cycle

1. *Business Understanding*: The first and most important step in data mining is asking the right business questions. A question is a good one if answering it would lead to large payoffs for the organization, financially or otherwise. In other words, selecting a data mining project is like selecting any other project, in that it should show strong payoffs if the project is successful. There should be strong executive support for the data mining project, which means that the project aligns well with the business strategy. A related important step is to be creative and open in proposing imaginative hypotheses for the solution. Thinking outside the box is important, both in terms of a proposed model and in the data sets available and required.
2. *Data Understanding*: A related important step is to understand the data available for mining. One needs to be imaginative in scouring for many elements of data through many sources in helping address the hypotheses to solve a problem. Without relevant data, the hypotheses cannot be tested. Therefore, there is an implicit dance between steps 1 and 2. One needs to select a business problem for which relevant data can be available.
3. *Data Preparation*: The data should be relevant, clean, and of high quality. It is important to assemble a team that has a mix of technical and business skills, who understand the domain and the data. Data cleaning can take 80-90% of the time in a data mining project. It may be desirable to continue to experiment and add new data elements from external sources of data that could help improve predictive accuracy.
4. *Modeling*: This is the task of running many algorithms using the available data to discover if the hypotheses are supported. Patience is required in continuously engaging with the data until the data yields some good insights. A host of modeling tools and algorithms should be used. A tool could be tried with different options, such as running different decision tree algorithms.
5. *Model Evaluation*: One should not accept what the data says at first. It is better to triangulate the analysis by applying multiple data mining techniques, and conducting many what-if scenarios, to build confidence in the solution. One should evaluate and improve the model's predictive accuracy with more test data. When the accuracy has reached some satisfactory level, then the model should be deployed.
6. *Dissemination and rollout:* It is important that the data mining solution is presented to the key stakeholders, before it is deployed in the organization. Without deployment, the project will be a waste of time and will be a setback for establishing and supporting a data-based decision-process culture in the organization. The model should eventually be embedded in the organization's business processes.

MYTHS ABOUT DATA MINING

There are many myths about this area, scaring away many business executives from using data mining. Data mining is a mindset that presupposes faith in the ability to reveal insights. By itself, data mining is not too hard, nor is it too easy. It does require a disciplined approach and some cross-disciplinary skills.

Myth #1: Data Mining is about algorithms. Data mining is used by businesses to answer important and practical business questions. Formulating the problem statement correctly and identifying imaginative solutions for testing are far more important before the data mining algorithms are called in. Understanding the relative strengths of various algorithms is helpful but not mandatory.

Myth #2: Data Mining is about predictive accuracy. While important, predictive accuracy is a feature of the algorithm. As in Myth#1, the quality of output is a strong function of the right problem, the right hypothesis, and the right data. There are also unsupervised learning techniques where predictive accuracy is not relevant.

Myth #3: Data Mining requires a DW. While the presence of a DW assists in the gathering of cleansed information, sometimes the creation of the DW itself can benefit from some exploratory data mining. Some data mining problems may benefit from clean data available directly from the DW, but a DW is not mandatory.

Myth #4: Data Mining requires large quantities of data. Many interesting data mining exercises are done using small or medium sized data sets, at low costs, using end-user tools.

Myth #5: Data Mining requires a technology expert. Many interesting data mining exercises are done by end-users and executives using simple everyday tools like spreadsheets.

DATA MINING MISTAKES

Data mining is an exercise in extracting non-trivial useful patterns in the data. It requires a lot of preparation and patience to pursue the many leads that data may provide. Much domain knowledge, tools, and skills are required to find such patterns. Here are some of the more common mistakes in doing data mining that should be avoided.

Mistake #1: Selecting the wrong problem for data mining: Without the right goals or having no goals, data mining leads to a waste of time. Getting the right answer to an irrelevant question could be interesting, but it would be pointless from a business perspective. A good goal would be one that would deliver a good ROI to the organization.

Mistake #2: Buried under mountains of data without clear metadata: It is more important to be engaged with the data, than to have a lot of data. The relevant data required may be much less than initially thought. There may be insufficient knowledge about the data, or metadata. One should examine the data with a critical eye and not naively believe everything that one is told about the data.

Mistake #3: Disorganized data mining: Without clear goals, much time is wasted. Doing the same tests using the same mining algorithms repeatedly and blindly, without thinking about the next stage and without a plan, would lead to wasted time and energy. This can come from being sloppy about keeping track of the data mining procedure and results. Not leaving sufficient time for data acquisition, selection, and preparation can lead to data quality issues, and GIGO (or Garbage-In-Garbage-Out). Similarly, not providing enough time for testing the model, training the users and deploying the system, can make the project a failure.

Mistake #4: Insufficient business knowledge: Without a deep understanding of the business domain, the results would be uninterpretable and meaningless. Don't make erroneous assumptions, courtesy of experts. Don't rule out anything when observing data analysis results. Don't ignore suspicious (good or bad) findings and quickly move on. Be open to surprises. Even when insights emerge at one level, it is important to slice and dice the data at other levels to see if more powerful insights can be extracted.

Mistake #5: Incompatibility of data mining tools and datasets. All the tools from data gathering, preparation, mining, and visualization should work together. Use tools that can work with data from multiple sources in multiple industry standard formats. Much time can be spent in transforming data across tools.

Mistake #6: Looking only at aggregated results and not at individual records/predictions. It is possible that the right results at the aggregate level provide absurd conclusions at an individual record level. Diving into the data at the right angle can yield insights at any and many levels of data.

Mistake #7: Not measuring your results differently from the way your sponsor measures them. If the data mining team loses its sense of business objectives, and begins to mine data for its own sake, it will lose respect and executive support very quickly. The BIDM cycle (Figure 1.1) should be remembered.

CONCLUSION

Data Mining is like diving into the rough material to discover a valuable finished nugget. While the technique is important, domain knowledge is more important to provide imaginative solutions that can then be tested with data mining. The business objective should be well understood and should always be kept in mind to ensure that results are beneficial to the sponsor of the exercise. There are many data mining techniques that can be used for solving different problems.

REVIEW QUESTIONS

1. What is data mining?
2. What are supervised and unsupervised learning? What are the techniques?
3. Describe the key steps in the CRISP-DM process. Why is it important to follow these processes?
4. How can predictive accuracy be measured? What is a confusion matrix?
5. Why is data preparation so important and time consuming?
6. What are some of the most popular data mining techniques?
7. What are the major mistakes to be avoided when doing data mining?
8. What are the key requirements for a skilled data analyst?

TRUE/FALSE

1. Data mining seeks to identify patterns in the data.
2. Data mining is about using the algorithms with the highest predictive accuracy to model and solve a business problem.
3. Data cleansing and preparation for data mining takes about one-third of the time of the entire data mining project.
4. The first and most important practice in data mining is to understand the sources and quality of data.
5. The goal of supervised learning is to analyze the historical data stored in a database and automatically generate a model that can predict future behavior.
6. Regression equations are a good way of representing the output of clustering exercises.
7. Predictive Accuracy = Correct Predictions/Total Predictions
8. CRISP-DM is the name of a data modeling tool.
9. Neural networks are a versatile data mining technique.
10. Decision trees can generate knowledge from a few instances that can then be applied to a broad population.

CASELET

MAALA STORES Case Exercise: Step 3

Maala is constantly evaluating opportunities for improving efficiencies in its sales operations, including commercial operations.

1: *What data mining techniques would you use to analyze and predict sales patterns?*

2: *What data mining technique would you use to categorize its customer?*

CHAPTER 5

Data Visualization

Learning Objectives

LO 1 Understand the concept of data visualization and its critical role in decision-making

LO 2 Summarize the key rules for effective visualization

LO 3 Know the type and range of graphic devices available

LO 4 Appreciate the step-by-step process of telling a story with data visualizations

Data visualization is the art and science of making data easy to understand and consume, for the end user. Ideal visualization shows the right amount of data, in the right order, in the right visual form, to convey the high priority information. The right visualization requires an understanding of the consumer's needs, the nature of the data, and many tools and techniques available to present data. The right visualization arises from a complete understanding of the totality of the situation. One should use visuals to tell a true, complete, and fast-paced story.

Data visualization is the final step in the data life cycle. This is where the data is processed for presentation in an easy-to-consume manner to the right audience for the right purpose. The data should be converted into a language and format that is best preferred and understood by the consumer of data. The presentation should aim to highlight the insights from the data in an actionable manner. If the data is presented in too much detail, then the consumer of that data might lose interest and insight.

CASELET

Dr. Hans Gosling – Visualizing Global Public Health

Dr. Hans Rosling is a master at data visualization. He has perfected the art of showing data in novel ways to highlight unexpected truths. He has become an online star by using data visualization to make serious points about global health policy and development. Using novel ways to illustrate data obtained from UN agencies, he has helped demonstrate the progress that the world has made in improving public health on many dimensions. The best way to grasp the power of his work is to, where Life Expectancy is mapped along with Fertility Rate for all countries from 1962 to 2003.

"THE biggest myth is that if we save all the poor kids, we will destroy the planet," says Hans Rosling, a doctor and professor of international health at the Karolinska Institute in Sweden. "But you can't stop population growth by letting poor children die." He has computerized graphs to prove it: colorful visuals with circles that swarm, swell, and shrink like living creatures. Dr Rosling's mesmerizing graphics have been impressing audiences on the international lecture circuit, from the TED conferences to the World Economic Forum at Davos. Instead of bar charts and histograms, Dr Rosling uses Lego bricks, IKEA boxes, and data-visualization software developed by his Gapminder Foundation to transform reams of economic and public-health data into gripping stories. His aim is ambitious. "I produce a road map for the modern world," he says. "Where people want to drive is up to them. But I have the idea that if they have a proper road map and know what the global realities are, they'll make better decisions." (To know more visit economist.com).

Q1: *What are the business implications of data visualization?*

Q2: *How could these techniques be applied in your organization and work?*

EXCELLENCE IN VISUALIZATION

Data can be presented in the form of rectangular *tables*, or it can be presented in colorful graphs of various types. "Small, non-comparative, highly-labeled data sets usually belong in tables" (Ed Tufte, 2001, p 33). However, as the amount of data grows, graphs are preferable. Graphics help give shape to the data. Tufte, a pioneering expert on data visualization, presents the following objectives for graphical excellence:

1. *Show, and even reveal, the data*: The data should tell a story, especially a story hidden in large masses of data. However, reveal the data in context, so that the story is told correctly.
2. *Induce the viewer to think of the substance of the data*: The format of the graph should be so natural to the data that the format hides itself and lets the data shine.
3. *Avoid distorting what the data have to say*: Statistics can be used to lie. In the name of simplifying, some crucial context could be removed leading to distorted communication.
4. *Make large data sets coherent*: By giving shape to data, visualizations can help bring the data together to tell a comprehensive story.
5. *Encourage the eyes to compare different pieces of data*: Organize the chart in such ways that the eyes would naturally move to derive insights from the chart.
6. *Reveal the data at several levels of detail*: Graphs lead to insights, which raise further curiosity, and thus presentations should help to progressively get to the root cause.

7. *Serve a reasonably clear purpose*: Informing or decision-making, based on who is the target audience.
8. *Closely integrate with the statistical and verbal descriptions of the dataset*: There should be no separation of charts and text in the presentation. Each mode should tell a complete story. Intersperse text with the map/graphic to highlight the main insights.

Context is important in interpreting graphics. The perception of the chart is as important as the actual charts. Do not ignore the intelligence or the biases of the reader. Keep the template consistent, and only show variations in data. There can be many excuses for graphical distortion, for example, "just approximating." Quality of information transmission comes prior to aesthetics of chart. Leaving out contextual data can be misleading.

A lot of graphics are published because they serve a particular cause or a point of view. It is particularly important when in a for-profit or politically contested environment. Many related dimensions can be folded into a graph. The more the number of dimensions that are represented in a graph, the richer and more useful the chart becomes. The data visualizer should understand the client's objectives and present the data for accurate perception of the totality of the situation.

TYPES OF CHARTS

There are many kinds of data for graphing. Time series data is the most popular form of data. It helps reveal patterns over time. However, data could be organized around an alphabetical list of things, such as countries or products or salespeople. Figure 5.2 shows some of the popular chart types and their usage.

1. *Line graph*. This is a basic and most popular type of displaying information. It shows data as a series of points connected by straight line segments. If one is presenting time-series data, time is usually shown on the x-axis. Multiple variables can be represented on the same scale on y-axis to compare the line graphs of all the variables.
2. *Scatter plot:* This is another very basic and useful graphic form. It helps reveal the relationship between two variables. In the Roslingcaselet, it showed two dimensions: Life Expectancy and Fertility Rate. Unlike in a line graph, there are no line segments connecting the points.
3. *Bar graph:* A bar graph shows thin colorful rectangular bars with their lengths being proportional to the values represented. The bars can be plotted vertically or horizontally. The bar graphs use a lot more ink than the line graph and should be used when line graphs are inadequate.

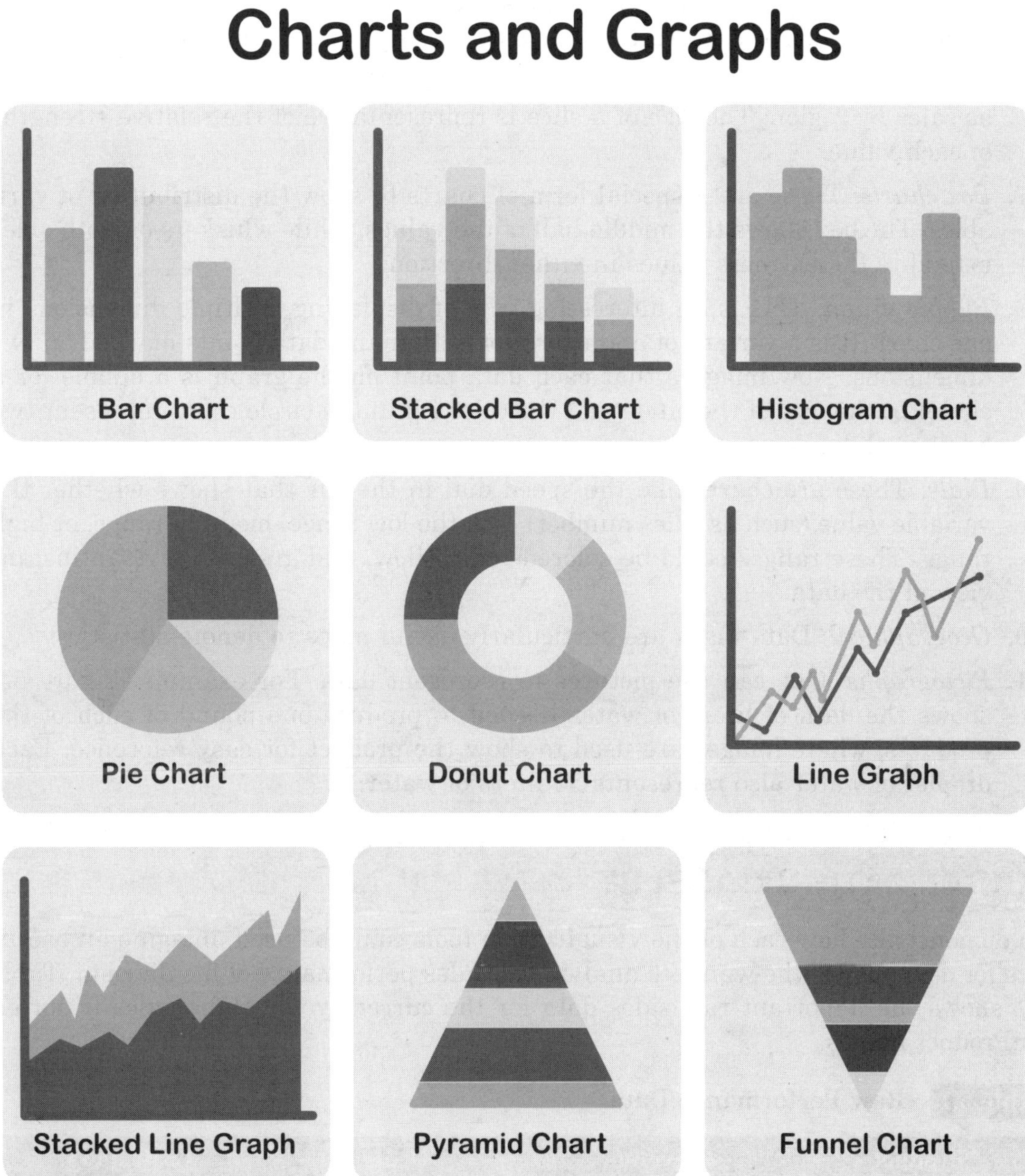

Figure 5.1 Different Types of Graphs

4. *Stacked bar graphs:* These are a particular method of doing bar graphs. Values of multiple variables are stacked one on top of the other to tell an interesting story. Bars can also be normalized such as the total height of every bar is equal, so it can show the relative composition of each bar.

5. *Histograms*: These are like bar graphs, except that they are useful in showing data frequencies or data values on classes (or ranges) of a numerical variable.
6. *Pie charts*: These are very popular to show the distribution of a variable, such as sales by region. The size of a slice is representative of the relative strengths of each value.
7. *Box charts:* These are a special form of charts to show the distribution of variables. The box shows the middle half of the values, while whiskers on both sides extend to the extreme values in either direction.
8. *Bubble graph*: This is an interesting way of displaying multiple dimensions in one chart. It is a variant of a scatter plot with many data points marked on two dimensions. Now imagine that each data point on the graph is a bubble (or a circle) ... the size of the circle and the color fill in the circle could represent two additional dimensions.
9. *Dials*: These are charts like the speed dial in the car that shows whether the variable value (such as sales number) is in the low range, medium range, or high range. These ranges could be colored red, yellow, and green to give an instant view of the data.
10. *Geographical*: Data maps are particularly useful maps to denote statistics.
11. *Pictographs*: One can use pictures to represent data. For example, Figure 5.2 shows the data of liters of water needed to produce one pound of each of the products, where images are used to show the product for easy reference. Each droplet of water also represents 50 liters of water.

VISUALIZATION CASELET

To demonstrate how each of the visualization tools could be used, imagine an executive for a company who wants to analyze the sales performance of his division. Table 5.1 shows the important raw sales data for the current year, alphabetically sorted by Product names.

Table 5.1 Raw Performance Data

Product	Revenue	Orders	SalesPers
AA	9731	131	23
BB	355	43	8
CC	992	32	6
DD	125	31	4
EE	933	30	7

Product	Revenue	Orders	SalesPers
FF	676	35	6
GG	1411	128	13
HH	5116	132	38
JJ	215	7	2
KK	3833	122	50
LL	1348	15	7
MM	1201	28	13

Phase 1

To reveal some meaningful pattern, a good first step would be to sort the table by Product revenue, with the highest revenue first. One could total up the values of Revenue, Orders, and Salespersons for all products. One can also add some important ratios to the right of the table (Table 5.2). Thus, the table expands with three new columns of computed values for comparability.

Table 5.2 Sorted Data, with Additional Ratios

Product	Revenue	Orders	SalesPers	*Rev/Order*	*Rev/SalesP*	*Orders/SalesP*
AA	9731	131	23	*74.3*	*423.1*	*5.7*
HH	5116	132	38	*38.8*	*134.6*	*3.5*
KK	3833	122	50	*31.4*	*76.7*	*2.4*
GG	1411	128	13	*11.0*	*108.5*	*9.8*
LL	1348	15	7	*89.9*	*192.6*	*2.1*
MM	1201	28	13	*42.9*	*92.4*	*2.2*
CC	992	32	6	*31.0*	*165.3*	*5.3*
EE	933	30	7	*31.1*	*133.3*	*4.3*
FF	676	35	6	*19.3*	*112.7*	*5.8*
BB	355	43	8	*8.3*	*44.4*	*5.4*
JJ	215	7	2	*30.7*	*107.5*	*3.5*
DD	125	31	4	*4.0*	*31.3*	*7.8*
Total	**25936**	**734**	**177**	*35.3*	*146.5*	*4.1*

One could start by visualizing the revenue as a pie-chart. The revenue proportion drops significantly from the first product to the next (Figure 5.2). It is interesting to note that the top three products produce almost 75% of the revenue.

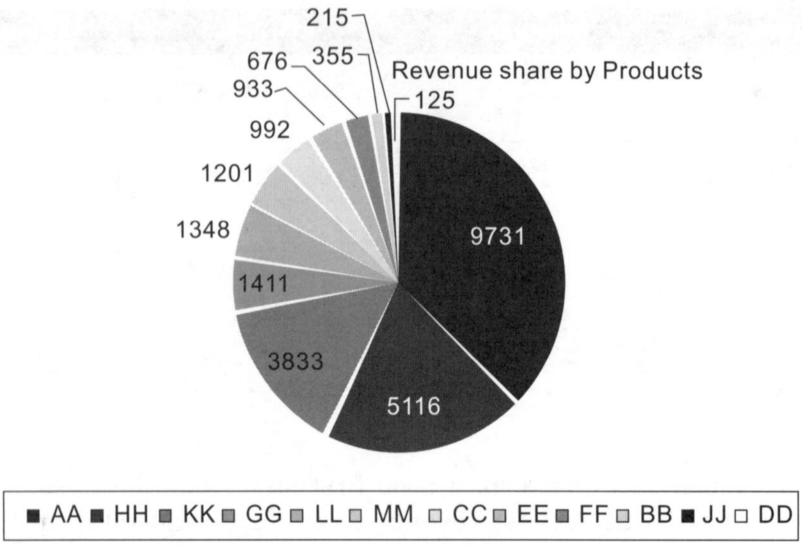

Figure 5.2 Revenue Share by Product

The number of orders for each product can be plotted as a bar graph (Figure 5.3). It is interesting that the top four products have a large and approximately the same number of orders. The orders for the remaining products are miniscule in comparison.

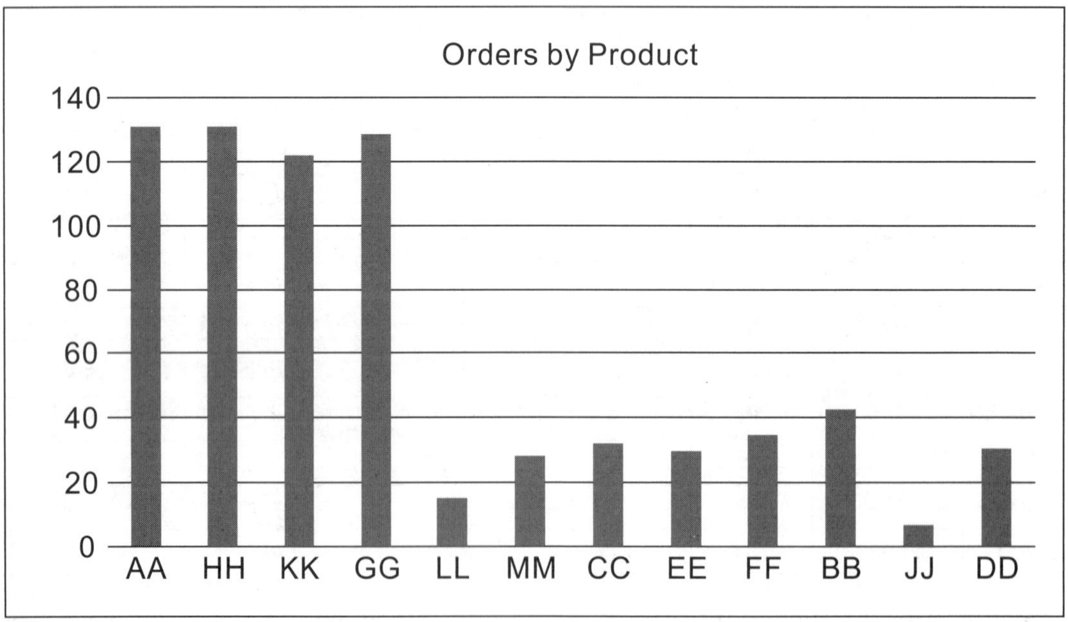

Figure 5.3 Orders by Products

Phase 2

The executive may want to understand the productivity of salespersons. This analysis could be done both in terms of the number of orders, or revenue, per salesperson. There could be two separate graphs, one for the number of orders per salesperson, and the other for the revenue per salesperson. However, an interesting way would be to plot both measures on the same graph to give a more complete picture. This can be done even when the two data have different scales. The data is here resorted by a number of orders per salesperson.

Figure 5.4 shows two line graphs superimposed upon each other. One line shows the revenue per salesperson, while the other line shows the number of orders per salesperson. It shows that the highest productivity of 5.3 orders per salesperson, down to 2.1 orders per salesperson. The second line, the blue line, shows the revenue per salesperson for each of the products. The revenue per salesperson is highest at 630, while it is lowest at just 30.

And thus, additional layers of data visualization can go on for this data set.

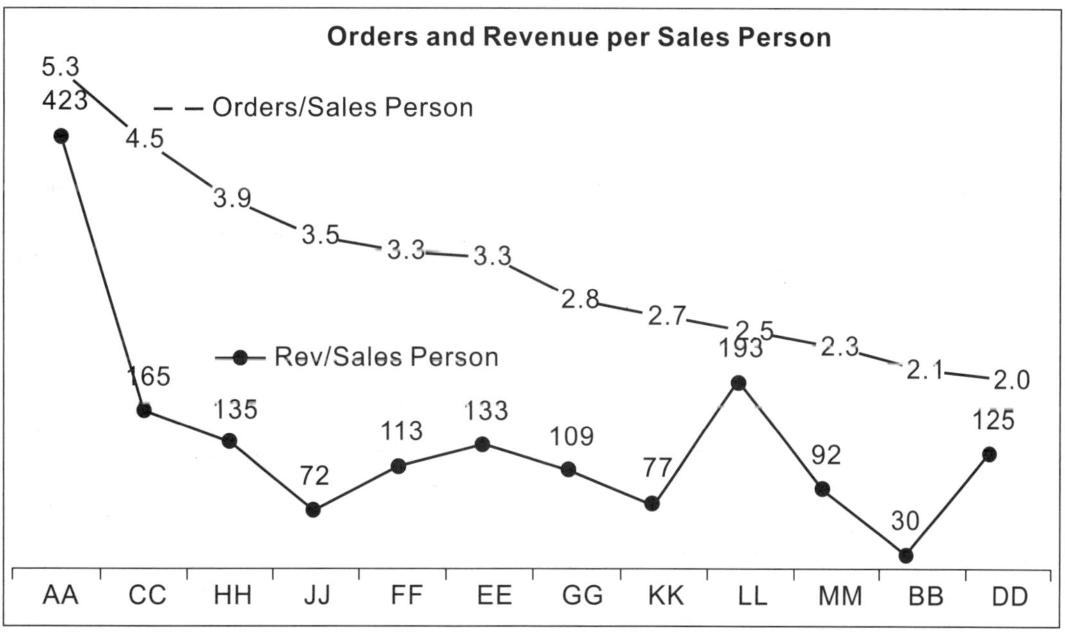

Figure 5.4 Salesperson Productivity by Product

Phase 3

The orders data could be investigated further to examine order patterns. Suppose additional data has been made available for Orders by their size. Suppose the orders are chunked into four sizes: Tiny, Small, Medium, and Large. Additional data is shown in Table 5.3.

Table 5.3 Additional Data on Order Sizes

Product	Total Orders	Tiny	Small	Medium	Large
AA	131	5	44	70	12
HH	132	38	60	30	4
KK	122	20	50	44	8
GG	128	52	70	6	0
LL	15	2	3	5	5
MM	28	8	12	6	2
CC	32	5	17	10	0
EE	30	6	14	10	0
FF	35	10	22	3	0
BB	43	18	25	0	0
JJ	7	4	2	1	0
DD	31	21	10	0	0
Total	734	189	329	185	31

Figure 5.5 is a stacked bar graph that shows the percentage of orders by size for each product. This chart (Figure 5.5) brings a different set of insights. It shows that the product HH has a larger proportion of tiny orders. The products at the far right have a large number of tiny orders and very few large orders.

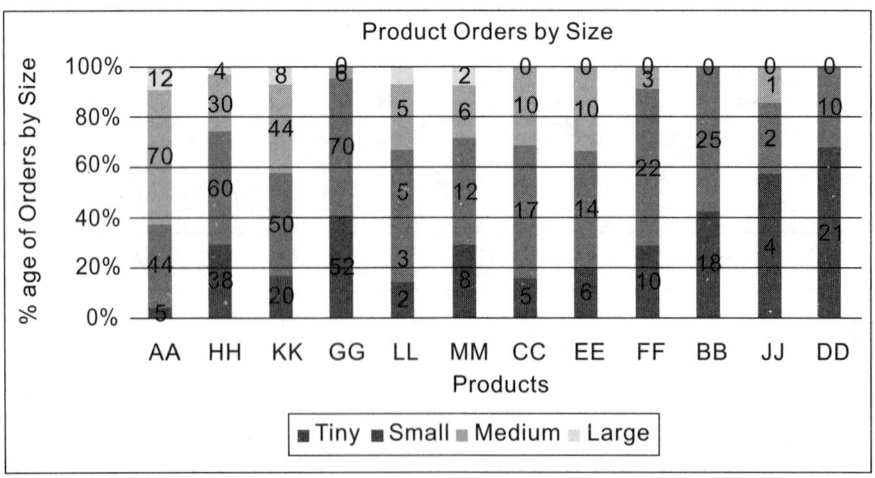

Figure 5.5 Product Orders by Order Size

TIPS FOR DATA VISUALIZATION

To help the client in understanding the situation, the following considerations are important:

1. *Fetch appropriate and correct data for analysis.* This requires some understanding of the domain of the client and what is important for the client. For example, in a business setting, one may need to understand the measures of profitability and productivity.
2. *Sort the data in the most appropriate manner.* It could be sorted by numerical variables, or alphabetically by name.
3. *Choose an appropriate method to present the data.* The data could be presented as a table, or it could be presented as any of the graph types.
4. *The data set could be pruned* to include only the more significant elements. More data is not necessarily better unless it makes the most significant impact on the situation.
5. *The visualization could show additional dimensions for reference* such as the expectations or targets with which to compare the results.
6. *The numerical data may need to be binned into a few categories.* For example, the orders per person were plotted as actual values, while the order sizes were binned into four categorical choices.
7. *High-level visualization could be backed by more detailed analysis.* For the most significant results, a drill-down may be required.
8. *There may be a need to present additional textual information* to tell the whole story. For example, one may require notes to explain some extraordinary results.

CONCLUSION

Data Visualization is the final phase of the data lifecycle and leads to the consumption of data by the end user. It should tell an accurate, complete, and simple story backed by data, while keeping it insightful and engaging. There are innumerable types of visual graphing techniques available for visualizing data. The choice of the right tools requires a good understanding of the business domain, the dataset, and the client's needs. There is ample room for creativity to design ever more compelling data visualizations to convey the insights most efficiently from the data.

REVIEW QUESTIONS

1. What is data visualization?
2. How would you judge the quality of data visualizations?
3. What are key data visualization principles?
4. When would you use tables or graphs?
5. Describe the key steps in data visualization.
6. Describe your favorite data visualization, from popular press or a book that you read, etc.

TRUE/FALSE

1. Data visualization leads to consumption of data.
2. Good graphics are independent of the context of the data.
3. Any data that can be presented in the form of tables can also be presented in colorful graphs.
4. Any particular data visualization should reveal the data at the aggregate level or the detail level, but not at both.
5. A scatter plot is the most popular type of displaying information.
6. A bubble chart can display more dimensions than a pie chart.
7. One should use data visualizations to tell a true, complete and fast-paced story.
8. When presenting results, the analyst should focus on the data and the analysis, and not draw any conclusions.
9. A good visualization should maximize the amount of data that can be packed into it.
10. A decision tree is a form of data visualization.

CASELET

MAALA STORES Case Exercise: Step 4

Maala is constantly evaluating its performance for improving efficiencies in all its operations, including commercial operations as well as charitable activities.

1: *What data visualization techniques would you use to help understand sales patterns?*

2: *What data visualization technique would you use to categorize its customers?*

Section 2
Popular Data Mining Techniques

This section covers five important data mining techniques.

The first three techniques are examples of supervised learning, consisting of classification techniques.

- Chapter 6 covers decision trees, which are the most popular form of data mining techniques. There are many algorithms to develop decision trees.
- Chapter 7 describes regression modeling techniques. These are statistical techniques.
- Chapter 8 covers artificial neural networks, which are machine learning techniques.

The next two techniques are examples of unsupervised learning, consisting of data exploration techniques.

- Chapter 9 covers Cluster Analysis. This is also called Market Segmentation analysis.
- Chapter 10 covers the Association Rule Mining technique, also called Market Basket Analysis.

CHAPTER

6 Decision Trees

Learning Objectives

LO 1	Understand the concept of Decision Trees
LO 2	Know the importance of decision trees in data mining
LO 3	Learn how to construct a decision tree from a given dataset
LO 4	Know about algorithms for making decision trees, and their comparative features

Decision trees are a simple way to guide one's path to making decisions. Decision trees are hierarchically branched structures that help one come to a decision based on asking certain questions in a particular sequence. A good decision tree should be short, clear, balanced, and ask only a few meaningful questions. Decision trees are one of the most widely used techniques for classification. Decision trees are very efficient to use, easy to explain, and their classification accuracy is competitive with other methods. Decision trees can generate knowledge from a few test instances that can then be applied to a broad population. They are used mostly to answer relatively simple binary decisions.

CASELET

Predicting Heart Attacks Using Decision Trees

A study was done at UC San Diego concerning heart disease patient data. The patients were diagnosed with a heart attack from chest pain, diagnosed by EKG, high enzyme levels in their heart muscles, etc. The objective was to predict which of these patients was at risk of dying from a second heart attack within the next 30 days. The prediction would determine the treatment plan, such as whether to keep the patient in intensive care or not. For each patient, more than 100 variables were collected, including demographics, medical history, and lab data. Using that data, and the CART algorithm, a decision tree was constructed.

The decision tree showed that if Blood Pressure was low (<=90), the chance of another heart attack was very high (70%). If the patient's BP was ok, the next question to ask was the patient's age. If the age was low (<=62), then the patient's survival was almost guaranteed (98%). If the age was higher, then the next question to ask was about sinus problems. If their sinus was ok, the chances of survival were 89%. Otherwise, the chance of survival dropped to 50%. This decision tree predicts 86.5% of the cases correctly. (To know more see: Salford Systems).

Q1: *Is a decision tree good enough in terms of accuracy, design, readability, for this data, etc.*

Q2: *Identify the benefits of creating such a decision tree. Can these be quantified?*

DECISION TREE PROBLEM

Imagine a conversation between a doctor and a patient. The doctor asks questions to determine the cause of the ailment. The decision may be a binary one, such as whether to admit the patient or not. Or it may be a complex multi-valued decision, as to what may be the diagnosis for a particular set of medical symptoms. The doctor would continue to ask questions, till they are able to arrive at a reasonable decision. If nothing seems plausible, they might recommend some tests to generate more data and options.

This is essentially how experts in any field solve problems. They use decision trees or decision rules. For every question they ask, the potential answers eliminate some possibilities, and create separate branches of logic for further questioning. For each branch, the expert would know how to proceed ahead. The process continues until the end of the tree is reached, which means a leaf node is reached, which will announce a decision.

Human experts learn from past experiences or data points. Similarly, a machine can be trained to learn from past data points and extract some knowledge or rules from them. Decision trees use simple iterative algorithms to abstract knowledge from data. A decision tree's predictive accuracy would depend upon how often it makes correct decisions. Here are some general insights:

1. The more data is available for training the decision tree, the more accurate its knowledge extraction will be, and thus, it will make more accurate decisions. However, conflicting data can also generate noise and make a decision tree impossible.
2. The more variables the tree can choose from, the greater is the likely accuracy of the decision tree.
3. In addition, a good decision tree should also be frugal so that it takes the least number of questions, and thus, the least amount of effort, to get to the right decision.

DECISION TREE EXERCISE

Here is an exercise to create a decision tree that helps make decisions about approving the play of an outdoor game. The objective is to predict the play decision given the atmospheric conditions out there. The decision is: Should the game be allowed or not? Here is the decision problem.

Outlook	Temp	Humidity	Windy	Play
Sunny	Hot	Normal	True	??

To answer that question, one should look at past experiences, and see what decision was made in a similar instance, if such an instance exists. One could look up the database of past decisions to find the answer and try to come to an answer. Here is a list of the decisions taken in 14 instances of past soccer game situations. (Dataset courtesy: Witten, Frank, and Hall, 2010).

Temp	Outlook	Humidity	Windy	Play
Hot	Sunny	High	False	*No*
Hot	Sunny	High	True	*No*
Hot	Overcast	High	False	*Yes*
Mild	Rainy	High	False	*Yes*
Cool	Rainy	Normal	False	*Yes*
Cool	Rainy	Normal	True	*No*
Cool	Overcast	Normal	True	*Yes*
Mild	Sunny	High	False	*No*
Cool	Sunny	Normal	False	*Yes*
Mild	Rainy	Normal	False	*Yes*
Mild	Sunny	Normal	True	*Yes*
Mild	Overcast	High	True	*Yes*
Hot	Overcast	Normal	False	*Yes*
Mild	Rainy	High	True	*No*

Source: Witten et al., "Weather Data", Data Mining

If there were a row for *Sunny/Hot/Normal/Windy* condition in the data table, it would match the current problem; and the decision from that row could be used to answer the current problem. However, there is no such past instance in this case. There are three disadvantages of looking up the data table:

1. It is not possible to decide if there isn't a row that corresponds to the exact situation today. If there is no exact matching instance available in the database, past experience cannot accurately guide the decision.
2. Searching through the entire past database may be time consuming, depending on the number of variables and the organization of the database.
3. If the data values are not available for all the variables, then the lookup becomes difficult. In this instance, if the data for humidity variable was not available, looking up the past data would not help.

A better way of solving the problem may be to abstract the knowledge from the past data into decision trees or rules. These rules can be represented in a decision tree, and then that tree can be used to make the decisions. The decision tree may not need values for all the variables.

DECISION TREE CONSTRUCTION

A decision tree is a hierarchically branched structure. What should be the first question asked in creating the tree? One should ask the more important question first, and the less important questions later. What is the most important question that should be asked to solve the problem? How is the importance of the questions determined? Thus, how should the root node of the tree be determined?

Determining root node of the tree: In this example, there are four choices based on the four variables. One could begin by asking one of the following questions: what is the outlook, what is the temperature, what is the humidity, or what is the wind speed? A criterion should be used to evaluate these choices. The key criterion would be to choose the variable which one of these questions gives the most insight about the situation. Another way to look at it would be the criterion of frugality. That is, which question will provide us the shortest ultimate decision tree. Another way to look at this is that if one is allowed to ask one and only one question, which one would one ask. In this case, the most important question should be the one that, by itself, helps make the most correct decisions with the fewest errors. The four choices can now be systematically compared, to see which variable by itself will help make the most correct decisions. One should systematically calculate the correctness of decisions based on each question. Then, one can select the question with the most correct predictions, or the fewest errors.

Start with the first variable, in this case outlook. It can take three values, sunny, overcast, and rainy.

Start with the sunny value of outlook. There are five instances where the outlook is sunny. In two of the five instances, the *play* decision was *yes*, and in the other three, the decision was No. Thus, if the decision rule was that Outlook:sunny → No, then three out of five decisions would be correct, while two out of five such decisions would be incorrect. There are two errors out of five. This can be recorded in Row 1.

Attribute	Rules	Error	Total Error
Outlook	Sunny→No	2/5	

Similar analysis would be done for other values of the outlook variable. There are four instances where the outlook is overcast. In all four out of four instances, the Play decision was yes. Thus, if the decision rule was that Outlook:overcast → Yes, then four out of four decisions would be correct, while none of the decisions would be incorrect. There are 0 errors out of 4. This can be recorded in the next row.

Attribute	Rules	Error	Total Error
Outlook	Sunny→No	2/5	
	Overcast →yes	0/4	

There are five instances where the outlook is rainy. In three of the five instances, the *play* decision was *yes*, and in the other three, the decision was *no*. Thus, if the decision rule was that Outlook:rainy→ Yes, then three out of five decisions would be correct, while two out of five decisions would be incorrect. There will be 2/5 errors. This can be recorded in the next row.

Attribute	Rules	Error	Total Error
Outlook	Sunny→No	2/5	4/14
	Overcast →yes	0/4	
	Rainy →yes	2/5	

Adding up errors for all values of outlook, there are four errors out of 14. In other words, Outlook gives 10 correct decisions out of 14, and four incorrect ones.

A similar analysis can be done for the other three variables. At the end of that analytical exercise, the following Error table will be constructed.

Attribute	Rules	Error	Total Error
Outlook	Sunny→No	2/5	4/14
	Overcast →yes	0/4	
	Rainy →yes	2/5	
Temp	Hot →No	2/4	5/14
	Mild →Yes	2/6	
	Cool → Yes	1/4	
Humidity	High → No	3/7	4/14
	Normal →Yes	1/7	
Windy	False →Yes	2/8	5/14
	True →No	3/6	

The variable that leads to the least number of errors (and thus the largest number of correct decisions) should be chosen as the first node. In this case, two variables have the least number of errors. There is a tie between outlook and humidity, as both have four errors out of 14 instances. The tie can be broken using another criterion, the purity of resulting sub-trees.

If all the errors were concentrated in a few of the sub-trees, and some of the branches were completely free of error, that is preferred from a usability perspective. Outlook has one error-free branch, for the overcast value, while there is no such pure sub-class for the humidity variable. Thus, the tie is broken in favor of outlook. The decision tree will use outlook as the first node, or the first splitting variable. The first question that should be asked to solve the Play problem, is "What is the value of outlook"?

Splitting the Node: From the root node, the decision tree will be split into three branches or sub-trees, one for each of the three values of outlook. Data for the root node (the entire data) will be divided into three segments, one for each of the values of outlook. The sunny branch will inherit the data for the instances that had sunny as the value of outlook. These will be used for further building of that sub-tree. Similarly, the rainy branch will inherit data for the instances that had rainy as the value of outlook. These will be used for further building of that sub-tree. The overcast branch will inherit the data for the instances that had overcast as the outlook. However, there will be no need to build further on that branch. There is a clear decision, *yes*, for all instances when the outlook value is overcast.

The decision tree will look like this after the first level of splitting.

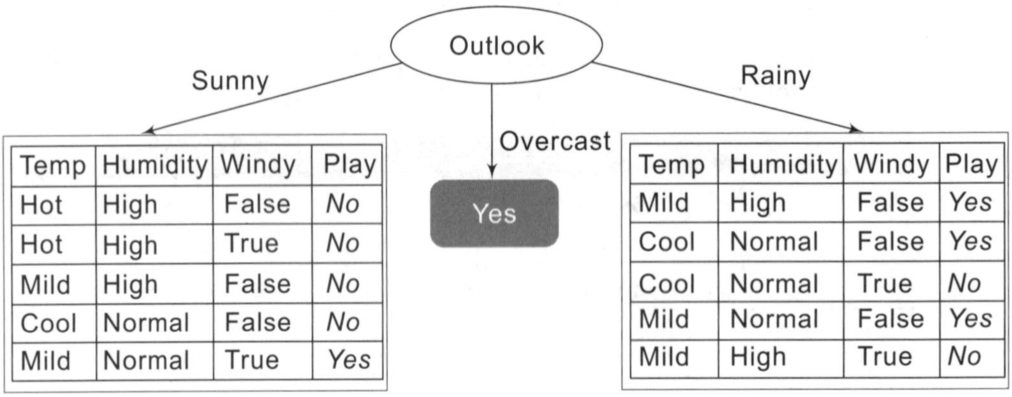

Temp	Humidity	Windy	Play
Hot	High	False	*No*
Hot	High	True	*No*
Mild	High	False	*No*
Cool	Normal	False	*No*
Mild	Normal	True	*Yes*

Temp	Humidity	Windy	Play
Mild	High	False	*Yes*
Cool	Normal	False	*Yes*
Cool	Normal	True	*No*
Mild	Normal	False	*Yes*
Mild	High	True	*No*

Determining the next nodes of the tree: A similar recursive logic of tree building should be applied to each branch. For the sunny branch on the left, error values will be calculated for the three other variables – Temp, Humidity, and Windy. The final comparison looks like this:

Attribute	Rules	Error	Total Error
Temp	Hot->No	0/2	1/5
	Mild->No	1/2	
	Cool->Yes	0/1	
Humidity	High->No	0/3	0/5
	Normal->Yes	0/2	
Windy	False->No	1/3	2/5
	True->Yes	1/2	

The variable of humidity shows the least amount of error, that is, zero error. The other two variables have non-zero errors. Thus, the Outlook:sunny branch on the left will use humidity as the next splitting variable.

Similar analysis should be done for the "rainy" value of the tree. The analysis would look like this.

Attribute	Rules	Error	Total Error
Temp	Mild->Yes	1/3	2/5
	Cool->yes	1/2	
Humidity	High->No	1/2	2/5
	Normal->Yes	1/3	
Windy	False->Yes	0/3	0/5
	True-No	0/2	

For the Rainy branch, it can similarly be seen that the variable Windy gives all the correct answers, while neither of the other two variables makes all the correct decisions.

This is how the final decision tree looks like. Here, it is shown as produced using Weka open-source data mining platform (Figure 6.1). This is the model that abstracts the knowledge of the past data.

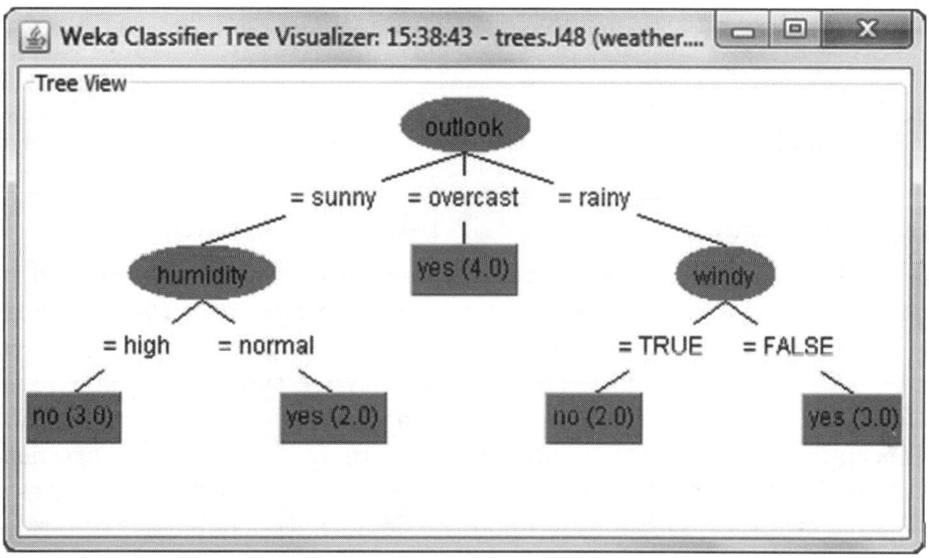

Figure 6.1 Decision Tree for the Weather Problem

This decision tree can be used to solve the current problem. Here is the problem again.

Outlook	Temp	Humidity	Windy	Play
Sunny	Hot	Normal	True	??

According to the tree, the first question to ask is about Outlook. In this problem, the Outlook is Sunny. So, the decision problem moves to the Sunny branch of the tree.

The node in that sub-tree is Humidity. In the problem, Humidity is Normal. That branch leads to an answer Yes. Thus, the answer to the play problem is Yes.

Outlook	Temp	Humidity	Windy	Play
Sunny	Hot	Normal	True	*Yes*

LESSONS FROM CONSTRUCTING TREES

Table 6.1 shows the benefits of using this decision tree compared with looking up the answers from the data table.

Table 6.1 Comparing Decision Tree with Table Look-up

	Decision Tree	Table Lookup
Accuracy	Varied level of accuracy	100% accurate
Generality	General. Applies to all situations	Applies only when a similar case had occurred earlier
Frugality	Only three variables needed	All four variables are needed
Simple	Only one, or max two variable values are needed	All four variable values are needed
Easy	Logical and easy to understand	Can be cumbersome to look up; no understanding of the logic behind the decision

Here are a few observations about how the tree was constructed:

1. The final decision tree in our example has zero errors in mapping to the prior data. In other words, the tree has a *predictive accuracy of 100%*. The tree completely fits the data. In real-life situations, such perfect predictive accuracy may not be possible when making decision trees. When there are larger, complicated data sets, with many more variables, a perfect fit is often unachievable. This is especially true in business and social contexts, where things are not always fully clear and consistent. Thus, one can produce a tree with the highest level of predictive accuracy. Depending upon the domain, trees above 80–90 % accuracy may be quite useful.
2. The decision tree algorithm *selected the minimum number of variables* that are needed to solve the problem. Thus, one can start with all available data variables, and let the decision-tree algorithm select the variables that are useful, and discard the rest.
3. This tree is *almost symmetric* with all branches being of almost similar lengths. However, in real-life situations, some of the branches may be much longer than others, and the tree may need to be pruned to make it more balanced and usable.

4. It may be possible to *increase predictive accuracy by making more sub-trees* and making the tree longer. However, the marginal accuracy gained from each subsequent level in the tree will be less, and it may not be worth the loss in ease and interpretability of the tree. If the branches are long and complicated, it will be difficult to understand and use. The longer branches may need to be trimmed to keep the tree easy to use.
5. A perfectly fitting tree has the *danger of over-fitting the data*, thus capturing all the random variations in the data. It may fit the training data well but may not do well in predicting the future real instances.
6. There was a *single best tree* for this data. There could however be two or more equally efficient decision trees of similar length with similar predictive accuracy for the same data set. Decision trees are *based strictly on patterns within the data*, and do not rely on any underlying theory of the problem domain. When multiple candidate trees are available, one could choose whichever is easier to understand, communicate, or implement.

DECISION TREE ALGORITHM

As we saw, decision trees employ the divide and conquer method. The data is branched at each node, starting with the root node, according to certain criteria until all the data is assigned to leaf nodes. It recursively divides a training set until each division consists of examples from one class.

The following is a pseudo code for making decision trees:

1. Create a root node and assign all the training data to it.
2. Select the best splitting attribute according to certain criteria, such as least error or most information gain.
3. Add a branch to the root node for each value of the split.
4. Split the data from the node into mutually exclusive subsets along the lines of the specific split.
5. Repeat steps 2 and 3 for each and every leaf node until a stopping criterion is reached.

There are many algorithms for making decision trees. Decision tree algorithms differ on three key elements:

1. Splitting criteria
   a. Which variable should be used for the first split? How should one determine the most important variable for the first branch, and subsequently, for each sub-tree?

Algorithms use different measures like least errors, information gain, Gini's coefficient, etc. To compute the splitting variable, the provides the most benefit. Information gain is a mathematical construct to compute the reduction in information entropy from a prior state to the next state that takes some information as given. The greater is the reduction in entropy, the higher is the information gain. The Gini coefficient is a statistical concept that measures the inequality among values of a frequency distribution. The lower is the Gini's coefficient, the better is the decision.

b. What values to use for the split? If the variables have continuous values such as for age or blood pressure, what value-ranges should be used to make bins for splitting the values of that variable? The answer lies in trying out some values based on certain best practices.

c. How many branches should be allowed for each node? There could be binary trees, with just two branches at each node. Or there could be more branches allowed.

2. Stopping criteria: When should one stop building the tree? There are two major ways to make that determination. The tree building could be stopped when a certain depth of the branches has been reached and the tree becomes unreadable after that. The tree could also be stopped when the error level at the lowest nodes is within predefined tolerable levels.

3. Pruning: This is the act of reducing the size of decision trees by removing sections of the tree that provide little additional value. The decision tree could be trimmed to make it more balanced, general, and easily usable. The symptoms of an over-fitted tree are that it is too deep, with too many branches, which may reflect anomalies due to random noise or outliers instead of mainly the underlying relationship. The pruning is often done after the tree is constructed. There are two approaches to avoid over-fitting.

- Pre-pruning means to halt the tree construction early, when certain criteria are met. The downside is that it is difficult to decide what criteria to use for halting the construction, because one does not know what may happen subsequently, if one keeps growing the tree.
- Post-pruning: Remove branches or sub-trees from a "fully grown" tree. This method is commonly used. C4.5 algorithm uses a statistical method to estimate the errors at each node for pruning. A validation set may be used for pruning as well.

The most popular decision tree algorithms are C5, CART, and CHAID (Table 6.2).

Table 6.2 Comparing Popular Decision Tree Algorithms

Decision-Tree	C4.5	CART	CHAID
Full Name	Iterative Dichotomiser (ID3)	Classification and Regression Trees	Chi-square Automatic Interaction Detector
Basic algorithm	Hunt's algorithm	Hunt's algorithm	adjusted significance testing
Developer	Ross Quinlan	Bremman	Gordon Kass
When developed	1986	1984	1980
Types of trees	Classification	Classification & Regression trees	Classification & regression
Serial implementation	Tree-growth & Tree-pruning	Tree-growth & Tree-pruning	Tree-growth & Tree-pruning
Type of data	Discrete & Continuous; Incomplete data	Discrete and Continuous	Non-normal data also accepted
Types of splits	Multi-way splits	Binary splits only; Clever surrogate splits to reduce tree depth	Multi-way splits as default
Splitting criteria	Information gain	Gini's coefficient, and others	*Chi*-square test
Pruning Criteria	Clever bottom-up technique avoids overfitting	Remove weakest links first	Trees can become very large
Implementation	Publicly available	Publicly available in most packages	Popular in market research, for segmentation

TOOLS FOR MAKING DECISION TREES

Decision trees are the most popular, versatile, and easy to use data mining technique. There are many successful decision tree algorithms. Therefore, almost all publicly available data mining software platforms offer decision tree algorithm implementations. This includes languages such as R and Python (see examples in the Appendices), and GUI tools such as Weka (see example in Appendix), or commercial tools such as SPSS Modeler of SAP tools, and even as add-on tools on Microsoft Excel.

CONCLUSION

Decision trees are the most popular, versatile, and easy-to-use data mining technique with high predictive accuracy. They are also very useful as communication tools with executives. There are many successful decision tree algorithms. All publicly available data mining software platforms offer multiple decision tree implementations.

REVIEW QUESTIONS

1. What is a decision tree? Why are decision trees the most popular classification technique?
2. What is a splitting variable? Describe three criteria for choosing a splitting variable.
3. What is pruning? What are pre-pruning and post-pruning? Why choose one over the other?
4. What are Gini's coefficient and information gain? (Hint: google it).

DECISION TREE EXERCISE

Create a decision tree for the following data set. The objective is to predict the class category. (loan approved or not).

Age	Job	House	Credit	Loan Approved
Young	False	No	Fair	*No*
Young	False	No	Good	*No*
Young	True	No	Good	*Yes*
Young	True	Yes	Fair	*Yes*
Young	False	No	Fair	*No*
Middle	False	No	Fair	*No*
Middle	False	No	Good	*No*
Middle	True	Yes	Good	*Yes*
Middle	False	Yes	Excellent	*Yes*
Middle	False	Yes	Excellent	*Yes*
Old	False	Yes	Excellent	*Yes*
Old	False	Yes	Good	*Yes*
Old	True	No	Good	*Yes*
Old	True	No	Excellent	*Yes*
Old	False	No	Fair	*No*

Then solve the following problem using the model.

Age	Job	House	Credit	Loan Approved
Young	False	False	Good	??

TRUE/FALSE

1. Decision trees are essentially a hierarchy of if-then statements.
2. Decision trees apply only to strategic decisions made by executives.
3. A good decision tree should be short and ask only a few meaningful questions.
4. A decision tree should be balanced so it can make accurate predictions.
5. Decision trees use statistical techniques to abstract knowledge from data.
6. A good decision tree does not need to be colorful.
7. A decision tree can have any number of branches at any of the nodes.
8. It is desirable to have a 100% predictive accuracy of the tree, even if the tree becomes very long.
9. Making a decision tree is a recursive process.
10. The way of selecting the most important variable in constructing a decision tree is called the splitting criteria.

CASELET

MAALA STORES Case Exercise: Step 5

Maala is constantly evaluating requests for opening new stores. They would like to formalize the process for handling many requests, so that the best candidates are selected for detailed evaluation.

Develop a decision tree for evaluating new store options. Here is the training data:

City-size	Avg Income	Local Investors	LOHAS Awareness	Decision
Metro	High	Many	Cosmic	Yes
Midsize	Med	Few	Decent	No
Town	Low	Many	Little	No
Metro	High	Few	Cosmic	Yes
Town	Med	Many	Cosmic	No
Midsize	High	Many	Decent	Yes
Midsize	Med	Many	Decent	No
Metro	Med	Few	Decent	No
Midsize	High	Many	Little	No

City-size	Avg Income	Local Investors	LOHAS Awareness	Decision
Town	High	Few	Cosmic	Yes
Town	Med	Few	Cosmic	No
Midsize	High	Few	Decent	No

Use the decision tree to answer the following question?

City-size	Avg Income	Local investors	LOHAS awareness	Decision
Midsize	Med	Few	Decent	??

CHAPTER 7

Regression

Learning Objectives

LO 1 Understand the basic concept of correlation and regression

LO 2 Learn how to do a regression exercise

LO 3 Learn how to do a nonlinear regression exercise

LO 4 Know about logistic regression as a technique for classification

LO 5 Know advantages and disadvantages of regression

Regression is a well-known statistical technique to model the predictive relationship between several independent or predictor variables (DVs) and one dependent or predicted variable. The objective is to find the best fitting curve to predict the values of a dependent variable in a multidimensional space, with each independent variable being a dimension. The regression curve could be a straight line, or it could be a nonlinear curve. The quality of fit of the curve to the data can be measured by the coefficient of correlation (r), which is the square root of the amount of variance (R^2) explained by the curve.

The key steps for regression are simple:

1. List all the variables available for making the model.
2. Establish a Dependent Variable (DV) of interest.
3. Examine visual (if possible) relationships between variables of interest.
4. Find a way to predict DV using the other variables.

CASELET

Data driven Prediction Markets

Traditional pollsters still seem to be using methodologies that worked well a decade or two ago. Nate Silver is a new breed of data-based political forecasters who are seeped in big data and advanced analytics. In the 2012 elections, he predicted that Barack Obama would win the election with 291 electoral votes, compared to 247 for Mitt Romney, giving the President a 62% lead and re-election. He stunned the political forecasting world by correctly predicting the Presidential winner in all 50 states, including all nine *swing states. He also correctly predicted the winner in 31 of the 33 US Senate races.*

Nate Silver brings a different view to the world of forecasting political elections, viewing it as a scientific discipline. State the hypothesis scientifically, gather all available information, analyze the data, and extract insights using sophisticated models and algorithms and, finally, apply human judgment to interpret those insights. The results are likely to be much more grounded and successful. (To know more see The Signal and the Noise: Why Most Predictions Fail but Some Don't, by Nate Silver, 2012)

Q1: *What is the impact of this story on traditional pollsters & commentators?*

Q2: *Could one predict the chance of business success from customer polls?*

CORRELATIONS AND RELATIONSHIPS

Statistical relationships are about which elements of data 'hang" or move together, and which ones "hang" separately. It is about categorizing variables that have a close relationship with one another, and discovering the strength of the relationships. It is about describing significant positive relationships and significant negative differences.

The first and foremost measure of the strength of a relationship is co-relation (or correlation). The strength of a correlation is a quantitative measure that is measured in a normalized range between 0 (zero) and 1. A correlation of 1 indicates a perfect relationship, where the two variables are in perfect sync. A correlation of 0 indicates that there is no relationship between the variables.

The relationship can be positive, or it can be an inverse relationship, that is, the variables may move together in the same direction or in the opposite direction. Therefore, a good measure of correlation is the correlation coefficient, which is the square root of correlation. This coefficient, called r, can thus range from −1 to +1. An *r* value of 0 signifies no relationship. An *r* value of 1 shows a perfect relationship in the same direction, and an *r* value of −1 shows a perfect relationship but moving in opposite directions. The goal of regression is to find the set of independent variables that together can predict the dependent variable with a good correlation (R^2).

Given two numeric variables *x* and *y*, the coefficient of correlation *r* is mathematically computed by the following equation. $\overline{x}$ (called *x*-bar) is the mean of *x*, and $\overline{y}$ (*y*-bar) is the mean of *y*.

$$r = \frac{[(x - \overline{x}][y - \overline{y}]}{\sqrt{[(x - \overline{x})^2]\,[(y - \overline{y})^2]}}$$

VISUAL LOOK AT RELATIONSHIPS

A scatter plot (or scatter diagram) is a simple exercise for plotting all data points between two variables on a two-dimensional graph. It provides a visual layout of where all the data points are placed in that two-dimensional space. The scatter plot can be useful for graphically intuiting the relationship between two variables.

Here is a picture (Figure 7.1) that shows many possible patterns in scatter diagrams.

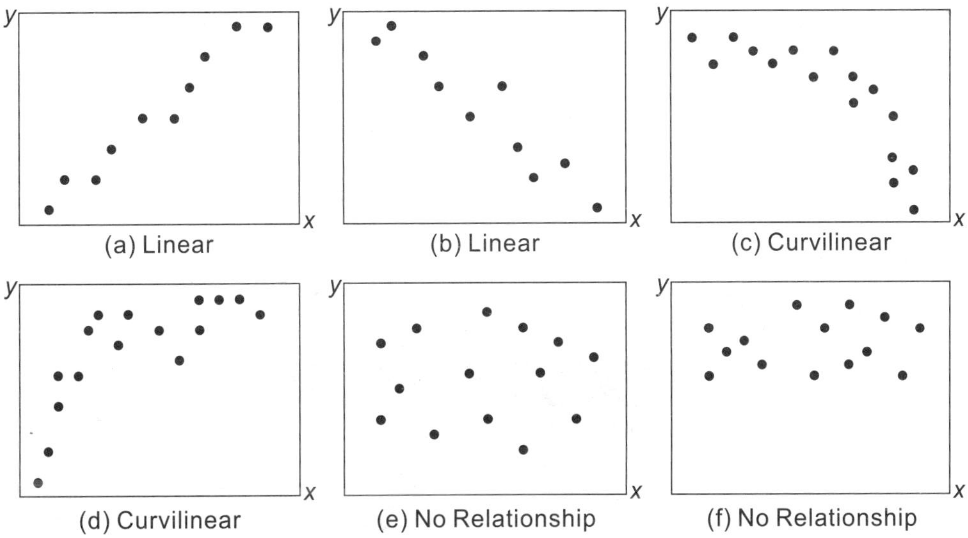

Figure 7.1 Scatter Plots showing Types of Relationships among Two Variables

Chart (a) shows a very strong linear relationship between the variables x and y. That means the value of y increases proportionally with x. Chart (b) also shows a strong linear relationship between the variables x and y. Here, it is an inverse relationship. That means the value of y decreases proportionally with x.

Chart (c) shows a curvilinear relationship. It is an inverse relationship, which means that the value of y decreases proportionally with x. However, it seems a relatively well-defined relationship, like an arc of a circle, which can be represented by a simple quadratic equation (quadratic means the power of two, that is, using terms like x^2 and y^2). Chart (d) shows a positive curvilinear relationship. However, it does not seem to resemble a regular shape, and thus would not be a strong relationship. Charts (e) and (f) show no relationship. That means variables x and y are independent of each other.

Charts (a) and (b) are good candidates that model a simple linear regression model (the terms regression model and regression equation can be used interchangeably). Chart (c) too could be modeled with a little more complex, quadratic regression equation. Chart (d) might require an even higher order polynomial regression equation to represent the data. Charts (e) and (f) have no relationship; thus, they cannot be modeled together, by regression or using any other modeling tool.

SAMPLE REGRESSION EXERCISE

The regression model is described as a linear equation that follows. y is the dependent variable, that is, the variable being predicted. x is the independent variable, or the predictor variable. There could be many predictor variables (such as $x_1, x_2, \ldots$) in a regression equation. However, there can be only one dependent variable (y) in the regression equation.

$$y = \beta_0 + \beta_1 x + \varepsilon$$

Where β_0 and β_1 are the constant, and the co-efficient for the x variable; and ε *is the random error variable.*

A simple example of a regression equation would be to predict a house price from the size of the house. Here is a sample house prices data:

House Price	Size (sqft)
$229,500	1850
$273,300	2190
$247,000	2100
$195,100	1930
$261,000	2300
$179,700	1710
$168,500	1550
$234,400	1920
$168,800	1840
$180,400	1720
$156,200	1660
$288,350	2405
$186,750	1525
$202,100	2030
$256,800	2240

The two dimensions of (one predictor, one outcome variable) data can be plotted on a scatter diagram. A scatter plot with a best-fitting line looks like the graph that follows (Figure 7.2).

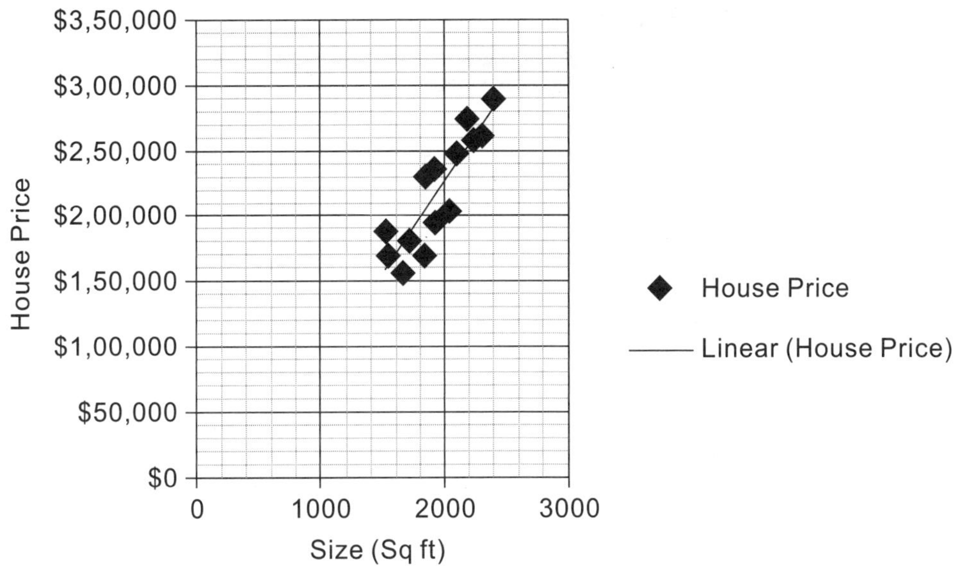

Figure 7.2 Scatter Plot and Regression Equation between House Price and House Size.

Visually, one can see a positive correlation between House Price and Size (sqft). The relationship is strong but not perfect. Running a regression model between the two variables produces the following output (truncated).

Regression Statistics	
r	**0.891**
r^2	**0.794**
Coefficients	
Intercept	**-54191**
Size (sqft)	**139.48**

It shows that the coefficient of correlation is 0.891. r^2, the measure of total variance explained by the equation, is 0.794, or 79%. That means the two variables are highly positively correlated. Regression coefficients help create the following model for predicting house prices.

House Price ($) = 139.48 * Size(sqft) – 54191

This equation explains only 79% of the variance in house prices.

Suppose other predictor variables are made available, such as the number of rooms in the house. It might help improve the regression model. When there are more than one independent variable, it is called a multiple regression model.

The house data now looks like this:

House Price	Size (sqft)	#Rooms
$229,500	1850	4
$273,300	2190	5
$247,000	2100	4
$195,100	1930	3
$261,000	2300	4
$179,700	1710	2
$168,500	1550	2
$234,400	1920	4
$168,800	1840	2
$180,400	1720	2
$156,200	1660	2
$288,350	2405	5
$186,750	1525	3
$202,100	2030	2
$256,800	2240	4

While it may be possible to make a three-dimensional scatter plot, one can alternatively examine the correlation matrix among the variables.

	House Price	Size (sqft)	#Rooms
House Price	1		
Size (sqft)	0.891	1	
Rooms	0.944	0.748	1

It shows that the House price has a strong correlation with the number of rooms (0.944) as well. Thus, it is likely that adding this variable to the regression model will add to the strength of the model.

Running a regression model between these three variables produces the following output (truncated).

Regression Statistics	
r	**0.984**
r^2	**0.968**
	Coefficients

Regression Statistics	
Intercept	12923
Size(sqft)	65.60
Rooms	23613

It shows that the coefficient of correlation of this regression model is 0.984. R^2, the total variance explained by the equation, is 0.968 or 97%. That means the variables are positively and very strongly correlated. Adding a new relevant variable has helped improve the strength of the regression model.

Using the regression coefficients helps create the following equation for predicting house prices.

House Price ($) = 65.6 * Size (sqft) + 23,613 * Rooms + 12,924

This equation shows a 97% goodness of fit with the data, which is very good for business and economic data. There is always some random variation in naturally occurring business data, and it is not desirable to overfit the model to the data.

This predictive equation could be used for future transactions. Given the regression situation above, it will be possible to predict the price of the house with 2000 sq ft and 3 rooms.

House Price	Size (sqft)	#Rooms
??	2000	3

House Price ($) = 65.6 * 2000 (sqft) + 23,613 * 3 + 12,924 = $214,963

The predicted values should be compared with the actual values to see how close the model is able to predict the actual value. As new data points become available, there could be opportunities to fine-tune and improve the model.

NON-LINEAR REGRESSION EXERCISE

The relationship between the variables may also be curvilinear. For example, given past data from electricity consumption (kWh) and temperature (temp), the objective is to predict the electrical consumption from the temperature value. Here are a few past observations.

kWatt	Temp (F)
12,530	46.8
10,800	52.1

kWatt	Temp (F)
10,180	55.1
9730	59.2
9750	61.9
10,230	66.2
11,160	69.9
13,910	76.8
15,690	79.3
15,110	79.7
17,020	80.2
17,880	83.3

In two dimensions (one predictor, one outcome variable), data can be plotted on a scatter diagram. A scatter plot with a best-fitting line looks like the graph below (Figure 7.3).

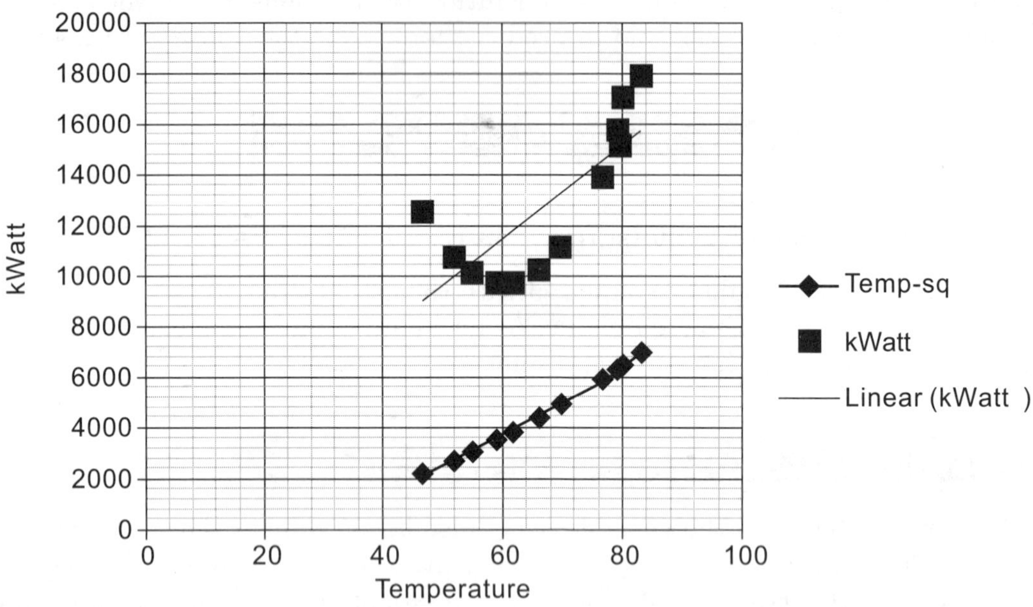

Figure 7.3 Scatter Plots showing Regression between (a) kWatt and temp, and (b) kWatt and temp square

It is visually clear that the linear relationship between temp and kWatt does not fit the data well. The relationship between temperature and kWatt follows a curvilinear model, where it hits the bottom at a certain value of temperature. The second line is the relationship between KWH and $Temp^2$. The scatter plot shows that the energy consumption shows a strong linear relationship with $Temp^2$. Thus, the regression model can be enhanced by introducing a non-linear variable (such as a quadratic variable $Temp^2$) in the equation. Computing the regression model after adding the $Temp^2$ variable leads to the following results:

Regression Statistics	
r	0.992
r^2	0.984
	Coefficients
Intercept	**67245**
Temp (F)	**-1911**
Temp-sq	**15.87**

It shows that the coefficient of correlation of the regression model is 0.99. R^2, or the total variance explained by the equation is 0.985, or 98.5%. That means the variables are very strongly and positively correlated. The regression coefficients help create the following equation for

Energy Consumption (kWatt) = 15.87 × Temp² – 1911 × Temp + 67,245

This equation shows a 98.5% fit, which is very good for business and economic contexts. Now one can predict the kWatt value for when the temperature is 72°.

Energy consumption = $(15.87 \times 72^2) - (1911 \times 72) + 67{,}245 = 11{,}923$ kWatt

LOGISTIC REGRESSION

Regression models traditionally work with continuous numeric value data for dependent and independent variables, as seen in the examples above. Regression models have evolved to work with categorical variables too. These are called Logistic regression. The dependent variable could be a binary variable such as whether a loan is approved (yes or no). Logistic regression measures the relationship between a categorical dependent variable and one or more independent variables. For example, Logistic regression might be used to predict whether a patient has a given disease (e.g., diabetes), based on observed characteristics of the patient (age, gender, body mass index, results of blood tests, etc.).

Logistical regression models use probability scores as the predicted values of the dependent variable. Logistic regression takes the natural logarithm of the probability of the dependent variable being a case (referred to as the logit function or transformation), and creates a continuous criterion as a transformed version of the dependent variable. Thus, a logit transformation of the dependent variable is (automatically) used in logistic regression. The net effect is that although the dependent variable in logistic regression is binomial (or categorical, i.e., has only two possible values), the logit value is a continuous function using which a linear regression is conducted. Here is the general logistic function, with the independent variable on the horizontal axis and the logit dependent variable on the vertical axis (Figure 7.4).

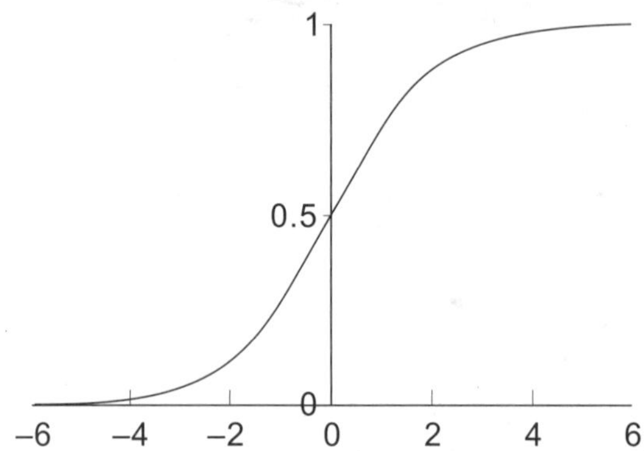

Figure 7.4 General Logit Function

All popular data mining platforms provide support for regular multiple regression models, as well as options for Logistic Regression.

ADVANTAGES AND DISADVANTAGES OF REGRESSION

Regression Models are very popular because they offer many advantages.

1. Regression models are easy to understand, as they are built upon basic statistical principles such as correlation and least square error.
2. Regression models provide simple algebraic equations that are easy to understand and use.
3. The strength (or the goodness of fit) of the regression model is measured in terms of the correlation coefficients, and other related statistical parameters that are well understood.
4. Regression models can match and beat the predictive power of other modeling techniques.
5. Regression models can include all the variables that one wants to include in the model.
6. Regression analysis is widely used in many fields, such as economics, finance, marketing, and more.

7. Regression modeling tools are pervasive. They are found in all statistical packages as well as data mining packages. MS Excel also provides regression modeling capabilities.

Regression models can however prove inadequate under many circumstances.

1. First and foremost, one should not assume that there would be a linear equation that will fit the data. Regression models do not automatically take care of non-linearity. A series of scatter plots can help determine the relationships between independent and dependent variables. The user needs to imagine the kind of additional terms that would be needed to be added to the regression model to improve its fit.
2. Regression models cannot cover poor data quality. If the data is not prepared well to remove missing values, or is not well-behaved in terms of a normal distribution, the validity of the model suffers. If the data has many outliers (or values outside a normal distribution), that would impact the regression model.
3. Regression models suffer from collinearity problems (meaning strong linear correlations among some independent variables). If the independent variables have strong correlations among themselves, then they will "eat" into each other's predictive power and the regression coefficients will lose their ruggedness. Regression models will not automatically choose between highly collinear variables, although some packages attempt to do that.
6. Regression models can be unwieldy and unreliable if a large number of variables are included in the model. All variables entered into the model will be reflected in the regression equation, irrespective of their contribution to the predictive power of the model. There is no concept of automatic pruning of the regression model, although some packages attempt to do that.
7. Regression models work only with numeric data and not with categorical variables. There are ways to deal with categorical variables though by creating multiple new variables with a yes/no value.
8. Just as with decision trees, a regression model may be overfitted to the data. This means that the model may be too closely fitted to the current dataset that it may not be able to represent the general relationship very accurately.
9. Regression analysis can reveal a correlation between two variables, but it does not prove causality. It is possible that the relationship between the variables is due to another intermediating factor that has not been considered in the model.

TIME SERIES ANALYSIS

Time series analysis is a special case of regression analysis where the key independent variable is time. The dependent variables may be continuous variables such as sales, stock prices, or population. A time series would be gathered at equally spaced time intervals, which could be any daily, weekly, monthly, quarterly, or yearly, etc. Time has special characteristics such as seasonality and cyclicality. For example, one may want to compare the Spring season's past years of data to project Spring season's data for subsequent years.

The goal of time series analysis is to understand the underlying patterns and trends in the data at various granularities, and to use this information to make predictions for future points in time. The major methods used in time series analysis are trend analysis, seasonality analysis, and forecasting. Trend analysis is used to identify the overall pattern in the data, such as an upward or downward trend. Seasonality analysis identifies repeating patterns in the data, such as an hour of day or day or week fluctuations. Forecasting is used to make predictions about future values based on the patterns and trends identified in the data, with a different level of confidence in the range of predicted values.

ARIMA, (Auto Regressive Integrated Moving Average), is a particularly popular time series forecasting model for seasonality or trend analysis. ARIMA is a linear regression model that includes some additional terms for autoregression (AR), differencing (I for "Integrated"), and moving average (MA) terms to smooth out the model for the underlying patterns and trends in the data. Autoregression (AR) is a statistical technique used to model the relationship between a variable and its own lagged values from previous time points (t-1, t-2, etc.). Integrated (I) refers to the property of a time series where the mean, variance, and covariance of the data do not change over time. Moving average (MA) models the behavior of a time series by using the average of past "q" values, where "q" is the order of the moving average. It can help smooth out the fluctuations in the data, making it easier to identify patterns and trends.

CONCLUSION

Regression models are simple, versatile, visual/graphical tools with high predictive ability. Regression models produce a relative regression equation that can be used to predict future values. They include non-linear as well as binary predictions. One should be careful of the many limitations of the regression model to ensure that the models are accurate. Time Series analysis is a particularly popular regression method used in economic predictions, using underlying seasonal trends in data.

REVIEW EXERCISES

1. What is a regression model? What is multiple regression? What is non-linear regression? What is logistic regression?

2. What is correlation? What is the coefficient of correlation? What is the range of values for correlation and correlation coefficient?
3. What is a scatter plot? How does it help with regression modeling?
4. What are the advantages and disadvantages of regression modeling?
5. Compare and contrast decision trees with regression models for predictions.
6. What is Time Series Analysis? How is it different from regression analysis?

REGRESSION HANDS-ON EXERCISE

Run a Regression Model for the data table below, to predict C using A and B.

(a) Create regression analysis using Excel, Weka, R, and Python. Examine the full details of the regression analysis. Are the results identical?

(b) Write the regression equation and predict the value of C for A = 40 and B = 240.

A	B	C
22	200	240
53	199	252
32	162	180
66	380	410
33	200	210
52	220	310
63	350	380
51	216	270
37	188	280
49	300	305
37	200	275
29	240	245
50	250	330
47	240	245
28	250	240

TRUE/FALSE

1. Regression is an artificial intelligence technique.
2. In regression, a dependent variable is predicted using many independent variables.

3. Correlation coefficient (*R*) can take only positive values from zero to 1.
4. The best-fitting regression line can be straight or a curved one.
5. Regression model can automatically adjust the model to take into account any nonlinear relationship.
6. There can be only one dependent variable in one regression equation.
7. Regression models can be used for time-series analysis.
8. Regression models traditionally work with continuous numeric data.
9. Regression model is uniquely determined by the data.
10. Regression modeling tools are found in almost all statistical as well as data mining packages.

CASELET

MAALA STORES Case Exercise: Step 6

Liberty wants to forecast its sales for next year, for financial budgeting.

Year	Global GDP Index per Capita	# Cust Serv Calls('000s)	# Employees ('000)	# Items ('000)	Revenue ($M)
1	100	25	45	11	2000
2	112	27	53	11	2400
3	115	22	54	12	2700
4	123	27	58	14	2900
5	122	32	60	14	3200
6	132	33	65	15	3500
7	143	40	72	16	4000
8	126	30	65	16	4200
9	166	34	85	17	4500
10	157	47	97	18	4700
11	176	33	98	18	4900
12	180	45	100	20	5000

Check the correlations. Which variables are strongly correlated?

Create a regression model that best predicts the revenue.

Do a Time Series analysis of all the variables, and project for the next year.

[Hint: Exclude the Year column/variable from Regression analysis]

CHAPTER 8

Artificial Neural Networks

Learning Objectives

LO 1 Understand what are ANNs and why they are useful

LO 2 Know the design principles of ANN

LO 3 Learn about the representation of the elements of an ANN

LO 4 Know architectures of ANNs

LO 5 Understand how ANNs are developed and trained

LO 6 Know advantages and disadvantages of ANNs

Artificial Neural Networks (ANNs) are inspired by the information processing model of the mind/brain. The human brain consists of about 100 billion neurons that link with one another in an intricate pattern. Every neuron receives information from many other neurons, processes it, gets excited or not, and passes its state information to other neurons. ANNs are the force behind Deep Learning, Machine Learning, and Artificial Intelligence systems.

Just like the brain is a multipurpose system, the ANNs are also very versatile systems. They can be used for many kinds of pattern recognition and prediction. They are also used for classification, regression, clustering, association, and optimization activities. They are used in finance, marketing, manufacturing, operations, information systems applications, and so on.

ANNs are composed of a large number of highly interconnected processing elements (neurons) working in multi-layered structures that receive inputs, process the inputs, and produce an output. An ANN is typically designed for a specific application, such as pattern recognition or data classification, and trained through a learning process. Just like in biological systems, ANNs make adjustments to the strengths of the synaptic connections with each new learning instance.

ANNs are like a black box that is trained into solving a particular type of problem, and they can develop high predictive powers. Their intermediate synaptic parameter values evolve as the system obtains feedback on its predictions, and thus, an ANN learns from more training data (Figure 8.1).

Figure 8.1 General ANN Model

CASELET

IBM Watson – Analytics in Medicine

The amount of medical information available is doubling every five years and much of this data is unstructured. Physicians simply don't have time to read every journal that can help them keep up to date with the latest advances. Mistakes in diagnosis are likely to happen and clients have become more aware of the evidence. Analytics will transform the field of medicine into Evidence-based medicine. How can healthcare providers address these problems?

IBM's Watson cognitive computing system can analyze large amounts of unstructured text and develop hypotheses based on that analysis. Physicians can use Watson to assist in diagnosing and treating patients. First, the physician might describe symptoms and other related factors to the system. Watson can then identify the key pieces of information and mine the patient's data to find relevant facts about family history, current medications, and other existing conditions. It combines this information with current findings from tests, and then forms and tests a hypothesis by examining a variety of data sources—treatment guidelines, electronic medical record data and doctors' and nurses' notes, as well as peer-reviewed research and clinical studies. From here, Watson can provide potential treatment options and its confidence rating for each suggestion.

Watson has been deployed at many leading healthcare institutions to improve the quality and efficiency of healthcare decisions; to help clinicians uncover insights from patient information in electronic medical records (EMR); among other benefits.

Q1: *How would IBM Watson change medical practices in the future?*

Q2: *In what other industries & functions could this technology be applied?*

BUSINESS APPLICATIONS OF ANN

Artificial neural networks are used most often when the objective function is complex, and where there exists plenty of data, and the model is expected to improve over a period of time. A few sample applications:

1. ANNs are used in stock price prediction where the rules of the game are extremely complicated, and a lot of data needs to be processed very quickly.
2. ANNs are used for character recognition, as in recognizing hand-written text, or damaged or mangled text. They are used in recognizing fingerprints. These are complicated patterns and are unique for each person. They are also used for visual recognition, such as face recognition systems. Layers of neurons can progressively clarify the pattern leading to a remarkably accurate result.
3. They are also used in traditional classification problems, like approving a financial loan application.

DESIGN PRINCIPLES OF ANN

1. A neuron is the basic processing unit of the network. The neuron (or processing element) receives inputs from its preceding neurons (or PEs), does some non-linear weighted computation on the basis of those inputs, transforms the result into its output value, and then passes on the output to the next neuron in the network (Figure 8.2). X's are the inputs, w's are the weights for each input, and y is the output.

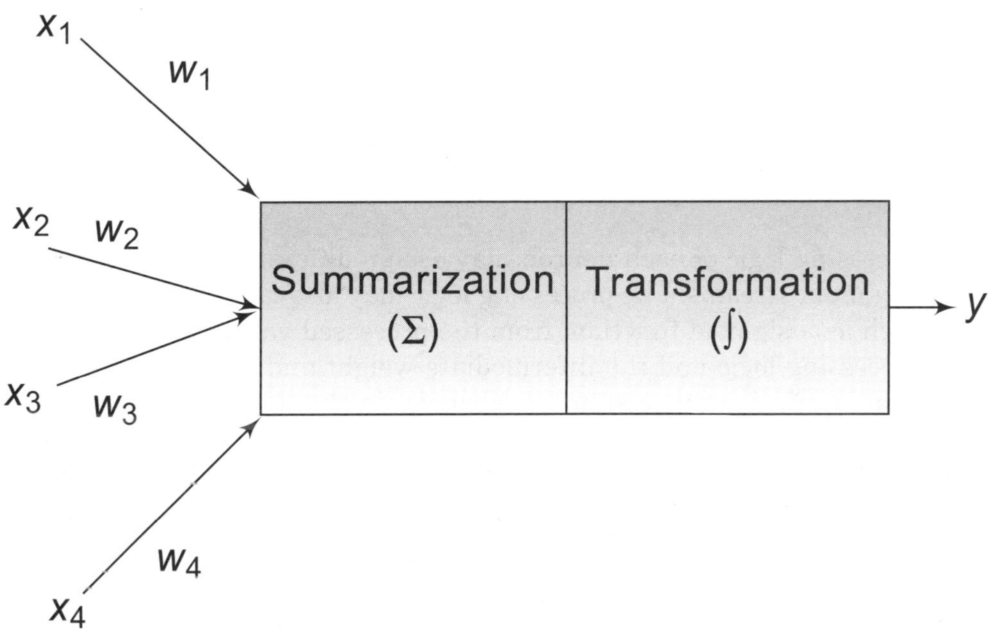

Figure 8.2 Model for a Single Artificial Neuron

2. An ANN is usually a multi-layered model. There is at least one input neuron, one output neuron, and at least one processing neuron. An ANN with just this basic structure would be a simple, single-stage computational unit. A simple task may be processed by just that one neuron and the result may be communicated soon. ANNs, however, may have multiple layers of processing elements in sequence. There could be many neurons involved in a sequence depending upon the complexity of the predictive action. The layers of PEs could work in sequence, or they could work in parallel (Figure 8.3).

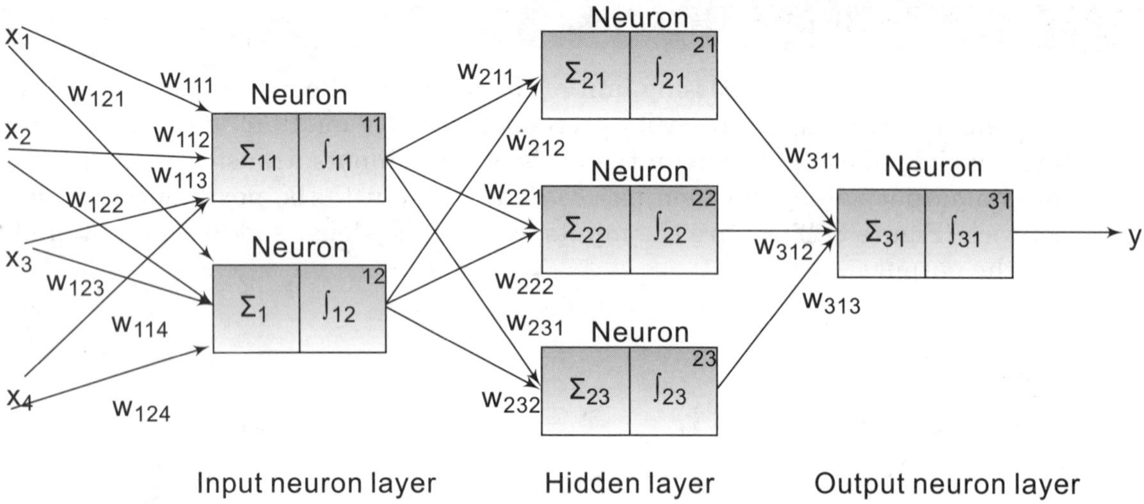

Figure 8.3 Model for a Multi-layer ANN

3. The processing logic of each neuron may assign different weights to the various incoming input streams. The processing logic may also use non-linear transformation, such as a sigmoid function, from the processed values to the output value. This processing logic and the intermediate weight and processing functions are just what works for the system as a whole, in its objective of solving a problem collectively. They do not have significance or interpretability as individual weights. Thus, ANNs are considered to be an opaque and black-box system.
4. The ANN can be trained by making similar decisions over and over again with many training cases. It will continue to learn by adjusting its internal computation and communication based on feedback about its previous decisions. Thus, ANNs become better at making a decision, as they handle more and more decisions over time.

Depending upon the nature of the problem being solved, and the availability of good training data, at some point, the neural network will learn enough and begin to match the predictive accuracy of a human expert. In many practical situations, the predictions of ANN, trained over a long period of time with a large number of training data, have begun to decisively become more accurate than human experts. At that point, ANN can begin to be seriously considered for deployment in real situations in real time.

REPRESENTATION OF A NEURAL NETWORK

A neural network is a series of neurons that receive inputs from other neurons. They do a weighted summation function of all the inputs, using different weights (or importance) for each input. The weighted sum is then transformed into an output value using a transfer function.

Learning in ANN occurs when the various processing elements in the neural network adjust the underlying relationship (weights, transfer function, etc.) between input and outputs, in response to the feedback on their predictions. If the prediction made was correct, then the weights would remain the same, but if the prediction was incorrect, then the parameter values would change.

The Transformation (Transfer) Function is any function suitable for the task at hand. The transfer function for ANNs is usually a non-linear sigmoid function. Thus, if the normalized computed value is less than some value (say 0.5), then the output value will be zero. If the computed value is at the cut-off threshold, then the output value will be a 1. It could be a non-linear hyperbolic function in which the output is either a -1 or a 1. Many other functions could be designed for any or all of the processing elements.

Thus, in an ANN, every processing element can potentially have a different number of input variables, a different set of weights for those inputs, and a different transformation function. All those parameter values support and compensate for one another until the neural network as a whole learns to provide the correct output, as desired by the user.

ARCHITECTING A NEURAL NETWORK

There are many ways to architect the functioning of an ANN using fairly simple and open rules with a tremendous amount of flexibility at each stage. The most popular architecture is a *Feed-forward, multi-layered perceptron with a back-propagation learning* algorithm. Feedforward Networks are the simplest type of ANN and consist of input nodes, hidden nodes, and output nodes. The data flows in only one direction, from the input layer to the output layer, without looping back. That means there are multiple layers of PEs in the system and the output of neurons are fed forward to the PEs in the next layers. Backpropagation means that the feedback on the accuracy of the prediction is fed back into the neural network for learning to occur. This is the generic model that was essentially what was described in the earlier paragraphs. ANN architectures for different applications are shown in Table 8.1.

Table 8.1 ANN Architectures for Different Applications

Mining technique	ANN Architecture types
Classification	Feedforward networks (MLP), radial basis function, and probabilistic
Regression	Feedforward networks (MLP), radial basis function
Clustering	Adaptive resonance theory (ART), Self-organizing maps (SOMs)
Association Rule Mining	Hopfield networks

DEVELOPING AN ANN

It takes resources, training data, skill, and time to develop a neural network. Most data mining platforms offer at least the Multi-Layer-Perceptron (MLP) algorithm to implement a neural network. Other neural network architectures include Probabilistic networks and Self-organizing feature maps.

The steps required to build an ANN are as follows:

1. Gather data. Divide into training data and test data. The training data needs to be further divided into training data and validation data.
2. Select the network architecture, such as the Feedforward network.
3. Select the algorithm, such as Multi-layer Perception.
4. Set network parameters.
5. Train the ANN with training data.
6. Validate the model with validation data.
7. Freeze the weights and other parameters.
8. Test the trained network with test data.
9. Deploy the ANN when it achieves good predictive accuracy.

Training an ANN requires that the training data be split into three parts (Table 8.2):

Table 8.2 ANN Training Datasets

Training set	This data set is used to adjust the weights on the neural network (~ 60%).
Validation set	This data set is used to minimize overfitting and verifying accuracy (~ 20%).
Testing set	This data set is used only for testing the final solution in order to confirm the actual predictive power of the network (~ 20%).
k-fold cross-validation	This approach means that the data is divided into k equal pieces, and the learning process is repeated k-times with each piece becoming the training set. This process leads to less bias and more accuracy, but is more time consuming.

ADVANTAGES AND DISADVANTAGES OF USING ANNs

There are many benefits of using ANN.

1. ANNs impose very few restrictions on their use. ANN can deal with (identify/model) highly nonlinear relationships on its own, without much work from the

user or analyst. They help find practical data-driven solutions where algorithmic solutions are non-existent or too complicated.

2. There is no need to program neural networks, as they learn from examples. They get better with use, without much programming effort.
3. They can handle a variety of problem types, including classification, clustering, associations, etc.
4. ANN is tolerant of data quality issues and they do not restrict the data to follow strict normality and/or independence assumptions.
5. They can handle both numerical and categorical variables.
6. ANNs can be much faster than other techniques.
7. Most importantly, they usually provide better results (prediction and/or clustering) compared to statistical counterparts, once they have been trained enough.

The key disadvantages arise from the fact that they are not easy to interpret or explain or compute.

1. They are deemed to be black-box solutions, lacking explainability. Thus, they are difficult to communicate about, except through the strength of their results.
2. Optimal design of ANN is still an art: it requires expertise and extensive experimentation.
3. It can be difficult to handle a large number of variables (especially the rich nominal attributes).
4. It takes large data sets to train an ANN.

VARIANTS OF ANNs

Convolutional Neural Networks (CNNs) are specialized neural networks used for image and video recognition. They use a mathematical operation called convolution to analyze the relationships between pixels in an image by applying a set of filters to the input data to learn local features. The filters are designed to detect specific features in the input data, such as edges or textures. By stacking multiple convolutional layers, CNNs can learn increasingly complex features and representations of the input data. CNNs use pooling layers to reduce the dimensionality of the feature maps to reduce overfitting and make the model more computationally efficient.

Recurrent Neural Networks (RNNs) are neural networks that are designed to process sequences of data, such as time series or sequences of words in a sentence. RNNs use feedback connections to allow information to persist and be used later in the processing of the sequence. Transformers are a related type of deep learning model that has become popular for natural language processing tasks, such as GPT (Generative

Pre-Trained Transformer). They are based on the self-attention mechanism, which allows the model to focus on different parts of the input sequence when making predictions. Transformers can process input sequences of any length in parallel, rather than sequentially. This allows transformers to be trained on large amounts of data much more efficiently than RNNs.

Generative Adversarial Networks (GANs) are neural networks that are used for generative modeling. They consist of two parts: a generator network that generates new data, and a discriminator network that determines whether the generated data is real or fake. The generator and the discriminator are trained to play against each other and help each other learn. GANs were used to design the AlphaGo model that beat the world champion in the game of Go. The generator network generates new data that is similar to a given training dataset. The discriminator network is trained to distinguish between real data from the training dataset and fake data generated by the generator network. For example, the generator network would generate fake realistic images. The discriminator tries to accurately distinguish between real and fake images. Over time, the generator becomes better at generating data and the discriminator becomes better at distinguishing between real and fake data. GANs are useful for facial recognition, image synthesis, and more.

CONCLUSION

Artificial neural networks are complex systems that model the functioning of the human brain. Each neuron receives inputs from connected neurons, processes them, and decides whether to send a signal to the other neurons, or not. ANNs are versatile enough to solve many data mining tasks with high accuracy. However, they are like black boxes, and they provide little guidance CNNs for image processing, RNNs for speech processing, and GNNs for game playing.

REVIEW EXERCISES

1. What is an artificial neural network? How does it work?
2. Compare an artificial neural network with a decision tree.
3. What makes an artificial neural network versatile enough for supervised as well as non-supervised learning tasks?
4. Examine the steps in developing a neural network for predicting stock prices. What kind of objective function and what kind of data would be required for a good stock price predictor system using ANN?
5. What are some of the advanced forms of Neural Networks? How do they differ from each other?

TRUE/FALSE

1. ANN is a machine learning technique.
2. ANNs are like a black box trained into solving a particular type of problem.
3. ANNs can be used for Classification, Clustering, Association Rules, and Optimization activities.
4. The processing logic of each neuron may assign different weights to the various incoming input streams.
5. A neural network is a multilayered model.
6. An ANN should have at least one input neuron, one output neuron, and at least three processing neurons.
7. ANN can deal with (identify/model) nonlinear relationships but with much work from the user or analyst.
8. Learning in ANN occurs when the various processing elements in the neural network adjust the underlying relationship (weights, transfer function, etc.) between inputs and outputs.
9. The most popular ANN architecture is self-organizing maps based learning algorithm.
10. IBM Watson is a form of a neural network.

CHAPTER

9 Cluster Analysis

Learning Objectives

LO 1 Understand cluster analysis and its applications

LO 2 Learn the types of clusters and how they are represented

LO 3 Learn how the clustering technique works in practice

LO 4 Understand the K-means technique and its pseudocode

LO 5 Discuss the advantages and disadvantages of ANNs

Cluster analysis is used for automatic identification of natural groupings of things. It is also known as the segmentation technique. In this technique, data instances that are similar to (or near) each other are categorized into one cluster. Similarly, data instances that are very different (or far away) from each other are moved into different clusters.

Cluster analysis is an unsupervised learning technique, as there is no output or dependent variable for which a right or wrong answer can be computed. The correct number of clusters or the definition of those clusters is not known ahead of time. Clustering techniques can only suggest to the user how many clusters would make sense from the characteristics of the data. The user can specify a different, larger or smaller, number of desired clusters based on their making business need. The cluster analysis technique will then define many distinct clusters from analysis of the data, with cluster definitions for each of those clusters. However, there are good or not so good cluster definitions, depending on how closely the cluster parameters fit the data.

CASELET

Cluster Analysis

A national insurance company distributes its personal and small commercial insurance products through independent agents. They wanted to increase their sales by better understanding their customers. They were interested in increasing their market share by doing some direct marketing campaigns, however without creating a channel conflict with the independent agents. They were also interested in examining different customer segments based on their needs, and the profitability of each of those segments.

They gathered attitudinal, behavioral, and demographic data using a mail survey of 2000 U.S. households that own auto insurance. Additional geo-demographic and credit information was added to the survey data. Cluster analysis of the data revealed five roughly equal segments:

- ***Non-Traditionals:*** *interested in using the Internet and/or buying insurance at work.*
- ***Direct Buyers:*** *interested in buying via direct mail or telephone.*
- ***Budget Conscious:*** *interested in minimal coverage and finding the best deal.*
- ***Agent Loyals:*** *expressed strong loyalty to their agents and high levels of personal service.*
- ***Hassle-Free:*** *similar to Agent Loyals but less interested in face-to-face service.*

(To know more visit: greenbook.org)

Q1. *Which customer segments would you choose for direct marketing? Will these create a channel conflict?*

Q2. *Could this segmentation apply to other service businesses? Which ones?*

APPLICATIONS OF CLUSTER ANALYSIS

Cluster analysis is used in almost every field where there is a large variety of transactions. It helps provide characterization, definition, and labels for sub-populations. It can help identify natural groupings of customers, products, patients, and so on. It can also help identify outliers in a specific domain and thus decrease the size and complexity of problems. A prominent business application of cluster analysis is in market research. Customers are segmented into clusters based on their characteristics—wants and needs, geography, price sensitivity, and so on. Here are some examples of cluster analysis:

1. *Market Segmentation:* Categorizing customers according to their similarities, for instance by their common wants and needs, and propensity to pay, can help with targeted marketing.
2. *Product portfolio:* People of similar sizes can be grouped together to make small, medium, and large sizes for clothing items.
3. *Text Mining:* Clustering can help organize a given collection of text documents according to their content similarities into clusters of related topics.

DEFINITION OF A CLUSTER

An operational definition of a cluster is that, given a representation of n objects, find K groups based on a measure of similarity, such that objects within the same group are alike, but the objects in different groups are not alike.

However, the notion of similarity can be interpreted in many ways. Clusters can differ in terms of their shape, size, and density. Clusters are patterns, and there can be many kinds of patterns. Some clusters are the traditional types, such as data points hanging together. However, there are other clusters, such as all points representing the circumference of a circle. There may be concentric circles with points of different circles representing different clusters. The presence of noise in the data makes the detection of the clusters even more difficult.

An ideal cluster can be defined as a set of points that is compact and isolated. In reality, a cluster is a subjective entity whose significance and interpretation require domain knowledge. In the sample data of 12 data points below (Figure 9.1), how many clusters can one visualize?

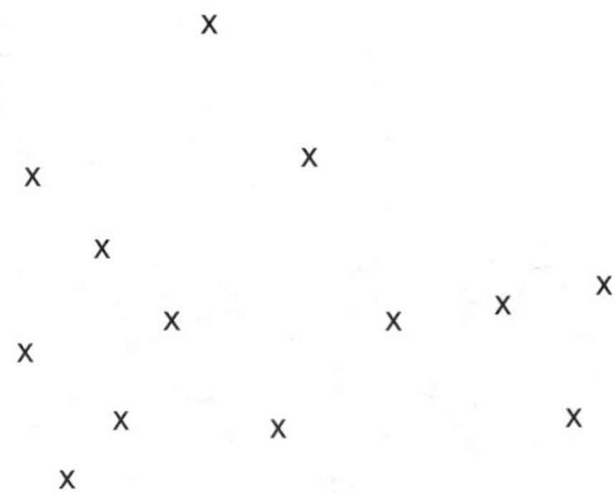

Figure 9.1 Visual Cluster Example

It seems like there are two clusters of approximately equal sizes. However, one can also see three clusters, depending on how we draw the dividing lines. There is no truly optimal way to calculate it. Heuristics are often used to define the number of clusters.

REPRESENTING CLUSTERS

The clusters can be represented by a central or modal value. A cluster can be defined by the *centroid* of the collection of points belonging to it. A *centroid* is a measure of the central tendency of the set of points. It is the point from where the least square distance from all the points is the minimum. A real-life equivalent would be the city center as that point that is considered the most easy to use by all constituents of the city. Just like all cities are defined by their centers or downtown areas, so also the clusters are defined by their centroids.

A cluster may also be represented by the most frequently occurring value in the cluster, that is, the cluster can be defined by its modal value. Thus, a particular cluster representing a social point of view could be called the “soccer moms”, even though not all members of that cluster need currently to be a mom with soccer-playing children.

CLUSTER ANALYSIS TECHNIQUES

Cluster analysis is an algorithmic machine-learning technique. The quality of a clustering result depends on the *algorithm*, the *distance* function, and the *application*. First, consider the distance function. Most cluster analysis methods use a distance measure to calculate the closeness between pairs of items. There are two major measures of distances: Euclidian distance ("as the crow flies" or straight line) is the most intuitive measure. The other popular measure is the Manhattan (rectilinear) distance, where one can go only in orthogonal directions. The Euclidian distance is the hypotenuse of a right triangle, while the Manhattan distance is the sum of the two legs of the right triangle. There are other measures of distance like Jacquard distance (to measure similarity of sets), or Edit distance (similarity of texts), and others.

In either case, the key objective of the clustering algorithm is the same:

- Inter-clusters distance ⇒ maximized; and
- Intra-clusters distance ⇒ minimized

There are many algorithms to produce clusters. There are top-down, hierarchical methods that start with creating a given number of best-fitting clusters. There are also bottom-up methods that begin with identifying naturally occurring clusters.

The most popular clustering algorithm is the K-means algorithm. It is a top-down, statistical technique, based on the method of minimizing the least squared distance from the center points of the clusters. Other techniques, such as neural networks, are also used for clustering. Comparing cluster algorithms is a difficult task, as there is no single right number of clusters. However, the speed of the algorithm and its versatility in terms of different datasets are important criteria.

Here is the generic pseudocode for clustering

1. *Pick an arbitrary number of groups/segments to be created*
2. *Start with some initial randomly-chosen center values for groups*
3. *Classify instances to closest groups*
4. *Compute new values for the group centers*
5. *Repeat steps 3 & 4 till groups converge*
6. *If clusters are not satisfactory, go to step 1 and pick a different number of groups/ segments*

The cluster analysis process can be continued with a different number of clusters and different locations of those points. Clusters are considered good if the cluster definitions stabilize, and the stabilized definitions prove useful for the purpose at hand. Else, repeat the clustering exercise with a different number of clusters, and different starting points for group means.

CLUSTERING EXERCISE

Here is a simple exercise to visually and intuitively identify clusters from data. X and Y are two dimensions of interest. The objective is to determine the number of clusters, and the center points of those clusters.

X	Y
2	4
2	6
5	6
4	7
8	3
6	6
5	2
5	7
6	3
4	4

A scatter plot of 10 items in two dimensions shows that they are distributed fairly randomly. As a bottom-up technique, the number of clusters and their centroids can be intuited (Figure 9.2).

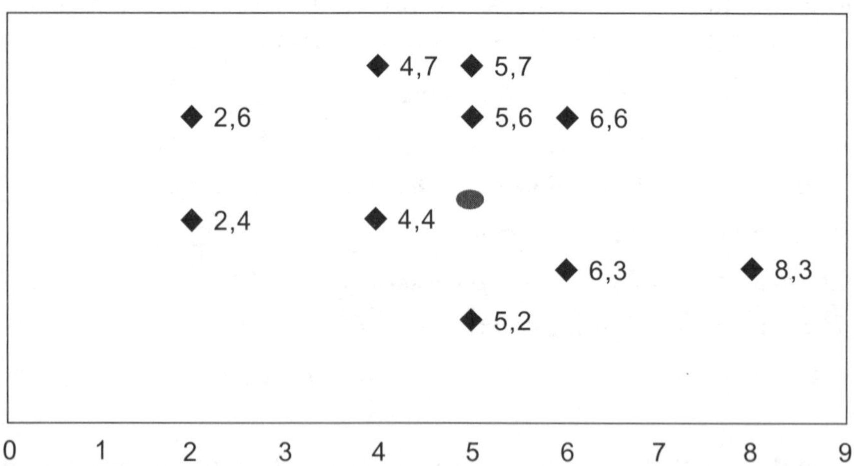

Figure 9.2 Initial Data Points and the Centroid (shown as Thick Dot)

The points are distributed randomly enough that it could be considered one cluster. The solid circle would represent the central point (centroid) of these points.

However, there is a big distance between points (2,6) and (8,3). So, this data could be broken into two clusters. The three points at the bottom right could form one cluster and the other seven could form the other cluster. The two clusters would look like this (Figure 9.3). The two circles will be the new centroids.

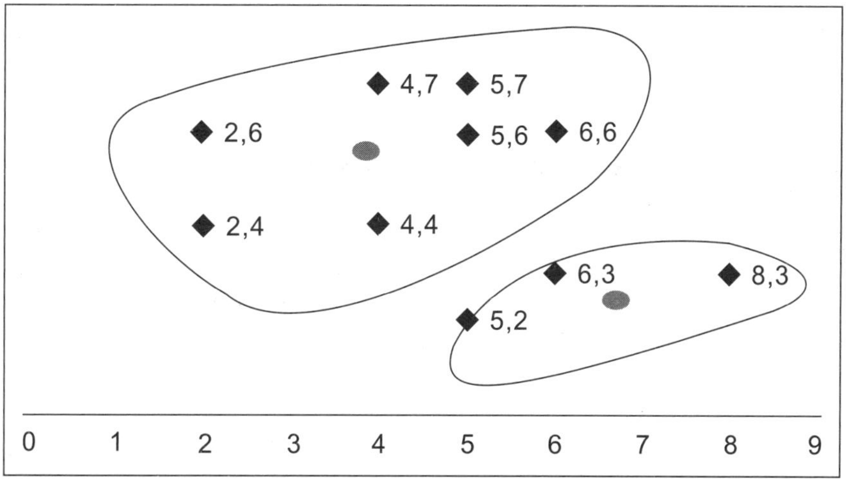

Figure 9.3 Dividing into two Clusters (Centroids shown as Thick Dots)

The bigger cluster seems too far apart. So, it seems like the 4 points on the top will form a separate cluster. The three clusters could look like this (Figure 9.4).

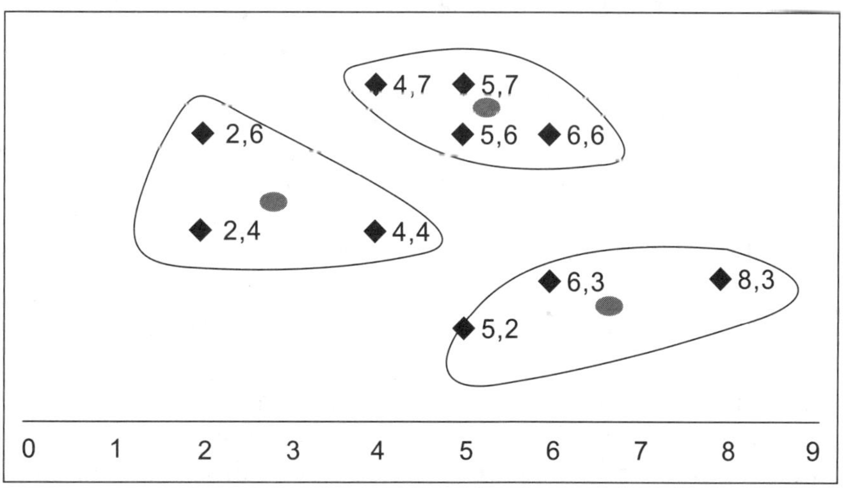

Figure 9.4 Dividing into three Clusters (Centroids shown as Thick Dots)

This solution has three clusters. The cluster on the right is far from the other two clusters. However, its centroid is not too close to all the data points. The cluster at the top looks very tight-fitting, with a nice centroid. The third cluster, at the left, is spread out and may not be of much usefulness.

This was a bottom-up exercise in visually producing three best-fitting cluster definitions from the given data. The right number of clusters will depend on the data and the application for which the data would be used.

K-MEANS ALGORITHM FOR CLUSTERING

K-means is the most popular clustering algorithm. It iteratively computes the clusters and their centroids. It is a top-down approach to clustering. Starting with a given number of K clusters, say three clusters. Thus, three random centroids will be created as starting points of the centers of three clusters. The circles are initial cluster centroids (Figure 9.5).

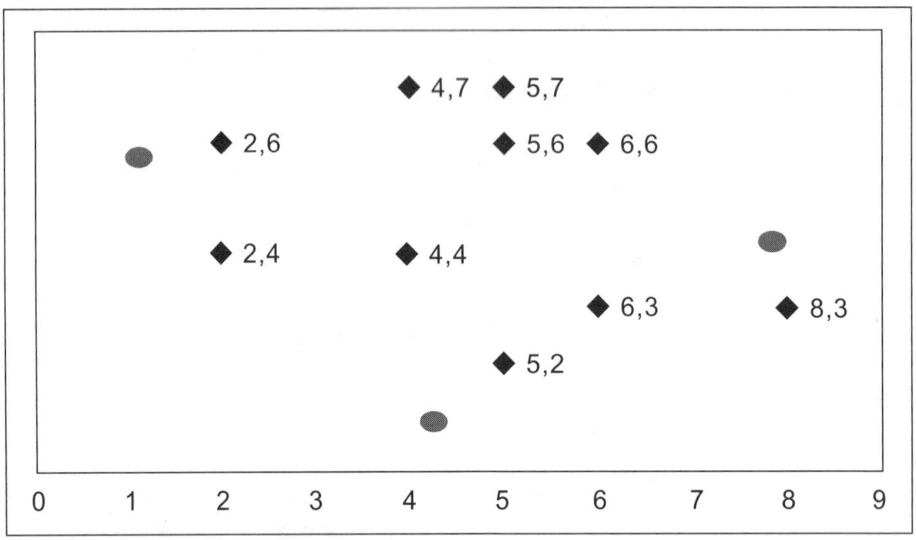

Figure 9.5 Randomly Assigning three Centroids for three Data Clusters

Step 1: For a data point, distance values will be from each of the three centroids. The data point will be assigned to the cluster with the shortest distance to the centroid. All data points will thus be assigned to one data point or the other (Figure 9.6). The arrows from each data element show the centroid that the point is assigned to.

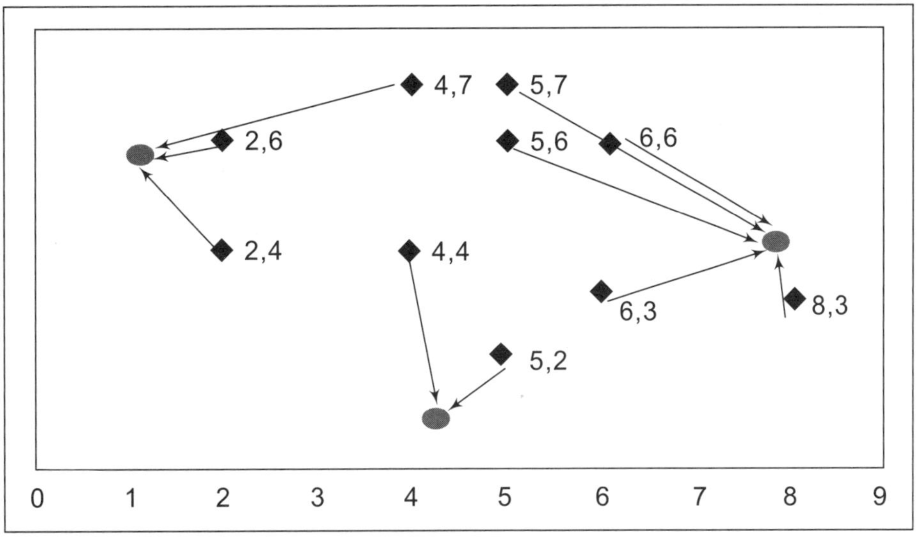

Figure 9.6 Assigning Data Points to the Closest Centroid

Step 2: The centroid for each cluster will now be recalculated such that it is closest to all the data points allocated to that cluster. The dashed arrows show the centroids being moved from their old (shaded) values to the revised new values (Figure 9.7).

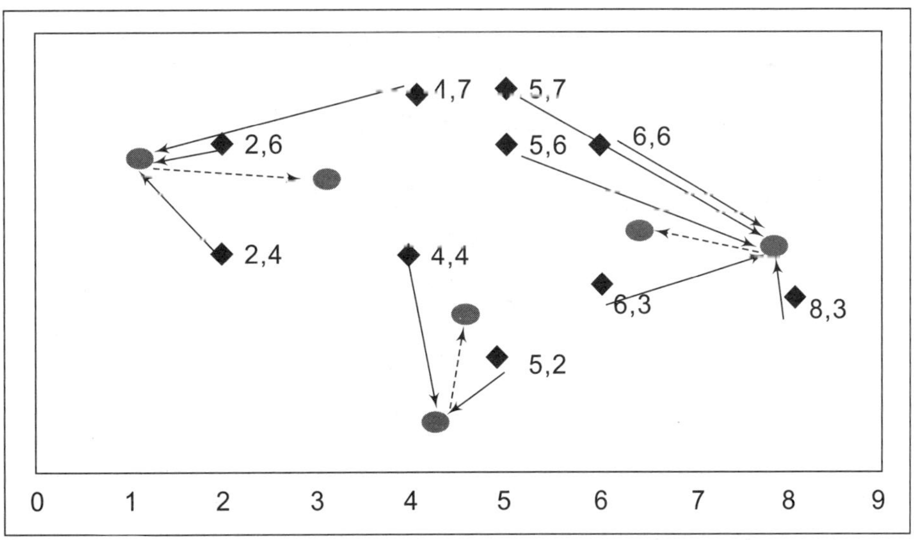

Figure 9.7 Recomputing Centroids for each Cluster

Step 3: Once again, data points are assigned to the three centroids closest to it (Figure 9.8).

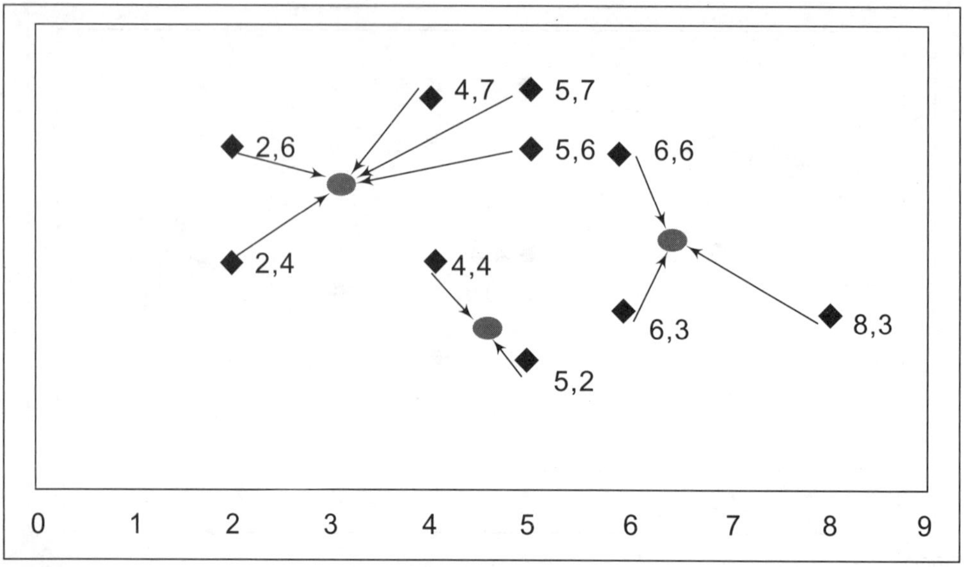

Figure 9.8 Assigning Data Points to Recomputed Centroids

The new centroids will be computed from the data points in the cluster until finally, the centroids stabilize in their locations. These are the three clusters computed by this algorithm.

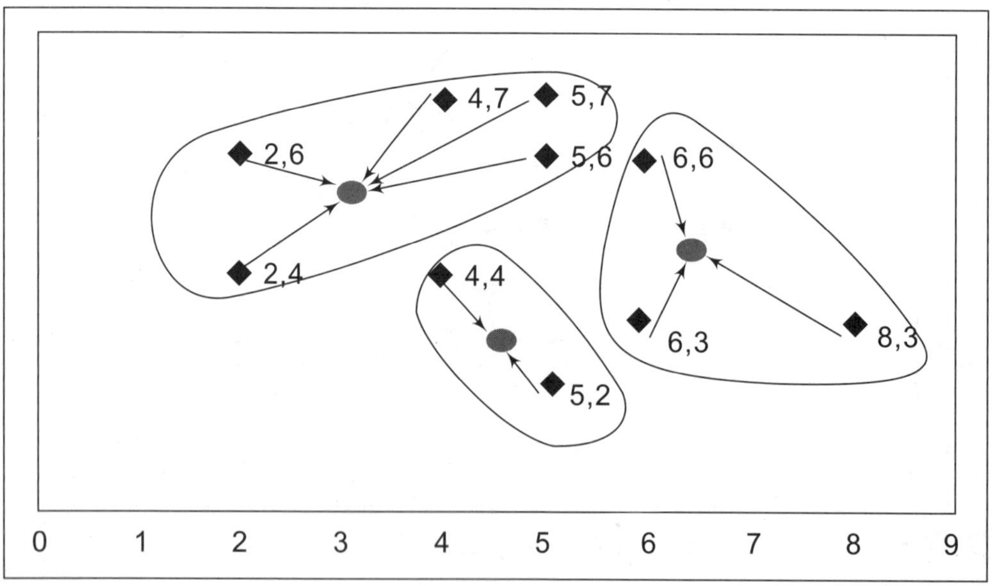

Figure 9.9 Recomputing Centroids for each Cluster till Clusters Stabilize

The three clusters shown are a 3-datapoints cluster with centroid (6.5,4.5), a 2-datapoint cluster with centroid (4.5,3), and a 5-datapoint cluster with centroid (3.5,3) (Figure 9.9).

These cluster definitions are different from the ones derived visually. This is a function of the random starting centroid values. The centroid points used earlier in the visual exercise were different from that chosen with the K-means clustering algorithm. The K-means clustering exercise should, therefore, be run again with this data, but with new random centroid starting values. With many iterations of the algorithm, the cluster definitions are likely to stabilize. If the cluster definitions do not stabilize, that may be a sign that the number of clusters chosen is too high or too low. The algorithm should be run again with different values of K.

Here is the pseudo-code for implementing a K-means algorithm.

Algorithm K-Means (K number of clusters, D list of data points)

1. Choose K number of random data points as initial centroids (cluster-centers)
2. Repeat till cluster-centers stabilize
   a. { Allocate each point in D to the nearest of K centroids;
   b. Compute centroid for the cluster using all points in the cluster}

SELECTING THE NUMBER OF CLUSTERS

The correct choice of the value of k is often ambiguous. It depends on the shape and scale of the distribution points in a data set and the desired clustering resolution of the user. Heuristics are needed to pick the right number. One can graph the percentage of variance explained by the clusters against the number of clusters (Figure 9.10). The first clusters will add more information (explain a lot of variances), but at some point, the marginal gain in variance will fall, giving a sharp angle to the graph, looking like an elbow. Beyond that elbow point, adding more clusters will not add much incremental value. That would be the desired K.

To engage with the data and to understand the cluster characteristics better, it is often preferable to start with a small number of clusters, such as 2 or 3, depending upon the data set and the application domain. This number can be increased subsequently, as needed from an application point of view. This helps us understand the data and the clusters progressively better.

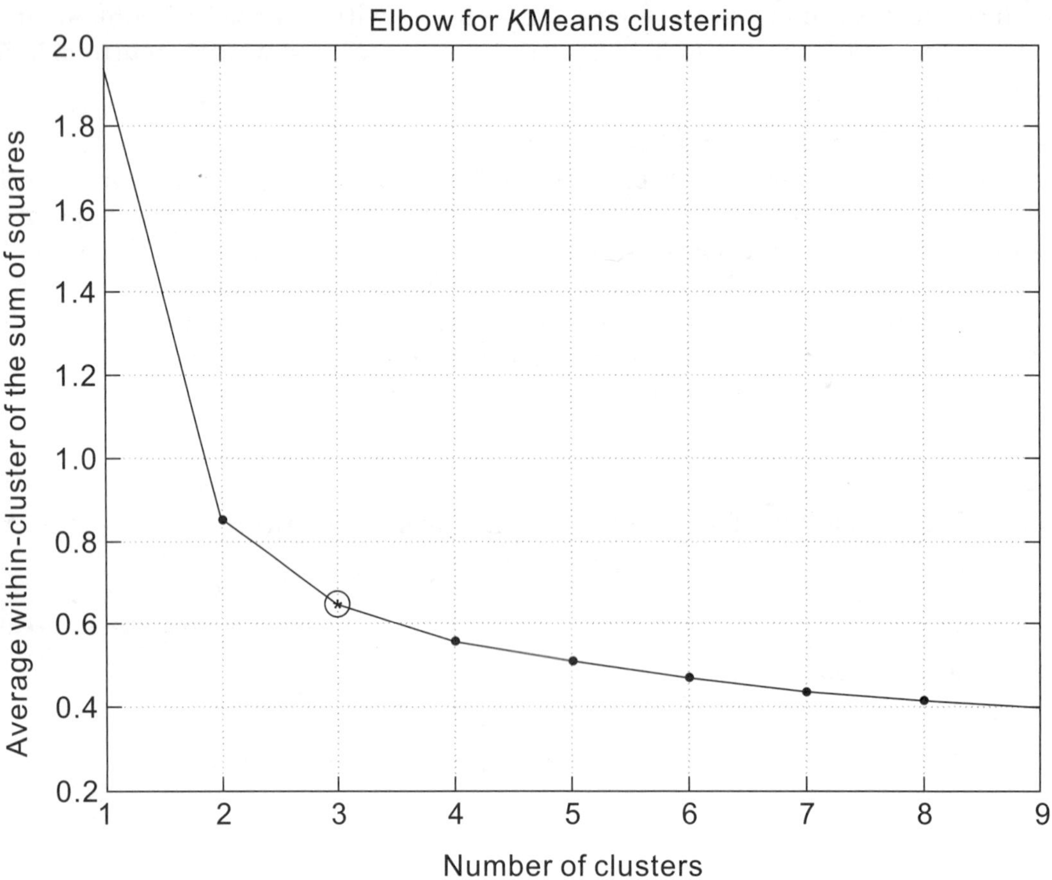

Figure 9.10 Elbow Method for Determining a number of Clusters in a Dataset

ADVANTAGES AND DISADVANTAGES OF K-MEANS ALGORITHM

There are many advantages of K-Means algorithm:

1. K-Means algorithm is simple, easy to understand, and easy to implement.
2. It is also efficient, in that the time taken to cluster k-means rises only linearly with the number of data points.
3. No other clustering algorithm performs better than K-Means, in general.

There are a few disadvantages too:

1. The user needs to specify an initial value of K.
2. The process of finding the clusters may not converge.

3. It is not suitable for discovering cluster shapes that are not hyper-ellipsoids (or hyper-spheres). For example, if there is a cluster of points that are on concentric circles at different radii from the center, K-Means will not be able to separate them.

Artificial neural networks can also be deployed for clustering, using the appropriate objective function. The neural network will produce the appropriate cluster centroids and cluster population for each cluster.

K-MODES ALGORITHM

K-Modes is a variant of the K-Means algorithm used for clustering with categorical data (such as names or colors). It groups similar objects into clusters based on the similarity of their categorical attributes. K-modes are capable of handling large numbers of categorical attributes and can be used for large datasets. Like in K-means, the "k" in k-modes refers to the number of clusters that are formed. The k-modes algorithm starts by randomly selecting initial centroids for each cluster, and then iteratively updates the centroids and assigns objects to clusters until the centroids stabilize.

CONCLUSION

Cluster analysis is a useful, unsupervised learning technique that is used in many business situations to segment the data into meaningful small groups. K-Means algorithm is an easy statistical technique to iteratively segment the data. However, there is only a heuristic technique to select the right number of clusters. K-Modes is a variant to use with categorical data. However, there are many irregular kinds of similarities that require special clustering techniques.

REVIEW EXERCISES

1. What is unsupervised learning? When is it used?
2. Describe three business applications in your industry where cluster analysis will be useful.
3. What is the centroid of a cluster? How is it computed?
4. Describe the pseudocode of the K-means algorithm. And of K-Modes.
5. Data about height and weight for a few volunteers is available. Create a set of clusters for the following data, to decide how many sizes of T-shirts should be ordered.

Height	Weight
71	165
68	165
72	180
67	113
72	178
62	101
70	150
69	172
72	185
63	149
69	132
61	115

TRUE/FALSE

1. Cluster analysis is used for market segmentation.
2. A good set of clusters should be of significantly different sizes.
3. Usually the clusters can each be represented by a central point, or the modal point, also called the 'centroid'.
4. A decision tree can help in determining the likely number of clusters in a given dataset.
5. The key objective of all clustering algorithms is the same, i.e.,inter-cluster distance is maximized and intra-cluster distance is minimized.
6. There are multiple ways of measuring the distance between data points.
7. An unlimited number of variables can be used for cluster analysis.
8. *K*-means is the most popular clustering algorithm.
9. *K*-means automatically produces the right number of clusters in the data.
10. Amazon uses clustering technique to recommend new products for its customers to buy.

CASELET

MAALA STORES Case Exercise: Step 7

Maala wants to find a suitable number of segments for its customers, for targeted marketing. Here is a list of representative customers.

Customer	Number of Transactions	Total Purchase ($)	Income ($ K)
1	5	450	90
2	10	800	82
3	15	900	77
4	2	50	30
5	18	900	60
6	9	200	45
7	14	500	82
8	8	300	22
9	7	250	90
10	9	1000	80
11	1	30	60
12	6	700	80

1: *What is the right number of customer segments for Maala?*

2: *What are their centroids for the segment clusters?*

CHAPTER 10 Association Rule Mining

Learning Objectives

LO 1 Understand Association Rule Mining and its business applications

LO 2 Learn how association rules are represented

LO 3 Know Apriori algorithm and its pseudocode

LO 4 Learn how the association rule technique works in practice

Association rule mining is a popular, unsupervised learning technique, used in business to help identify shopping patterns. It is also known as market basket analysis. It helps find interesting relationships (affinities) between variables (items or events). Thus, it can help cross-sell related items and increase the size of a sale.

All data used in this technique is of categorical type. There is no dependent variable. It uses machine learning algorithms. The fascinating "relationship between sales of diapers and beers" is how it is often explained in popular literature. This technique accepts as input the raw point-of-sale transaction data. The output produced is the description of the most frequent affinities among items. An example of an association rule would be, "A Customer who bought a flight ticket and a hotel reservation also bought a rental car plan 60 percent of the time".

CASELET

Netflix suggestions and recommendation engines are powered by a suite of algorithms using data about millions of customer ratings about thousands of movies. Most of these algorithms are based on the premise that similar viewing patterns represent similar user tastes. This suite of algorithms, called CineMatch, instructs Netflix's servers to process information from its databases to determine which movies a customer is likely to enjoy. The algorithm takes into account many factors about the films themselves, the customers' ratings, and the combined ratings of all Netflix users. The company estimates that a whopping 75 percent of viewer activity is driven by recommendations. According to Netflix, these predictions were valid around 75 percent of the time and half of Netflix users who rented CineMatch-recommended movies gave them a five-star rating.

To make matches, a computer

1. *Searches the CineMatch database for people who have rated the same movie - for example, "The Return of the Jedi".*

2. *Determines which of those people have also rated a second movie, such as "The Matrix".*
3. *Calculates the statistical likelihood that people who liked "Return of the Jedi" will also like "The Matrix".*
4. *Continues this process to establish a pattern of correlations between subscribers' ratings of many different films.*

Netflix launched a contest in 2006 to find an algorithm that could beat CineMatch. The contest, called the Netflix Prize, promised $1 million to the first person or team to meet the accuracy goals for recommending movies based on users' personal preferences. Each of these algorithm submissions was required to demonstrate a 10 percent improvement over CineMatch. Three years later, the $1 million prize was awarded to a team of seven people (To know more visit: http://electronics.howstuffworks.com).

Q1: *Are Netflix customers being manipulated into seeing what Netflix wants them to see?*

Q2: *Compare this story with Amazon's recommendation engine.*

BUSINESS APPLICATIONS OF ASSOCIATION RULES

In business environments, a pattern or knowledge can be used for many purposes. In sales and marketing, it is used for cross-marketing and cross-selling, catalog design, e-commerce site design, online advertising optimization, product pricing, and sales/promotion configurations. This analysis can suggest that one should not put one item on sale at a time, and instead, one should create a bundle of products that were promoted as a package to sell other non-selling items.

In retail environments, this technique can be used for store design. Strongly associated items could be kept close together for customer convenience. Or they could be placed far apart so that the customer has to walk the aisles and in doing so is potentially exposed to other items.

In medicine, this technique can be used for relationships between symptoms and illnesses; diagnosis and patient characteristics/treatments; genes and their functions; etc.

REPRESENTING ASSOCIATION RULES

A generic association rule is represented between a set X and Y: $X \Rightarrow Y$ **[S%, C%]**

X, Y: Products and/or services

X: Left-hand-side (LHS)

Y: Right-hand-side (RHS)

S: Support: How often *X* and *Y* go together in the dataset, i.e., $P(X \cup Y)$

C: Confidence: How often *Y* is found, given *X*, i.e., $P(Y \mid X)$

Example: {Hotel booking, Flight booking} ⇒ {Rental Car} [30%, 60%]

Computation example:

[Note: *P*(*X*) is the mathematical representation of the probability or chance of *X* occurring in the data set.}

Suppose there are 1000 transactions in a data set. There are 300 occurrences of *X*, and 150 occurrences of (*X*, *Y*) in the data set.

Support *S* for $X \Rightarrow Y$ will be $P(X \cup Y) = 150/1000 = 15\%$.

Confidence for $X \Rightarrow Y$ will be $P(Y \mid X)$; or $P(X \cup Y) / P(X) = 150/300 = 50\%$

ALGORITHMS FOR ASSOCIATION RULE

Not all association rules are interesting and useful, only those that are strong rules and also those that occur frequently. In association rule mining, the goal is to find all rules that satisfy the user-specified minimum support and minimum confidence. The resulting sets of rules are all the same irrespective of the algorithm used, that is, given a transaction data set T, a minimum support and a minimum confidence, the set of association rules existing in T is uniquely determined.

Fortunately, there are a large number of algorithms that are available for generating association rules. The most popular algorithms are Apriori, Eclat, FP-Growth, along with various derivatives and hybrids of the three. All the algorithms help identify the frequent item sets, which are then converted into association rules.

APRIORI ALGORITHM

This is the most popular algorithm used for association rule mining. The objective is to find subsets that are common to at least a minimum number of itemsets. A frequent itemset is an itemset whose support is greater than or equal to the minimum support threshold. It uses a bottom-up approach; and the size of frequent subsets is gradually increased, from one-item subsets to two-item subsets, then three-item subsets, and so on. Groups of candidates at each level are tested for minimum support. The Apriori property is a downward closure property, which means that any subsets of a frequent itemset are also frequent itemsets. Thus, if (A,B,C,D) is a frequent itemset, then any subset such as (A,B,C) or (B,D) are also frequent itemsets.

ASSOCIATION RULES MINING EXERCISE

Here are a dozen sales transactions. There are six products being sold: Milk, Bread, Butter, Eggs, Cookies, and Ketchup. Transaction#1 sold Milk, Eggs, Bread, and Butter. Transaction#2 sold Milk, Butter, Egg & Ketchup, and so on. The objective is to use this transaction data to find affinities between products, that is, which products sell together often.

Suppose that the business requirements need the support level to be set at 33 percent, and the confidence level to be set at 50 percent. That means that we have decided to consider rules from only those itemsets that occur at least 33 percent of the time in the total set of transactions. Confidence level means that within those itemsets, the rules of the form X → Y should be such that there is at least 50 percent chance of Y occurring based on X occurring.

Transactions List				
1	Milk	Egg	Bread	Butter
2	Milk	Butter	Egg	Ketchup
3	Bread	Butter	Ketchup	
4	Milk	Bread	Butter	
5	Bread	Butter	Cookies	
6	Milk	Bread	Butter	Cookies
7	Milk	Cookies		
8	Milk	Bread	Butter	
9	Bread	Butter	Egg	Cookies
10	Milk	Butter	Bread	
11	Milk	Bread	Butter	
12	Milk	Bread	Cookies	Ketchup

First step is to compute one-item Itemsets, that is, how often does any product individually sell.

1-item Sets	Frequency
Milk	9
Bread	10
Butter	10

1-item Sets	Frequency
Egg	3
Ketchup	3
Cookies	5

Thus, Milk sells in 9 out of 12 transactions. Bread sells in 10 out of 12 transactions. And so on.

At every point, there is an opportunity to select itemsets of interest, and thus further analysis. Other itemsets that occur very infrequently may be removed. If itemsets that occur 4 or more times out of 12 are selected, that corresponds to meeting a minimum support level of 33 percent (4 out of 12). Only four items make the cut. The frequent items that meet the support level of 33 percent are:

Frequent 1-item Sets	Frequency
Milk	9
Bread	10
Butter	10
Cookies	5

The next step is to go for the next level of itemsets using items selected earlier:

2-item Sets	Frequency
Milk, Bread	7
Milk, Butter	7
Milk, Cookies	3
Bread, Butter	9
Butter, Cookies	3
Bread, Cookies	4

Thus, (Milk, Bread) sell 7 times out of 12. (Milk, Butter) sell together seven times, (Bread, Butter sell) together nine times, and (Bread, Cookies) sell our times.

However, only four of these transactions meet the minimum support level of 33%.

2-item Sets	Frequency
Milk, Bread	7
Milk, Butter	7
Bread, Butter	9
Bread, Cookies	4

The next step is to list the next higher level of itemsets: three-item itemsets.

3-item Sets	Frequency
Milk, Bread, Butter	6
Milk, Bread, Cookies	1
Bread, Butter, Cookies	3

Thus, (Milk, Bread, Butter) sell 6 times out of 12. (Bread, Butter, Cookies) sell three times out of 12. One three-item itemset meets the minimum support requirements.

3-item Sets	Frequency
Milk, Bread, Butter	6

There is no possibility to create a four-item itemset for this support level.

CREATING ASSOCIATION RULES

The most important association rules start top-down with the most frequent itemsets of higher sized itemsets. Association rules are created that meet the minimum support level and confidence level requirements.

The highest level itemset that meets the support requirements is the three-item itemset. The following itemset has a support level of 50% (6 out of 12).

Milk, Bread, Butter	6

This itemset could lead to three possible candidate Association rules.

(Bread, Butter) → Milk; (Milk, Butter) → Bread; (Bread, Milk) → Butter.

Start with evaluating the first rule: (Bread, Butter) → Milk.

There are a total of total 12 transactions. $T = 12$.

X (in this case Bread, Butter) occurs nine times;

X, Y (in this case Bread, Butter, Milk) occurs six times.

The support level for this rule is $X / T = 6/12 = 50\%$.

The confidence level for this rule is $X / Y = 6/9 = 67\%$.

This rule meets our thresholds for support (>33%) and confidence (>50%).

Thus, the first valid Association rule from this data is:

(Bread, Butter) → Milk {$S = 50\%$, $C = 67\%$}.

In exactly the same way, other rules can be considered for their validity.

Consider the rule: (Milk, Bread) → Butter. Out of total 12 transactions, (Milk, Bread) occurs seven times; and (Milk, Bread, Butter) occurs six times. The support level for this rule is 6/12 = 50%. The confidence level for this rule is 6/7 = 86%. This rule meets our thresholds for support (>33%) and confidence (>50%). Thus, the second valid Association rule from this data is: **(Milk, Bread) →Butter {*S* = 50%, *C* = 67%}**.

Consider the rule (Milk, Butter) → Bread. Out of total 12 transactions, (Milk, Butter) occurs seven times, while (Milk, Butter, Bread) occurs six times. The support level for this rule is 6/12 = 50%. The confidence level for this rule is 6/7 = 86%. This rule meets our thresholds for support (>33%) and confidence (>50%). Thus, the next valid Association rule is: **Milk, Butter → Bread {*S* = 50%, *C* = 86%}**.

Thus, there were only three possible rules at the three-item itemset level, and all were found to meet the stated requirements.

One can get to the next lower level and generate association rules at the two-item itemset level.

Consider the rule Milk → Bread. Out of total 12 transactions, Milk occurs nine times, while (Milk, Bread) occurs seven times.

The support level for this rule is 7/12 = 58%. The confidence level for this rule is 7/9 = 78%. This rule meets our thresholds for support (>33%) and confidence (>50%).

Thus, the next valid Association rule is:

Milk -> Bread {58%, 78%}.

Many such rules could be derived if needed. However, not all such association rules are interesting. The client may be interested in only the top few rules that they want to implement. The number of association rules accepted depends upon the business's need. Implementing every rule in business will require cost and effort, with some potential gains. The strongest of rules, with the highest support and confidence rates, should be implemented first, and the others should be progressively implemented later.

OTHER ALGORITHMS

FP-Growth algorithm is an improvement over the Apriori algorithm, as it uses a different data structure to represent the transactions and reduces the number of candidate itemsets that need to be generated.

ECLAT algorithm uses a "top-down" approach, starting with all possible itemsets and then pruning itemsets that are not frequent enough to generate rules.

RECOMMENDATION ENGINES

A recommendation engine or system analyzes user purchase data to make suggestions for what that user might be interested in next, such as a book, a video, a message, or a job. These systems can improve revenue and satisfaction by encouraging cross-selling, and upselling by suggesting product alternatives. They can also use items abandoned in a digital shopping cart as a potential set of affinities.

There are two main types of recommendation engines: collaborative filtering and content-based filtering. There are hybrid filtering versions combining features from both of the above. The collaborative filtering technique is about finding common interests among people with similar behavior patterns. This means that users of a certain common profile may purchase similar content. Those that bought this also bought that. Content-based filtering is about categorizing content based on common interests. For example, products that are commonly bought together can be served next. Netflix is a great example of a hybrid recommendation engine. It considers both the interests of the user (collaborative) and the descriptions or features of the movie or show (content-based).

CONCLUSION

Association Rules help discover affinities between products in transactions. It helps make cross-selling recommendations much more targeted and effective. The Apriori technique is the most popular technique, and it is a machine learning technique. It works by identifying frequent itemsets. The most frequent itemsets can be converted into association rules, with the minimum support and confidence levels.

REVIEW EXERCISES

1. What are association rules? How do they help?
2. How many association rules should be used?
3. What are frequent item sets?
4. How does the Apriori algorithm work?

5. What are support and confidence levels?
6. What are recommendation engines, and how do they work?

TRUE/FALSE

1. Also known as Market Basket Analysis, Association Rule Mining is a machine learning algorithm.
2. Association rule mining is an unsupervised learning technique that helps find frequent patterns.
3. Not all association rules are interesting. The client may be interested in implementing only the top few rules.
4. All the data used in association rules technique is of ratio (numeric) type.
5. Given a transaction dataset *T*, a minimum support and a minimum confidence, the goal is to determine a set of rules that meet those support and confidence conditions.
6. The set of association rules existing in *T* depends upon the algorithm used.
7. A generic association rule is represented between sets *X* and *Y* as ***X* ∅ *Y* [*S*%, *C*%]**.
8. A frequent itemset can contain any number of items.
9. Apriori is the name of the most popular association rule mining technique.
10. A suite of algorithms called CineMatch helps Netflix determine which movies a customer is likely to enjoy next.

CASELET

MAALA STORES Case Exercise: Step 8

Here is a list of Transactions from Maala's stores. Create association rules for the following data. With 33% support level and 66% confidence.

	Barley	Corn	Gram	Millet	Rice	Wheat
1	1	1	1	1	1	1
2		1		1	1	1
3	1		1		1	1
4		1	1		1	1
5	1		1	1	1	

	Barley	Corn	Gram	Millet	Rice	Wheat
6			1		1	1
7	1			1	1	1
8				1	1	1
9	1	1	1	1		
10	1	1	1		1	1
11		1		1	1	1
12	1	1		1	1	1

Section 3
Advanced Data Mining

This section covers advanced mining techniques that also include Text and Web Mining.

- Chapter 11 covers Text Mining, the art and science of generating insights from text. It is very important in the age of social media.
- Chapter 12 covers Naïve-Bayes classification technique used often for text data mining problems such as spam filtering. It includes two solved problems.
- Chapter 13 covers Support Vector Machines, a machine learning technique, also used often for text data mining problems such as spam filtering.
- Chapter 14 covers Web Mining, the art and science of generating insights from the worldwide web, its content and usage. It is very important in the digital age where a lot of advertising and selling is moving to the web.
- Chapter 15 covers Social Network Analysis, the art and science of discovering patterns of interaction and influence within the participants in a network. It can be applied in a wide range of situations from communication networks among human beings to the relative importance of websites with the worldwide web.

CHAPTER

11 Text Mining

CLearning Objectives

LO 1 Understand the concept of text mining and its applications

LO 2 Know the process of text mining, including the concept of Term-Document Matrix and how it can be mined

LO 3 Compare between text mining and data mining

LO 4 Learn some important best practices of text mining

Text mining is the art and science of discovering knowledge, insights, and patterns from an organized collection of textual databases. It involves the use of natural language processing (NLP) and machine learning techniques to analyze and make sense of text data. Text mining can help with frequency analysis of important terms, and their semantic relationships. Good text mining should produce relevant information with high accuracy and scalability.

Text is an important part of the growing data in the world. Social media technologies have enabled users to become producers of text and images and other kinds of information. Text mining can be applied to large-scale social media data for gathering preferences and measuring emotional sentiments. It can also be applied to societal, organizational, and individual scales.

Text mining is a rapidly evolving area of research. As the amount of social media and other text data grows, there is a need for efficient abstraction and categorization of meaningful information from the text. Artificial Intelligence tools have completely revolutionized text mining. Voice-based chat tools, such as Amazon's Alexa, Apple's Siri, and others, have developed remarkable accuracy in hearing and recognizing text, and acting upon it.

CASELET

WhatsApp and Private Security

Do you think that what you post on social media remains private? Think again. A new dashboard shows how much personal information is out there, and how companies are able to construct ways to make use of it for commercial benefits. Here is a dashboard of conversations between two people Jennifer and Nicole over 45 days.

There is a variety of categories that Nicole and Jennifer speak about such as computers, politics, laundry, desserts. The polarity of Jennifer's personal thoughts and tone is overwhelmingly

positive, and Jennifer responds to Nicole much more than vice versa, identifying Nicole as the influencer in their relationship.

The data visualization reveals the waking hours of Jennifer, showing that she is most active around 8:00 p.m. and heads to bed around midnight. Fifty-three percent of her conversation is about food – and 15% about desserts. Maybe she's a strategic person to push restaurant or weight loss ads.

The most intimate detail exposed during this conversation is that Nicole and Jennifer discuss right wing populism, radical parties, and conservative politics. It exemplifies that the amount of private information obtained from your WhatsApp conversations is limitless and potentially dangerous.

WhatsApp is the world's largest messaging service that has over 450 million users. Facebook recently bought this 3-year-old company for a whopping $19 billion. People share a lot of sensitive personal information on WhatsApp that they may not even share with their family members.

(To know more visit: What Facebook Knows About You From One WhatsApp Conv, by Adi Azaria, on Linked In, April 10, 2014).

Q1: *What are the business and social implications of this kind of analysis?*

Q2: *Are you worried? Should you be worried?*

Text mining works on texts from practically any kind of sources from any business or non-business domains, in any format including Word documents, PDF files, XML files, text messages, etc. Here are some representative examples:

1. In the *legal profession*, text sources would include laws, court deliberations, court orders, etc.
2. In *academic research*, it would include texts of interviews, published research articles, etc.
3. In the world of *finance*, it will include statutory reports, internal reports, CFO statements, and more.
4. In *medicine*, it would include medical journals, patient histories, discharge summaries, etc.
5. In *marketing*, it would include advertisements, customer comments, etc.
6. In the world of *technology* and search, it would include patent applications, the whole of information on the worldwide web, and more.

TEXT MINING APPLICATIONS

Text mining is a useful tool in the hands of knowledge officers to extract knowledge relevant to an organization. Text mining can be used across industry sectors and application areas, including decision support, sentiment analysis, fraud detection, survey analysis, and many more.

1. *Marketing:* The voice of the customer can be captured in its native and raw format and then analyzed for customer preferences and complaints.
   - **a.** Social personas are a clustering technique to develop customer segments of interest. Consumer input from social media sources, such as reviews, blogs, and tweets, contain numerous leading indicators that can be used toward anticipating and predicting consumer behavior.
   - **b.** A "listening platform" is a text mining application, that in real time, gathers social media, blogs, and other textual feedback, and filters out the chatter to extract true consumer sentiment. The insights can lead to more effective product marketing and better customer service.
   - **c.** The customer call center conversations and records can be analyzed for patterns of customer complaints. Decision trees can organize this data to create decision choices that could help with product management activities and to become proactive in avoiding those complaints.
2. *Business operations:* Many aspects of business functioning can be accurately gauged by analyzing text.
   - **a.** Social network analysis and text mining can be applied to emails, blogs, social media, and other data to measure the emotional states and the mood of employee populations. Sentiment analysis can reveal early signs of employee dissatisfaction, which can then be proactively managed.
   - **b.** Studying people as emotional investors and using text analysis of the social internet to measure mass psychology can help in obtaining superior investment returns.
3. *Legal:* In legal applications, lawyers and paralegals can more easily search case histories and laws for relevant documents in a particular case to improve their chances of winning.
   - **a.** Text mining is also embedded in e-discovery platforms that help in minimizing risk in the process of sharing legally mandated documents.
   - **b.** Case histories, testimonies, and client meeting notes can reveal additional information, such as morbidities in a healthcare situation that can help better predict high-cost injuries and prevent costs.
4. *Governance and Politics:* Governments can be overturned based on a tweet originating from a self-immolating fruit-vendor in Tunisia.
   - **a.** Social network analysis and text mining of large-scale social media data can be used for measuring the emotional states and the mood of constituent populations. Micro-targeting constituents with specific messages gleaned from

social media analysis can be a more efficient use of resources when fighting democratic elections.

b. In geopolitical security, internet chatter can be processed for real-time information and to connect the dots on any emerging threats.

c. In academics, research streams could be meta-analyzed for underlying research trends.

TEXT MINING PROCESS

The first level of text analysis is identifying frequent words. It begins with creating a bag of important words from all the documents at hand. Texts – documents or smaller messages – can then be ranked on how they match to a particular bag-of-words. However, there are challenges with this approach. For example, the words may be spelled a little differently. Or there may be different words with similar meanings.

The next level is the level of identifying meaningful phrases from words. Thus, "ice" and "cream" will be two different key words that often come together. However, there is a more meaningful phrase by combining the two words into "ice cream". There might be similarly meaningful phrases like "Apple Pie".

The next higher level is that of Topics. Multiple phrases could be combined into a Topic area. Thus, the two phrases of ice cream and apple pie above could be put into a common basket, and this bucket could be called "Desserts".

Text mining is a semi-automated process. Text data needs to be gathered, structured, and then mined, in a three-step process (Figure 11.1).

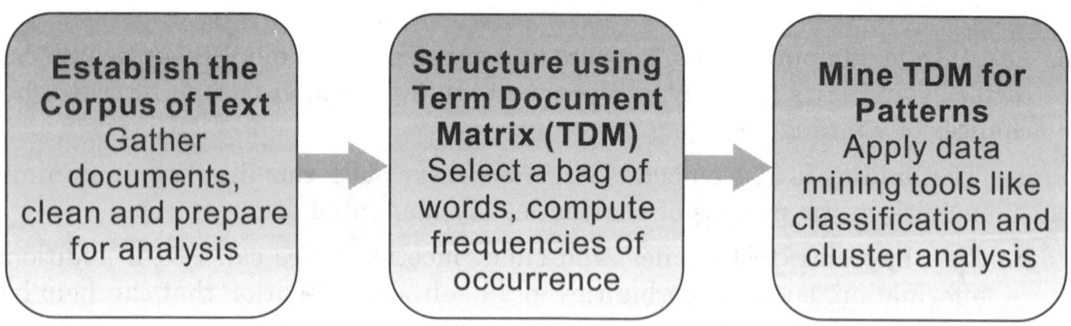

Figure 11.1 Text Mining Architecture

1. This involves collecting a large dataset of text data. The text and documents are first gathered into a corpus, and organized as a bag of words. Data is cleaned, such as by removing stop words, stemming, and lemmatizing the words.

2. The corpus is then formatted for structure. The raw text data is transformed into a numerical representation that can be used as input to machine learning algorithms. This can be done using techniques such as bag-of-words, n-grams, and term frequency-inverse document frequency (TF-IDF). The result is a matrix mapping important terms to source documents. This is called Term-document matrix or TDM.
3. The structured data in TDM can then be analyzed using different machine learning models for word structures, sequences, and frequency.

The process of text mining typically involves the following steps:

TERM DOCUMENT MATRIX

This is the heart of the structuring process. Free flowing text can be transformed into numeric data in a TDM, which can then be mined using regular data mining techniques.

1. There are several efficient techniques for identifying key terms from a text. There are less efficient techniques available for creating topics out of them. For the purpose of this discussion, one could call key words, phrases, or topics as a term of interest. This approach measures the frequencies of select important terms occurring in each document. This creates a t x d sized Term–by–Document Matrix (TDM) where t is the number of words/terms and d is the number of documents (Table 11.1).
2. Creating a TDM requires making choices of which terms to include. The terms chosen should reflect the stated purpose of the text mining exercise. The list of terms should be as extensive as needed but should not include unnecessary stuff that will serve to confuse the analysis, or slow the computation.

Table 11.1 Term-Document Matrix

	Term Document Matrix				
Document/Terms	**Investment**	**Profit**	**Happy**	**Success**	**...**
Doc 1	10	4	3	4	
Doc 2	7	2	2		
Doc 3			2	6	
Doc 4	1	5	3		
Doc 5		6		2	
Doc 6	4		2		
...					

Here are some considerations in creating a TDM.

1. A large collection of documents mapped to a large bag of words will likely lead to a very sparse matrix if they have few common words. Reducing the dimensionality of data will help improve the speed of analysis and the meaningfulness of the results. Therefore, some preprocessing would be useful. For example, synonyms, or terms with a similar meaning, should be combined and should be counted together, as a common term. This would help reduce the number of distinct terms of words or "tokens".
2. Data should be cleaned for spelling errors. Common spelling errors should be ignored, and the terms should be combined. Uppercase and lowercase terms should also be combined.
3. When many variants of the same term are used, just the stem of the word would be used to reduce the number of terms. For instance, terms like customer order, ordering, order data, should be combined into a single token word, called "Order". Similarly, for example, happy and happiness could be combined into one word.
4. On the other side, homonyms (terms with the same spelling but different meanings) should be counted separately. For example, the term order can mean a customer order, or the ranking of certain choices. These two should be treated separately. For example, "The boss ordered that the customer orders data analysis be presented in chronological order". This statement shows three different meanings for the word "order". Thus, there will be a need for a manual review of the TD matrix. This would enhance the quality of the analysis.
5. Terms with very few occurrences in very few documents should be eliminated from the matrix. This would help increase the density of the matrix and the quality of the analysis.
6. The measures in each cell of the matrix could be one of several possibilities. It could be a simple count of the number of occurrences of each term in a document. It could also be the log of that number. It could be the fraction number computed by dividing the frequency count by the total number of words in the document. Or there may be binary values in the matrix to represent whether a term is mentioned or not. The choice of value in the cells will depend upon the purpose of the text analysis.

At the end of this analysis and cleansing, a well-formed, densely populated, rectangular, TDM will be ready for analysis. The TDM could be mined using all the available data mining techniques.

MINING THE TDM

The TDM can be mined to extract patterns/knowledge. A variety of data mining techniques could be applied to the TDM to extract new knowledge.

A simple and unique text mining application will be to visualize the highest frequency terms. This can be done very attractively and colorfully in the form of a wordcloud. A wordcloud could be created after removing the common words like prepositions. It can be done for the top n words such as top 100 words, to focus on the key terms used in the document. The attached wordcloud represents the speech by US President Barack Obama on the topic of terrorism.

Figure 11.2 A Word Cloud of Factors in Education and Learning

Predictors of desirable terms could be discovered through predictive techniques, such as regression analysis. Suppose the word profit is a desirable word in a document. The number of occurrences of the word profit in a document could be regressed against many other terms in the TDM. The relative strengths of the coefficients of various predictor variables would show the relative impact of those terms on creating a profit discussion.

Predicting the chances of a document being liked is another form of analysis. For example, important speeches made by the CEO or the CFO to investors could be evaluated for quality. If the classification of those documents (such as good or poor speeches) was available, then the terms of TDM could be used to predict the speech class. A decision tree could be constructed that makes a simple tree with a few decision points that predict the success of a speech 80 percent of the time. This tree could be trained with more data to become better over time.

Clustering techniques can help categorize text documents by their common profile. For example, documents containing the words investment and profit more often could be bundled together. Similarly, documents containing the words, customer orders and marketing, more often could be bundled together. Thus, a few strongly demarcated bundles could capture the essence of the entire TDM. These bundles could thus help with further processing, such as handing over select documents to others for legal discovery.

Association rule analysis could show relationships of coexistence. Thus, one could say that the words, tasty and sweet, occur together often (say 5 percent of the time); and further, when these two words are present, 70 percent of the time, the word happy, is also present in the document.

COMPARING TEXT MINING AND DATA MINING

Text Mining is an advanced form of data mining, using unstructured textual data. There are many common elements between Text and Data Mining. However, there are some key differences (Table 11.2). The key difference is that text mining requires conversion of text data into frequency data, before data mining techniques can be applied.

Table 11.2 Comparing Text Mining and Data Mining

Dimension	Text Mining	Data Mining
Nature of data	Unstructured data: Words, phrases, sentences	Numbers; alphabetical and logical values
Language used	Many languages and dialects used in the world; many languages are extinct, new documents are discovered	Similar numerical systems across the world
Clarity and precision	Sentences can be ambiguous; sentiment may contradict the words	Numbers are precise.
Consistency	Different parts of the text can contradict each other	Different parts of data can be inconsistent, thus, requiring statistical significance analysis
Sentiment	Text may present a clear and consistent or mixed sentiment, across a continuum. Spoken words add further sentiment	Not applicable
Quality	Spelling errors. Differing values of proper nouns such as names. Varying quality of language translation	Issues with missing values, outliers, etc.
Nature of analysis	Keyword based search; co-existence of themes; Sentiment mining;	A full wide range of statistical and machine learning analysis for relationships and differences

TEXT MINING BEST PRACTICES

Many of the best practices that apply to the use of data mining techniques will also apply to text mining.

1. The first and most important practice is to ask the right business question. A good question is one which gives an answer and would lead to large payoffs for the organization. The purpose and the key question will define how and at what levels of granularity the TDM would be made. For example, TDM defined for simpler searches would be different from those used for complex semantic analysis or network analysis.
2. A second important practice is to be creative and open in proposing imaginative hypotheses for the solution. Thinking outside the box is important, both in the quality of the proposed solution and in finding high-quality data sets required to test the hypothesized solution. For example, a TDM of consumer sentiment data should be combined with customer order data in order to develop a comprehensive view of customer behavior. It is important to assemble a team that has a healthy mix of technical and business skills.
3. Another important element is to pursue the problem iteratively. Too much data can overwhelm the infrastructure and also befuddle the mind. It is better to divide and conquer the problem with a simpler TDM, with fewer terms and fewer documents and data sources. One can gradually expand as needed, in an iterative sequence of steps. In the future, one can add new terms to help improve predictive accuracy.
4. A variety of data mining tools should be used to test the relationships in the TDM. Different decision tree algorithms could be run alongside cluster analysis and other techniques. Triangulating the findings with multiple techniques, and many what-if scenarios, helps build confidence in the solution. Test the solution in many ways before committing to deploy it.

CONCLUSION

Text mining is diving into unstructured text to discover valuable insights about the business. The text is gathered and then structured into a term-document matrix based on the frequency of a bag of words in a corpus of documents. The TDM can then be mined for useful, novel patterns, and insights. While the technique is important, the business objective should be well understood and should always be kept in mind. Wordcloud is an important and unique text mining application.

REVIEW QUESTIONS

1. What is text mining? Why is text mining useful in the age of social media?
2. What kinds of problems can be addressed using text mining?
3. What kinds of sentiments can be found in the text? What is a wordcloud?

TRUE/FALSE

1. Text mining helps determine patterns within written text.
2. A corpus is the collection of all the documents selected for text mining.
3. TDM refers to TermDocument Method.
4. All data mining techniques can be applied to the TDM.
5. Creating a TDM involves creating a matrix for all the terms and words in the document.
6. Text sentiment analysis can reveal early signs of employee dissatisfaction.

CASELET

MAALA STORES Case Exercise: Step 9

Here are a few comments from customer service calls received by Liberty.

1. *I loved the design of the shirt. The size fitted me very well. However, the fabric seemed flimsy. I am calling to see if you can replace the shirt with a different one. Or please refund my money.*
2. *I was running late from work, and I stopped by to pick up some groceries. I did not like the way the manager closed the store while I was still shopping.*
3. *I stopped by to pick up flowers. The checkout line was very long. The manager was polite but did not open new cashiers. I got late for my appointment.*
4. *The manager promised that the product will be there, but when I went there, the product was not there. The visit was a waste. The manager should have compensated me for my trouble.*
5. *When there was a problem with my catering order, the store manager promptly contacted me and quickly got the kinks out to send me replacement food immediately. They are very courteous.*

Create a TDM with not more than six key terms. [Hint: Treat each comment as a document]

CHAPTER

12 Naïve Bayes Analysis

Learning Objectives

LO 1	Understand the concept of Naïve-Bayes analysis as a classification technique
LO 2	Learn how the NB model works
LO 3	Use the NB technique in different situations
LO 4	Know advantages and disadvantages of Naïve-Bayes analysis

Naïve Bayes (NB) technique is a supervised learning technique that uses probability-theory-based analysis. It is a probabilistic machine-learning technique that computes the probabilities of an instance belonging to each one of many target classes, given the prior probabilities of classification using individual factors. Naïve Bayes technique is a simple and fast algorithm that is commonly used often in classifying text documents into one of the multiple predefined categories such as for spam filtering.

CASELET

Fraud Detection in Government Contracts

OTCU, the Brazilian Court of Audit, wanted to use data mining for more efficient and effective use of resources for fraud detection in government transactions. They wanted to find ways to identify projects that had a high probability of fraud. An NB classifier was designed to assign a risk factor to each case.

The audit universe was the set of purchases, contracts, assets, programs, public employees or contractors. The audit universe was the set of pairs of public and private parties of all public contracts signed by the Brazilian federal administration between 1997 and 2011, totalizing almost 800,000 pairs. allowing, and assisting audit agencies in transitioning from reactive to proactive fraud detection models.

Second, the risk factors of an audit universe were identified that could relate to the entire entity set. The risk factors included the project related elements as well as external factors.

Naïve Bayes algorithm analysis was used to compute the probability distribution of entities belonging to risk classes. These probabilities were used to compute the conditional probability of fraud for the set of 800,000 pairs of public and private parties. The probability of high risk was used to sort the auditable units by total risk score. The result was that almost 2500 pairs had a high risk probability score of higher than 99%. The ranked audit universe was then used to develop an audit plan.

Q1: *What are the advantages to the government and people of Brazil from this analysis? How could this analysis be improved?*

Q2: *Identify another environment where a similar NB analysis could be beneficial.*

PROBABILITY

Probability is defined as a chance of something happening. The probability values thus range from zero to one, with a value of zero representing no chance, and one representing total certainty. Using past event records, the probability of something happening in the future can be reliably assessed. For example, one can assess the probability of dying from an airline accident, by dividing the total number of airline accident-related deaths in a time period by the total number of people flying during that period. These probabilities can then be compared to come to conclusions, such as the safety levels of various event types. For example, past data may show that the probability of dying from an airline accident is less than that of dying from being hit by lightning.

The Naïve-Bayes algorithm is special in that it takes into consideration the prior-probability of an instance belonging to a class, in addition to the recent track record of the instance belonging to that class.

(a) The word Naïve represents the strong assumption that all parameters/features of an instance are independent variables with little or no correlation. Thus, if people are identified by their height, weight, age, and gender, then all these variables are assumed to be independent of each other. This is generally not true, and one has to watch for this assumption being violated.

(b) The word Bayes refers to Bayesian analysis (based on the work of mathematician Thomas Bayes), which computes the probability of a new occurrence not only on the recent record, but also on the basis of prior experience.

NB algorithm is easy to understand and works fast. It also performs well in multiclass prediction, such as when the target class has multiple options beyond binary yes/no classification. NB can perform well even in the case of categorical input variables compared with numerical variable(s).

NAÏVE-BAYES MODEL

In the abstract, Naïve-Bayes is a conditional probability model for classification purposes.

The goal is to find a way to predict the class variable (Y) using a vector of independent variables (X), that is, find the function f : $X \rightarrow Y$. In probability terms, the goal is to find $P(Y|X)$, the probability of Y belonging to a certain class, given X. Y is generally assumed to be a categorical variable with two or more discrete values.

Given an instance to be classified, represented by a vector $X = (x_1,..., x_n)$ representing some n features (independent variables), the Naïve Bayes model assigns, to an instance, probabilities of belonging to any of K classes. The class k with the highest posterior probability is the label that is ultimately assigned to the instance.

The posterior probability (of belonging to a Class k) is calculated as a function of prior probabilities and current likelihood value, as shown in the equation below:

$$p(C_k | x) = \frac{p(C_k)p(x| C_k)}{p(x)}$$

$P(C_k | \boldsymbol{x})$ is the posterior probability of *class* k given *predictor* ***X***.

$P(C_k)$ is the prior probability of *class k*.

$P(\boldsymbol{x})$ is the prior probability of the *predictor*.

And $P(\boldsymbol{x} | C_k)$ is the current likelihood of *predictor* given *class*.

SIMPLE CLASSIFICATION EXAMPLE

Suppose a barber salon needs to predict the service required by the incoming customer. Suppose there are only two services offered: Cutting-Hair (R) and Manicure-Pedicure (M). Thus, the value to be predicted is whether the next customer will be for R or M. The number of classes (K) is 2.

The first step is to compute the prior probability. Suppose the data gathered for the last year showed that during that period, there were 2500 customers for R and 1500 customers for M. Thus, the default (or prior) probability for the next customer to be for R is 2500/4000 or 5/8. Similarly, the default probability for the next customer to be for M is 1500/4000 or 3/8. Based on this information alone, the default expectation is that the next customer would likely be for R.

Another way to predict the service requirement of the next customer would to be look at the most recent data. One could look at the last few (choose a number) customers, to predict the next customer. Suppose the last five customers were for the services … R, M, R, M, M, in that order. Thus, the data shows that the recent probability of R is 2/5 and the recent probability of M is 3/5. Based on just this information, the next customer will likely be for M.

Thomas Bayes suggested that the prior probability should be informed by the more recent data. Naïve Bayes posterior probability for a class is computed by multiplying the prior probability and the recent probability.

Thus, in this example, the *NB* posterior probability *P*(*R*) is 5/8 × 2/5 = 10/40. Similarly, the *NB* probability *P*(*M*) is 3/8 × 3/5 = 9/40. Since *P*(*R*) is greater than the *P* (*M*), there is a greater probability of the next customer to be for *R*. Thus, the expected class label assigned to the next customer would be *R*.

Suppose, however, that the next customer coming in was for *M* service. The last five customer sequence now becomes *M*, *R*, *M*, *M*, *M*. Thus, the recent data shows that the probability for *R* is 1/5 and the probability for M is 4/5.

Now, the *NB* probability for *R* is 5/8 × 1/5 = 5/40. Similarly, the *NB* probability for *M* is 3/8 × 4/5 = 12/40. Since *P*(*M*) is greater than the *P*(*R*), there is a greater probability of the next customer to be for *M*. Thus, the expected class label assigned to the next customer is *M*.

The NB predictor thus dynamically changes its prediction value based on recent data.

TEXT CLASSIFICATION EXAMPLE

The probability of document *d* being in class *c* is computed as

$$P(c \mid d) \propto P(c) \prod_{1 \leq k \leq n_d} P(t_k \mid c)$$

where $P(t_k \mid c)$ is the conditional probability of term t_k occurring in a document of class *c*.

Here are text classification training and test data. The goal is to classify the test data into the right class as *h* or ~*h* (read as not *h*).

Training Set	Document ID	Keywords in the Document	Class = *h* (Healthy)
	1	Love happy joy joy love	Yes
	2	Happy love kick joy happy	Yes
	3	Love move joy good	Yes
	4	love happy joy pain love	Yes
	5	joy love pain kick pain	No
	6	Pain pain love kick	No
Test Data	7	Love pain joy love kick	?

The prior probabilities of a document being classified using the six documents are:

$$P(h) = 4/6 = 2/3$$

$$P(\sim h) = 2/6 = 1/3$$

that is, there is 2/3 prior probability that a document will be classified as h and 1/3 probability of not *h*.

The conditional probability for each term is the relative frequency of the term occurring in each class of documents: the *h* class and the not *h* class.

Conditional Probabilities	
Class *h*	Class ~*h*
P (Love | *h*) = 5 / 19	*P* (Love | ~*h*) = 2 / 9
P (pain | *h*) = 1 / 19	*P* (pain | ~*h*) = 4 / 9
P (joy | *h*) = 5 / 19	*P* (joy | ~*h*) = 1 / 9
P (kick | *h*) = 1 / 19	*P* (kick | ~*h*) = 2 / 9

The probability of the test instance belonging to class *h* can be computed by multiplying the prior probability of the instance belonging to class *h*, with the conditional probabilities for each of the terms in the document for class h. Thus:

$P(h \mid d7) = P(h) * (P(\text{love} \mid h))\text{^}2 * P(\text{pain} \mid h) * P(\text{joy} \mid h) * P(\text{kick} \mid h)$

$= (2/3) * (5/19) * (5/19) * (1/19) * (5/19) * (1/19) = \sim 0.0000067$

Similarly, the probability of the test instance being (not *h*) can be computed using conditional probabilities for not *h*.

$P(\sim h \mid d7) = P(\sim h) * P(\text{love} \mid \sim h) * P(\text{love} \mid \sim h) * P(\text{pain} \mid \sim h) * P(\text{joy} \mid \sim h) * P(\text{kick} \mid \sim h)$

$= (1/3) * (2/9) * (2/9) * (4/9) * (1/9) * (2/9) = 0.00018$

The NB probability of the test instance being (not *h*) is much higher than its being *h*. Thus, the test document will be classified as (not *h*).

ADVANTAGES AND DISADVANTAGES OF NAÏVE BAYES

1. The NB logic is simple. The NB posterior probability computation process is also simple.
2. Conditional probabilities can be computed for discrete data and also for probabilistic distributions. When there is a number of variables in the vector *X*, then

the problem can be modeled using probability functions to simulate the incoming values. A variety of methods exist for modeling the conditional distributions of the X variables, including normal, lognormal, gamma, and Poisson.

3. Naive Bayes assumes that all the features are independent. For most instances, that works fine. However, it can be a limitation. If there are no joint occurrences at all of a class label with a certain attribute, then the frequency-based conditional probability will be zero. When all the probabilities are multiplied, it will make the entire posterior probability estimate to be zero. This can be rectified by adding 1 to all the numerators and by adding n, the number of variables in X, to all the denominators. This will be making those probabilities very small but not zero.
4. A limitation of NB is that the posterior probability computations are good for comparison and classification of the instances. However, the probability values themselves are not good estimates of the event happening.

SUMMARY

Naïve Bayes is a probability-based machine learning technique used for classifications. The idea is to compute the probabilities of each class for a given input and then choose the class with the highest probability. It is a mathematically simple way to include the contributions of many factors in predicting the class of the next data instance. It is often used for classifying texts.

REVIEW QUESTIONS

1. What is Naïve-Bayes technique? What do Naïve and Bayes stand for?
2. In what ways is NB better than other classification techniques? Compare with Decision trees.
3. What are the most popular applications of NB technique?

TRUE/FALSE

1. Naïve-Bayes is a statistical learning technique.
2. NB is popular for classifying text documents.
3. NB uses probability based analysis to predict future occurrences.
4. NB uses prior and recent probabilities to compute posterior probability.
5. NB assumes that the input variables are independent of each other.
6. NB requires discrete data values and not continuous distributions.

CHAPTER 13

Support Vector Machines

Learning Objectives

LO 1 Understand the concept of Support Vector Machines (SVM)

LO 2 Learn the algorithm for SVM

LO 3 Know about the Kernel method that makes SVM possible

LO 4 Know advantages and disadvantages of SVMs

Support Vector Machine (SVM) is a mathematical rigorous, machine learning technique to build a linear binary classifier. It creates a hyperplane in a high-dimensional space that can accurately slice a dataset into two segments according to the desired objective. The algorithms for developing the classifier can be mathematically challenging though. SVMs are popular since they are state-of-the-art for many practical problems, such as identifying spam emails and other text mining applications.

CASELET

Prostate Cancer Detection using Protein Biomarkers

Mass spectrometry technology is being used to generate a fast and efficient profile of the protein content of complex samples. It can generate data on up to 40,000 variables that constitute the profile for a protein sample. Data analytics can be used for narrowing the search space for protein biomarker candidates. These spectra can be used to identify peaks on certain biomarkers whose intensities correlate with a particular outcome variable, for example, prostate cancer. Thorough cross-validation studies and randomization tests are performed on a prostate cancer dataset with over 300 patients, obtained at the Eastern Virginia Medical School using SELDI-TOF mass spectrometry. A two-stage linear SVM-based procedure led to average classification accuracies of 87% on a four-group classification problem, using only 13 variables (or peaks).

Q1: *What can be said about the accuracy of various techniques? Does the accuracy increase by increasing the number of variables used in the analysis?*

Q2: *As the predictive models get more accurate, what will be the role of doctors? What other skills will they need to learn?*

SVM MODEL

An SVM is a classifier function in a high-dimensional space that defines the decision boundary between two classes. The support vectors are the data points that define the "gutters", or the boundary condition, on either side of the hyperplane, for each of the two classes. The SVM model is thus conceptually easy to understand.

Suppose there is a labeled set of points classified into two classes. The goal is to find the best classifier between the points of the two types.

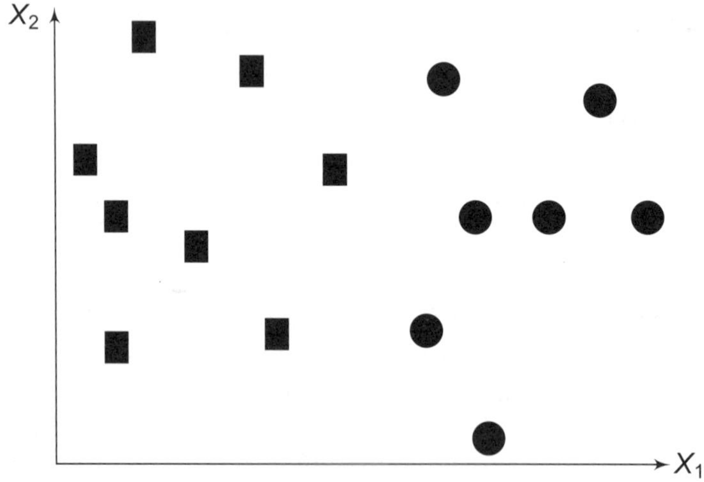

Figure 13.1 Data Points for Classification

SVM takes the widest "street" (a vector) approach to demarcate the two classes, and thus finds the hyperplane that has the widest margin: that is, the largest distance to the nearest training data points of the either class (Figure 13.1).

In Figure 13.2, the hard line is the optimal hyperplane. The dotted lines are the gutters on the sides of the two classes. The gap between the gutters is the maximum or widest margin. The classifier (hyperplane) is defined by only those points that fall on the gutters on both sides. These points are called the support vectors (shown in their bold shape). The rest of the data points that are safe in their class are irrelevant for defining the classifier (now shown unfilled).

Abstractly, suppose that the training data of n points is:

$$(\boldsymbol{X}_1, y_1) \text{ , ... , } (\boldsymbol{X}_n, y_n)$$

Where $\boldsymbol{X}_i$ represents the p-value vector for point i, and y_i is its binary class value of 1 or –1. Thus, there are two classes represented as 1 and –1.

Assuming that the data is indeed linearly separable, the classifier hyperplane is defined as a set of points (which is a subset of the training data), which satisfy the equation

$$\boldsymbol{W} \times \boldsymbol{X} + b = 0$$

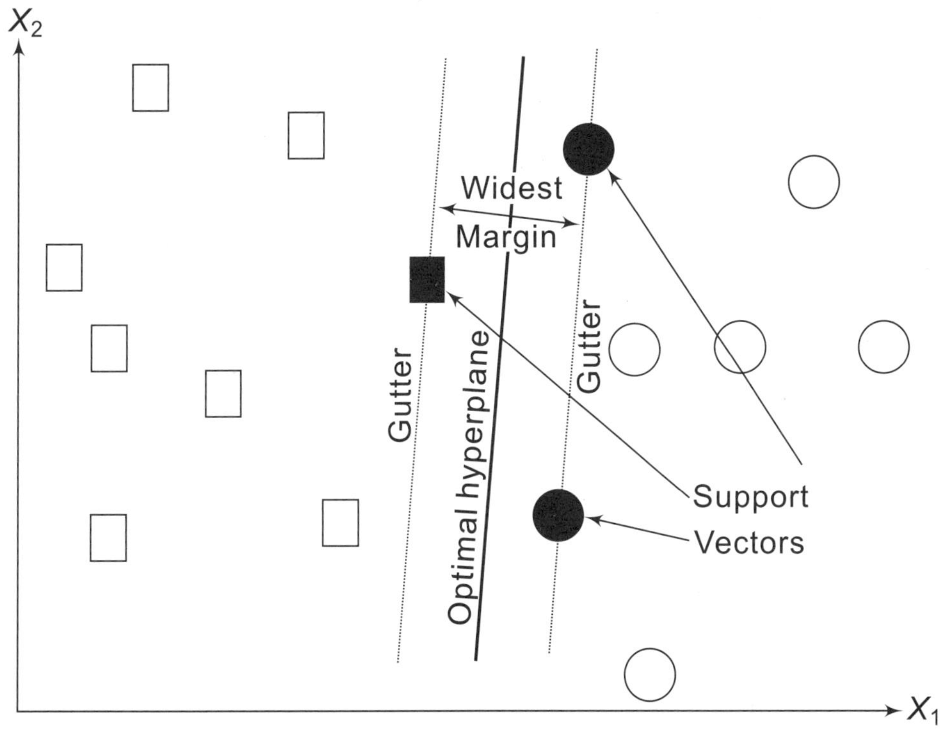

Figure 13.2 Support Vector Machine Classifier

Where $\boldsymbol{W}$ is the normal vector to the hyperplane.

The hard margins can be defined by the hyperplanes:

$$\boldsymbol{W} \times \boldsymbol{X} + b = 1 \qquad \text{and} \qquad \boldsymbol{W} \times \boldsymbol{X} + b = = -1$$

The width of the hard margin is $(2 \,/\, |\boldsymbol{W}|)$

For all points not on the hyperplane, they will be safe in their own class. Thus, the y values will have to be either greater than 1 (for points in class 1), or less than –1 (for points in class –1).

The SVM algorithm finds the weights vector (*W*) for the features, such that there is a widest margin between the two categories.

Computing an SVM using these equations is a hill-climbing process problem in a convex space. However, by working only with the points that are nearest to the classifying boundary, it reduces sharply the number of data instances to work with. This approach reduces its memory requirements for computation. This is possible because of using kernel methods.

THE KERNEL METHOD

The heart of an SVM algorithm is kernel methods. Most kernel algorithms are based on optimization in a convex space and are statistically well-founded.

Kernel stands for the core, or the germ in a fruit. Kernel methods operate using what is called the "kernel trick". This trick is to compute and work with the inner products of only the relevant pairs of data in the feature space; they do not need to compute all the data in a high-dimensional feature space. The kernel trick makes the algorithm much less demanding in computational and memory resources.

Kernel methods achieve this by learning from instances. They do not apply standard computational logic to all the features of each input. Instead, they remember each training example, and associate a weight representing its relevance to the achievement of the objective. This could be called instance-based learning. There are several types of Support Vector models, including linear, polynomial, RBF, and sigmoid.

SVM is somewhat akin to how human beings learn, especially about domains with a broad set of features, such as ethics. We learn lessons from only the "tough" situations and discard the "normal" instances. In kernel parlance, we assign high weights to abnormal situations, and very low weights to normal situations. The normal situations are almost completely forgotten.

SVMs have evolved to be more flexible and able to tolerate some amount of misclassification. The margin of separation between the categories is thus a "soft margin", as against a hard margin.

ADVANTAGES AND DISADVANTAGES

The main strength of SVMs is that they work well even when the number of features is much larger than the number of instances. It can work on datasets with huge feature space, such as is the case in spam filtering, where a large number of words could be potential signifiers of a message being spam.

Another advantage of SVMs is that even when the optimal decision boundary is a non-linear curve, the SVM transforms the variables to create new dimensions such that the representation of the classifier is a linear function of those transformed dimensions of the data.

SVMs are conceptually easy to understand. They create an easy-to-understand linear classifier. By working on only a subset of relevant data, they are computationally efficient. SVMs are now available with almost all data analytics toolsets.

The SVM technique has two major constraints. (a) It works well only with real numbers. That is, all the data points in all dimensions must be defined by numeric values only. (b) It works only with binary classification problems. One can make a series of cascaded SVMs to get around this constraint.

Training the SVMs is an inefficient and time-consuming process, when the data is large. It does not work well when there is much noise in the data, and thus has to compute soft margins. The SVMs will also not provide a probability estimate of classification, that is, the confidence level for classifying an instance.

SUMMARY

Support vector machines are a mathematically rigorous machine learning technique for classifying high-dimensional data into two classes. It creates a hyperplane, with the largest amount of separation between two classes. The classifier is made linear, by transforming the original features of input data into new features. SVMs use kernel methods to learn from specific instances that are close to the decision boundary. SVMs are used for text mining, such as spam filtering and outlier detection.

REVIEW QUESTIONS

1. What is a Support Vector Machine?
2. What are support vectors?
3. What is a kernel method?
4. Name two advantages and two limitations of SVMs.

TRUE/FALSE

1. SVM is a statistical learning technique.
2. SVMs are popular for classifying text documents.
3. SVMs use the entire dataset to develop the classifier.
4. Kernel methods use limited amount of data to facilitate faster processing.
5. SVMs can create a linear or curvilinear classifier.
6. SVMs can handle partial misclassifications.

CHAPTER 14 Web Mining

Learning Objectives

LO 1	Understand the concept of web mining
LO 2	Know the goals and process of web content mining
LO 3	Know the goals and process of web structure mining
LO 4	Learn about hub and authority pages
LO 5	Understand the goals, architecture, and process of web usage mining
LO 6	Compute PageRank manually for a small network

Web mining is the art and science of discovering patterns and insights from the world-wide web. The world-wide web is at the heart of the digital revolution. More data is posted on the web every day than was there on the whole web just 20 years ago. Billions of users are using it every day for a variety of purposes. The web is used for electronic commerce, business communication, and many other applications. Web mining analyzes data from the web and helps find insights that could optimize the web content and improve the user experience. Data for web mining is collected via Web crawlers, web logs, and other means.

Here are some characteristics of optimized websites:

1. *Appearance:* Aesthetic design. Well-formatted content, easy to scan, and navigate. Good color contrasts.
2. *Content:* Well-planned information architecture with useful content. Fresh content. Search-engine optimized. Links to other good sites.
3. *Functionality:* Accessible to authorized users. Fast loading times. Usable forms. Mobile enabled.

This type of content and its structure is of interest to ensure that the web is easy to use. The analysis of web usage provides feedback on the web content, and also the consumer's browsing habits. This data can be of immense use for commercial advertising, and even for social engineering.

The web could be analyzed for its structure as well as content. The usage pattern of web pages could also be analyzed. Depending upon objectives, web mining can be divided into three different types: Web usage mining, Web content mining, and Web structure mining (Figure 14.1).

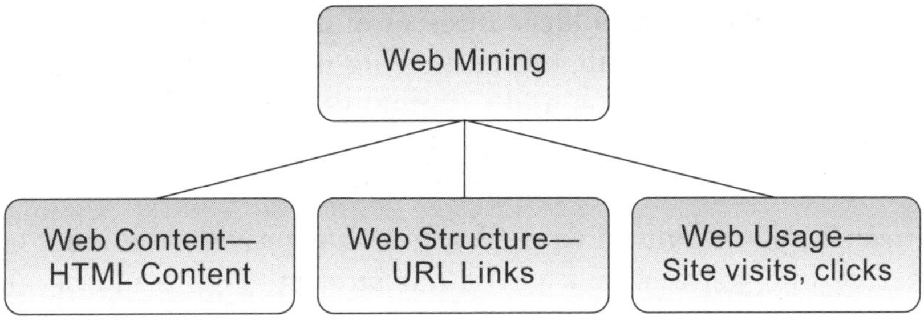

Figure: 14.1 Web Mining Structure

WEB CONTENT MINING

A website is designed in the form of pages with a distinct URL (universal resource locator). A large website may contain thousands of pages. These pages and their content are managed using specialized software systems called Content Management Systems. Every page can contain text, graphics, audio, video, forms, applications, and more kinds of content including user-generated content.

The websites keep a record of all requests received for its page/URLs, including the requester information using "cookies". The log of these webpage requests could be analyzed to gauge the popularity of those pages among different segments of the population. The text and application content on the pages could be analyzed for their usage by visit counts. The pages on a website themselves could be analyzed for the quality of content that attracts most users. Thus, unwanted or unpopular pages could be removed, or they can be transformed with different content and style. Similarly, more resources could be assigned to keep the more popular pages fresh and inviting.

In addition, there is a subset called Opinion mining. This involves extracting and analyzing opinions and sentiments from externally generated content such as customer reviews and social media posts posted on the websites. It can be used to extract information such as the overall sentiment toward a product or service, among others.

WEB STRUCTURE MINING

The Web works through a system of hyperlinks using the hypertext protocol (HTTP). Any page can create a hyperlink to any other page, and it can be linked to another page. The intertwined or self referral nature of the Web lends itself to some unique network analytical algorithms. The structure of Web pages could also be analyzed to examine the pattern of hyperlinks among pages. There are two basic strategic models for successful websites: Hubs and Authorities.

1. *Hubs:* These are pages with a large number of interesting links, especially outgoing links. They serve as a hub, or a gathering point, where people visit to access a variety of information. Media and e-commerce sites like Yahoo.com, google.com, and amazon.com are well-known hubs. Focused sites like Traveladvisor.com and yelp.com aspire to become hubs for new emerging areas.
2. *Authorities:* People gravitate toward pages that provide the most complete and authoritative information on a particular subject. This could be about general information, news, advice, user reviews, etc. These websites would have a large number of inbound links from other websites and visitors. Thus, Mayoclinic.com would serve as an authoritative page for expert medical opinion. NYtimes.com would serve as an authoritative page for daily news. Whitehouse.gov would serve as the authoritative page for the US government's policies.

WEB USAGE MINING

When a user clicks anywhere on a webpage or application, the action is recorded by many entities in many locations. The browser at the client machine will record the click, and also the web server providing the content will make a record of the pages served and the user activity on those pages. The entities connecting the client and the server, such as the router, proxy server, or ad server, too would record that click.

The goal of web usage mining is to extract useful information and patterns from data generated through Web page visits and transactions. The activity data comes from data stored in server access logs, referrer logs, agent logs, and client-side cookies. The user characteristics and usage profiles are also gathered directly, or indirectly, through syndicated data. Further, metadata, such as page attributes, content attributes, and usage data are also gathered.

The web content could be analyzed at multiple levels (Figure 14.2).

1. The *server side analysis* would show the relative popularity of the web pages accessed. Those websites could be hubs and authorities.
2. The *client side analysis* could focus on the usage pattern or the actual content consumed and created by users.
   a. Usage patterns could be analyzed using "clickstream" analysis, that is, analyzing web activity for patterns of a sequence of clicks, and the location and duration of visits on websites. Clickstream analysis can be useful for web activity analysis, software testing, market research, and analyzing employee productivity.
   b. Textual information accessed on the pages retrieved by users could be analyzed using text mining techniques. The text would be gathered and structured

using the bag-of-words technique to build a Term-document matrix. This matrix could then be mined using cluster analysis and association rules for patterns such as popular topics, user segmentation, and sentiment analysis.

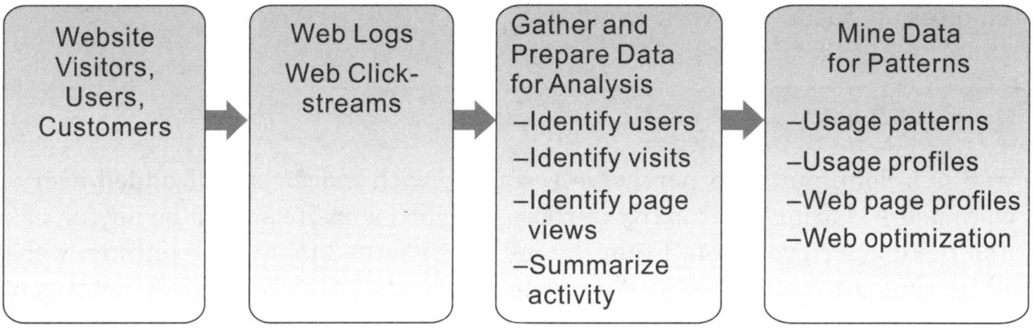

Figure 14.2 Web Usage Mining Architecture

Web usage mining has many business applications. It can help predict user behavior based on previously learned rules and users' profiles and can help determine the lifetime value of clients. It can also help design cross-marketing strategies across products, by observing association rules among the pages on the website. Web usage can help evaluate promotional campaigns and see if the users were attracted to the website and used the pages relevant to the campaign. Web usage mining could be used to present dynamic information to users based on their interests and profiles. This includes targeted online ads and coupons for user groups based on user access patterns.

WEB STRUCTURE MINING ALGORITHMS

Hyperlink-Induced Topic Search (HITS) is a link analysis algorithm that rates web pages as being hubs or authorities. Many other HITS-based algorithms have also been published. The most famous and powerful of these algorithms is called PageRank. Invented by Google co-founder Larry Page, this algorithm was originally used by Google to organize the results of its search function. This algorithm helps determine the relative importance of any particular web page by counting the number and quality of links to a page. The websites with more number of links, and/or more links from higher-quality websites, will be ranked higher. It works in a similar way as determining the status of a person in a society of people. Those with relations to more people and/or relations to people of higher status will be accorded higher status.

PageRank algorithm helps determine the order of pages listed upon a Google Search query. The original PageRank algorithm formulation has been updated in many ways and the latest tweaks in the algorithm are kept a secret so that other websites cannot take advantage of the algorithm and manipulate their website according to it. However, there are many standard elements that remain unchanged. These elements lead to the principles for a good website. This process is also called Search Engine Optimization (SEO). Web structure mining will be discussed further in the next chapter on Social Network Analysis.

CONCLUSION

The web is a dominant and pervasive resource, with more content added every day and more users visiting it for many purposes. A good website should be useful, easy to use, and flexible for evolution. From the insights gleaned using web mining, websites should be constantly optimized. Web usage mining can help discover what content users really like and consume and help prioritize that for improvement. Web structure can help improve traffic to those sites, by building authority for the sites.

REVIEW QUESTIONS

1. What are the three types of web mining?
2. What is clickstream analysis?
3. What are the two major ways that a website can become popular?
4. What are the privacy issues in web mining?
5. A user spends 60 minutes on the web, visiting 10 webpages in all. Given the clickstream data, what kind of analysis would you do?

TRUE/FALSE

1. The Web and the Internet are two names for the same thing.
2. The goal of web content mining is to look for broken URLs.
3. PageRank algorithm was created by Yahoo to determine the importance of webpages in relation to the overall structure of the web.
4. Hub pages are well-known websites which provide definitive information on a particular set of topics.
5. NYtimes.com is an example of a hub page.
6. A cookie is a piece of data stored on a web browser to keep track of a user's usage history.
7. Clickstream analysis is a part of web structure analysis.
8. All data mining techniques can be applied to web mining data.

CHAPTER

15 Social Network Analysis

Learning Objectives

LO 1	Understand the concepts of Social Networks and Social Network Analysis (SNA)
LO 2	Learn the applications of SNA
LO 3	Know the different network topologies
LO 4	Identify the techniques and algorithms for discovering subnetworks
LO 5	Understand the concept of a web page
LO 6	Learn about PageRank and how it is recursively computed
LO 7	Summarize differences between SNA and data mining

Social Networks are a graphical representation of a network of relationships among people and/or entities. Social network analysis (SNA) is the art and science of discovering patterns of interaction and influence within the participants in a network. These participants could be people, organizations, machines, concepts, or any other kind of entity. An ideal application of SNA will discover essential characteristics of a network including its central nodes and its sub-network structure. Sub-networks are clusters of nodes where the within-sub-network connections are stronger than the connections with nodes outside the sub-network. SNA is accomplished through graphically representing social relationships into a network of nodes and links and applying iterative computational techniques to measure the strengths of relationships. SNA ultimately helps understand the totality of network that is this entire universe, with infinite potential relationships among everything.

CASELET

The Social Life of Products

One of Amazon's value-added services is recommending the top products that were bought by individuals who also bought the product currently being browsed. Below is the network of products and the buying affinity of the books with each other. The most common measure in social networks is network centrality. To assess "positional advantage", we measure each node's network centrality. We have two parts of the network 1) the dense cluster in the center and 2) the four stand-alone clusters round the center cluster.

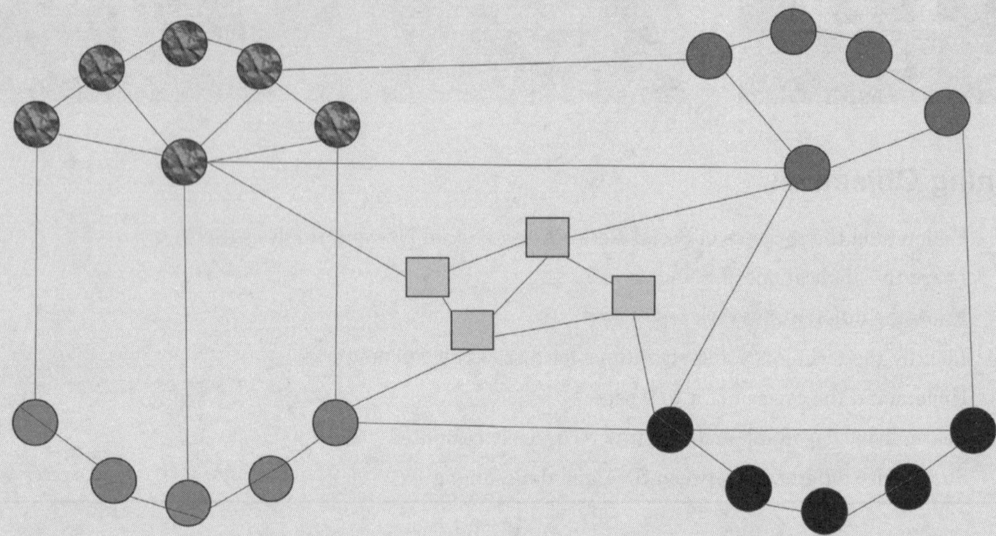

Questions:

Q1: *Can these maps provide an opportunity for the businesses that Amazon competes against? To authors and publicists?*

Q2: *Could a similar map of services be developed for a healthcare situation? How?*

APPLICATIONS OF SNA

Self-awareness: Visualizing his/her social network can help a person organize their relationships and support network. It can help them analyze the quality of their network.

Communities: Social Network Analysis can help identify, construct, and strengthen networks within communities to build wellness, comfort, and resilience. Analysis of joint authoring relationships and citations helps identify sub-networks of specializations of knowledge in an academic field. Researchers at Northwestern University found that the most determinant factor in the success of a Broadway play was the strength of relationships among the crew and cast.

Marketing: There is a popular network insight that any two people are related to each other through at most seven degrees of links. Organizations can use this insight to reach out with their message to large numbers of people, and to listen actively to opinion leaders as ways to understand their customers' needs and behaviors. Politicians can reach out to opinion leaders to get their message out.

Public Health: Awareness of networks can help identify the paths that certain diseases take to spread. Public health professionals can isolate and contain diseases before they expand to other networks.

NETWORK TOPOLOGIES

There are two primary types of network topologies: the ring-type and hub-spoke topologies. Each of the topologies has different characteristics and benefits.

In the ring network, nodes typically connect to their adjacent nodes in the network. Potentially all nodes can be connected to each other, through relationships with their nearest neighbors. A ring network could be dense where every node has a direct connection with practically every node. Or it could be sparse where every node connects to a small subset of the nodes. The number of connections needed to reach from one node to another could vary tremendously. A dense network, with more connections, will allow many direct connections between pairs of nodes. In a sparse network, one may need to traverse many connections to reach the desired destination. A peer-to-peer email (or messaging) network is an example of the ring model, as anyone can potentially directly connect with anyone else. In practice, email networks are sparse, as people connect directly with only a subset of people.

In the hub-spoke network, there is one central hub node to which all the other nodes are directly connected. There are no direct relationships between the nodes. Nodes connect with each other through the hub node. This is a hierarchical network structure since the hub node is central to the network. The hub node is structurally more important, as it is central to all communications between the other peripheral nodes. A good benefit of a hub-spoke network is that one could predictably reach from any node to any other node by traversing exactly just two connections. As an example, modern airlines operate on this model to maintain hub networks from which they operate flights to a large number of airports.

The density of a network can be defined as the average number of connections per node. For example, if a network with 10 nodes has 20 direct relationships among the entities, then the density would be two (20 divided by 10). The cohesiveness of the network is a related concept, which is the average number of connections needed to reach from one node to the other.

Another way of analyzing networks is to define the centrality (or importance) of every node. The number of links associated with a node is a sign of the centrality of the node. In the ring network Figure 15.1, each node has exactly two links. Thus, there is no central node. However, in the hub-spoke network, the hub-node N has eight links, while all other nodes have only one link each. Thus, the hub node N has a high centrality.

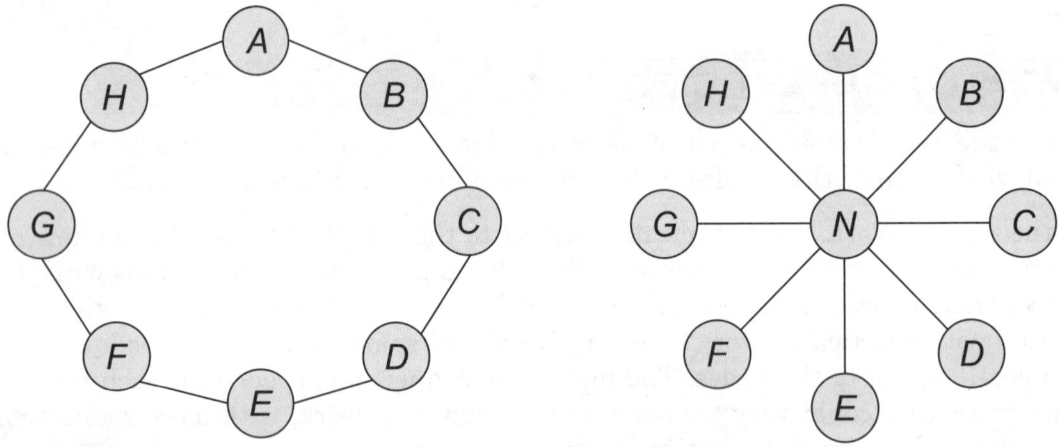

Figure 15.1 Network Topologies: Ring (left) and Hub-spoke (right)

A variant of network that combines both the above types is the network of networks, in which each participating network will connect with other networks at select points of contact. For example, the internet is a network of networks. Here, all the commercial and university and government and similar computer networks connect to one another at certain designated nodes (called gateways) to exchange information and conduct business.

TECHNIQUES AND ALGORITHMS

There are two major levels of SNA: discovering sub-networks within the network and ranking the nodes to find more important nodes or hubs.

Finding Sub-networks

A large network could be better analyzed and managed if it can be seen as an interconnected set of distinct sub-networks each with its own distinct identity and unique characteristics. This is like doing a cluster analysis of nodes. Nodes with strong ties between them would belong to the same sub-network, while those with weak or no ties would belong to separate sub-networks. This is an unsupervised learning technique, and *a priori*, there is no correct number of sub-networks in a network. The usefulness of the sub-network structure for decision-making is the main criterion for adopting a particular structure.

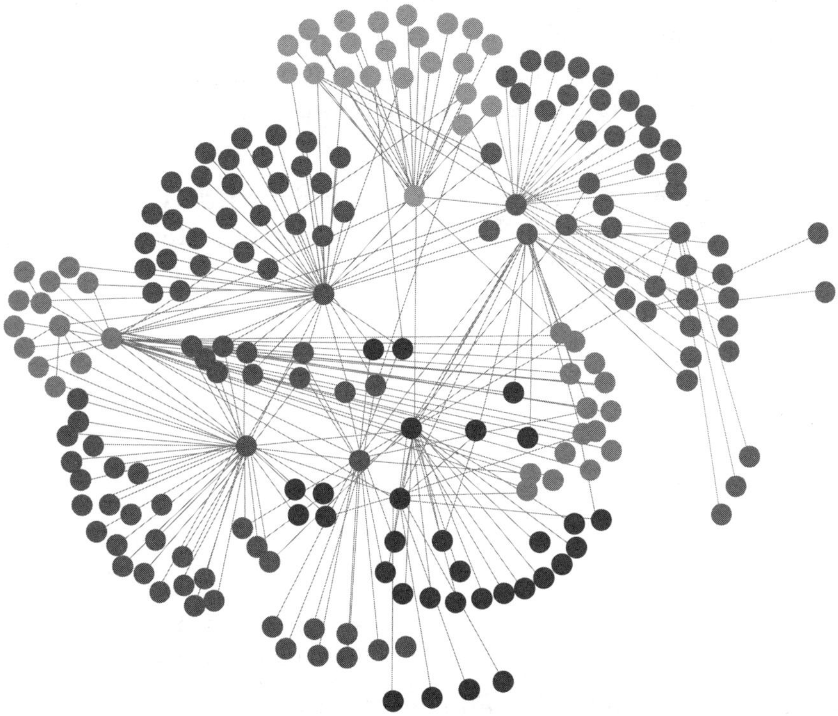

Figure 15.2 A Network with Distinct Sub-networks

Visual representations of networks can help identify sub-networks. The use of color can help differentiate different types of nodes. Representing strong ties with thicker or bolder lines could help visually identify the stronger relationships. A sub-network could be a collection of strong relationships around a hub node. In that case, the hub node could represent a distinct sub-network. A sub-network could also be a subset of nodes with dense relationships between them. In that case, one or more nodes will act as gateways to the rest of the network.

Computing Importance of Nodes

When the connections between nodes in the network have a directionality assigned to them, then the nodes can be compared for their relative influence or rank. (The terms importance and influence and rank of a node will be used interchangeably for the purpose of this discussion.) This is done using an "Influence Flow model". Every outbound link from a node can be considered an outflow of influence. Every incoming link is similarly an inflow of influence. More in-links to a node means greater importance of that node. Thus, there will be many direct and indirect flows of influence between any two nodes in the network.

Computing the relative influence of each node is done based on an input-output matrix of flows of influence among the nodes. Assume each node has an influence value. The computational task is to identify a set of rank values that satisfies the set of links between the nodes. It is an iterative task where we begin with some initial values and continue to iterate till the rank values stabilize.

Consider the following simple network with four nodes (*A*, *B*, *C*, *D*) and six directed links between them. Note that there is a bidirectional link. Here are the links:

Node *A* links into *B*.

Node *B* links into *C*.

Node *C* links into *D*.

Node *D* links into *A*.

Node *A* links into *C*.

Node *B* links into *A*.

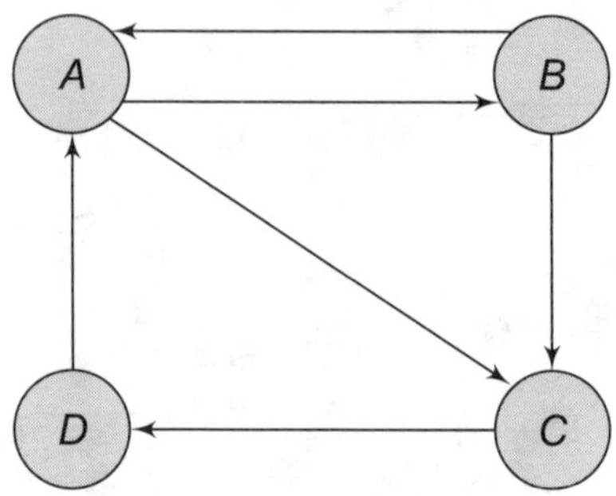

The goal is to find the relative importance, or rank, or every node in the network. This will help identify the most important node(s) in the network.

Begin by assigning the variables for influence (or rank) value for each node, as *Ra*, *Rb*, *Rc*, and *Rd*. The goal is to find the relative values of these variables.

There are two outbound links from node *A* to nodes *B* and *C*. Thus, both *B* and *C* receive half of node *A*'s influence. Similarly, there are two outbound links from node *B* to nodes *C* and *A*. Thus, both *C* and *A* receive half of node *B*'s influence. There is only one outbound link from node *D*, to node *A*. Thus, node *A* gets all the influence of node *D*. There is only one outbound link from node *C*, into node *D*. Thus, node *D* gets all the influence of node *C*.

Node *A* gets all of the influence of node *D*, and half the influence of node *B*.

Thus, $Ra = 0.5 \times Rb + Rd$

Node *B* gets half the influence of node *A*.

Thus, $Rb = 0.5 \times Ra$

Node *C* gets half the influence of node *A*, and half the influence of node *B*.

Thus, $Rc = 0.5 \times Ra + 0.5 \times Rb$

Node *D* gets all of the influence of node *C*, and half the influence of node *B*.

Thus, $Rd = Rc$

We have four equations using four variables. These can be solved mathematically.

We can represent the coefficients of these four equations in a matrix form as below. This is the Influence Matrix. The zero values represent that the term is not represented in an equation.

	Ra	Rb	Rc	Rd
Ra	0	0.50	0	1.00
Rb	0.50	0	0	0
Rc	0.50	0.50	0	0
Rd	0	0	1.00	0

For simplification, let us also state that all the Rank values add up to 1. Thus, the rank value of each node is a fraction, and all the rank values add up to 1. One can start with an initial set of Rank values, and then iteratively compute new Rank values till they stabilize. One can conveniently start with equal initial Rank values, such as 1/n or ¼ for each of the nodes.

Variable	InitVal
Ra	0.250
Rb	0.250
Rc	0.250
Rd	0.250

Computing the revised values using the equations stated earlier, we get a revised set of values shown as Iteration1. [This can be computed easily by creating formulae using the Influence matrix in a spreadsheet such as Excel].

Variable	InitVal	Iteration1
Ra	0.250	0.375
Rb	0.250	0.125
Rc	0.250	0.250
Rd	0.250	0.250

Using the Rank values from Iteration1 as the new starting values, we can compute new values for these variables, shown as Iteration 2. Rank values will continue to change.

Variable	InitVal	Iteration1	Iteration2
Ra	0.250	0.375	0.3125
Rb	0.250	0.125	0.1875
Rc	0.250	0.250	0.250
Rd	0.250	0.250	0.250

Working from values of Iteration2, and so, we can do a few more iterations till the values stabilize. Here are the final values after the 8th iteration.

Variable	InitVal	Iteration1	Iteration2	....	Iteration8
Ra	0.250	0.375	0.313	....	0.333
Rb	0.250	0.125	0.188	....	0.167
Rc	0.250	0.250	0.250	....	0.250
Rd	0.250	0.250	0.250	....	0.250

The final rank shows that Rank of node *A* is the highest at 0.333. Thus, the most important node is *A*. The lowest rank is 0.167, of *Rb*. Thus, *B* is the least important node. Nodes *C* and *D* are in the middle. In this case, their ranks did not change at all.

The relative scores of the nodes in this network would have been the same irrespective of the initial values chosen for the computations. It may take a longer or shorter number of iterations for the results to stabilize for different sets of initial values.

PAGERANK

PageRank is a particular application of the SNA techniques above to compute the relative importance of websites in the overall world-wide web. The data on websites and their links is gathered through web crawler bots that traverse through the webpages at frequent intervals. Every webpage is a node in a social network, and all the hyperlinks from that page become directed links to other webpages. Every outbound link from a webpage is considered an outflow of influence of that webpage. An iterative computational technique is applied to compute the relative importance of each page. That score is called PageRank, according to an eponymous algorithm invented by the founders of Google, the web search company.

PageRank is used by Google for ordering the display of websites in response to search queries. To be shown higher in the search results, many website owners try to artificially boost their PageRank by creating many dummy websites whose ranks can be made to flow into their desired website. Also, many websites can be designed with cyclical sets of links from where the web crawler may not be able to break out. These are called spider traps.

To overcome these and other challenges, Google includes a Teleporting factor in computing the PageRank. Teleporting assumed that there is a potential link from any node to any other node, irrespective of whether it really exists. Thus, the Influence matrix is multiplied by a weighting factor called Beta, with a typical value of 0.85 or 85%. The remaining weight of 0.15 or 15% is given to Teleportation. In the Teleportation matrix, each cell is given a rank of 1/n, where n is the number of nodes on the web. The two matrices are added to compute the final Influence matrix. This matrix can be used to iteratively compute the PageRanks of all the nodes, just as shown in the example earlier.

PRACTICAL CONSIDERATIONS

1. Network size: Most SNA research is done using small networks. Collecting data about large networks can be very challenging. This is because the number of links is the order of the square of the number of nodes. Thus, in a network of 1000 nodes, there are potentially 1 million possible pairs of links.
2. Gathering data: Electronic communication records (emails, chats, etc.) can be harnessed to gather social network data more easily. Data on the nature and quality of relationships needs to be collected using survey documents. Capturing and cleansing and organizing the data can take a lot of time and effort, just like in a typical data analytics project.
3. Computation and visualization: Modeling large networks can be computationally challenging and visualizing them also would require special skills. Big data analytical tools may be needed to compute large networks.
4. Dynamic networks: Relationships between nodes in a social network can be fluid. They can change in strength and functional nature. For example, there could be multiple relationships between two people ... they could simultaneously be co-workers, co-authors, and spouses. The network should be modeled frequently to see the dynamics of the network.

COMPARING SNA WITH DATA ANALYTICS

Table 15.1 Social Network Analysis vs Traditional Data Analytics

Dimension	Social Network Analysis	Traditional Data Mining
Nature of learning	Unsupervised learning	Supervised and unsupervised learning
Analysis goals	Hub nodes, important nodes, and sub-networks	Key decision rules, cluster centroids
Dataset structure	A graph of nodes and (directed) links	Rectangular data of variables and instances
Analysis techniques	Visualization with statistics; iterative graphical computation	Machine learning, statistics
Quality measurement	Usefulness is key criterion	Predictive accuracy for classification techniques

CONCLUSION

Social network analysis is a powerful method of analyzing relationships among entities to identify strong patterns. There could be sub-networks in a network based on strong ties within the network. A computationally rigorous set of techniques can be used to rank every node in a network for its influence and importance. PageRank is the implementation of this algorithm in the context of ranking websites.

REVIEW QUESTIONS

1. What is social network analysis? How is it different from other data mining techniques such as clustering or decision trees?
2. How can SNA help with improving the gross national happiness of any country or society?
3. What kind of pitfalls should one guard against in doing SNA? What are dense and sparse networks?
4. Data preparation takes more than 80–90% of the total time of an analytics project. Would that be true for SNA also? Why or why not?
5. Compute the rank values for the nodes for the following network which is a modified version of the exercise solved earlier. Which is the highest ranked node now?

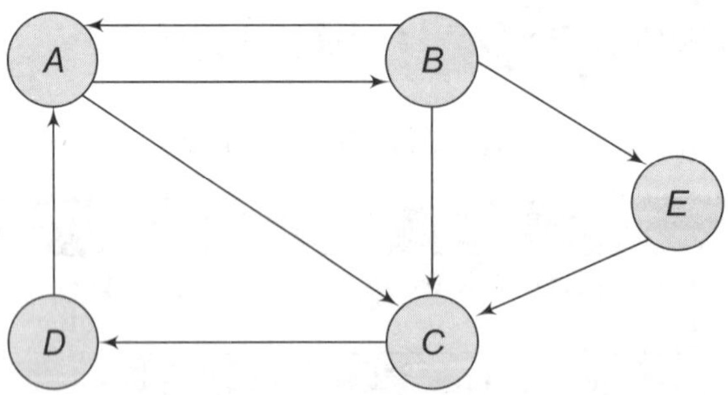

TRUE/FALSE

1. Social networks are a graphical representation of relationships among people and/or entities.
2. A social network represents social relationships into a network of nodes and links.

3. Social network analysis can be used to discover the subnetworks.
4. Subnetworks are clusters of nodes where the connections with nodes outside the subnetwork are stronger than within-subnetwork connections.
5. There are two essential network topologies – Ring-type and hub-spoke.
6. PageRank is a special type of network topology.
7. Teleporting is a way to enhance the PageRank of all the important websites.
8. All data mining techniques can be applied to SNA.

Section 4
Related Topics

This section covers high-level primes on additional topics.

- Chapter 16 covers big data. This is a new term created to describe the phenomenon of large amounts of data being generated from many data sources, which cannot be handled with traditional data management tools.
- Chapter 17 covers Artificial Intelligence. AI includes Machine learning, which is the source of many Data Mining techniques. AI also includes other fields like Natural language understand, Expert Systems, and more.
- Chapter 18 covers data privacy and the ethics issues related to gathering, analyzing, and using data.
- Chapter 19 covers Data Science careers and the skills needed. It also includes some additional data analytics case studies.
- Chapter 20 covers Data wrangling and dimensional reduction as preparation of data for a purpose. Ultimately, a good clean valuable dataset is necessary to help provide good valuable insights.
- Appendix A covers Data Modeling. This is useful as a ramp-up to data mining, especially for those who have not had much exposure to traditional data management or may need a refresher.
- Appendix B covers Statistics. This is useful as a ramp-up to data mining, for those who may not have had much exposure to statistics, or may need a refresher.
- Appendix C is a conclusion chapter to summarize the main points of Business Intelligence and Data Mining covered in this book.
- Appendix D includes a full report of an interesting Data Analytics project by an MBA students' team, to show the various phases and aspects of such a good project.
- Appendix P includes an extensive Python tutorial to help with many of the techniques shown in the book. No prior experience with Python is needed for using this tutorial.

- Appendix R includes an extensive R tutorial to help with many of the techniques shown in the book. No prior experience with R is needed for using this tutorial.
- Appendix W includes Weka tutorial for data mining. This tutorial will provide examples of solving certain data mining problems using Weka tool and the sample datasets provided with it.

CHAPTER 16

Big Data

Learning Objectives

LO 1 Understand what is big data

LO 2 Know the business benefits of big data

LO 3 Outline the technologies involved in big data

LO 4 Summarize how big data is managed

Big data is an all-inclusive term that refers to extremely large, very fast, highly diverse, and complex data that cannot be managed with traditional data management tools. Ideally, big data includes all kinds of data, and helps deliver the right information, to the right person, in the right quantity, at the right time, to help make the right decisions. Big data can be harnessed by developing infinitely scalable, totally flexible, and evolutionary data architectures, coupled with the use of cost-effective computing machines. The infinite potential knowledge embedded within this big data cosmic computer can help connect with and enjoy the support of all the laws of nature.

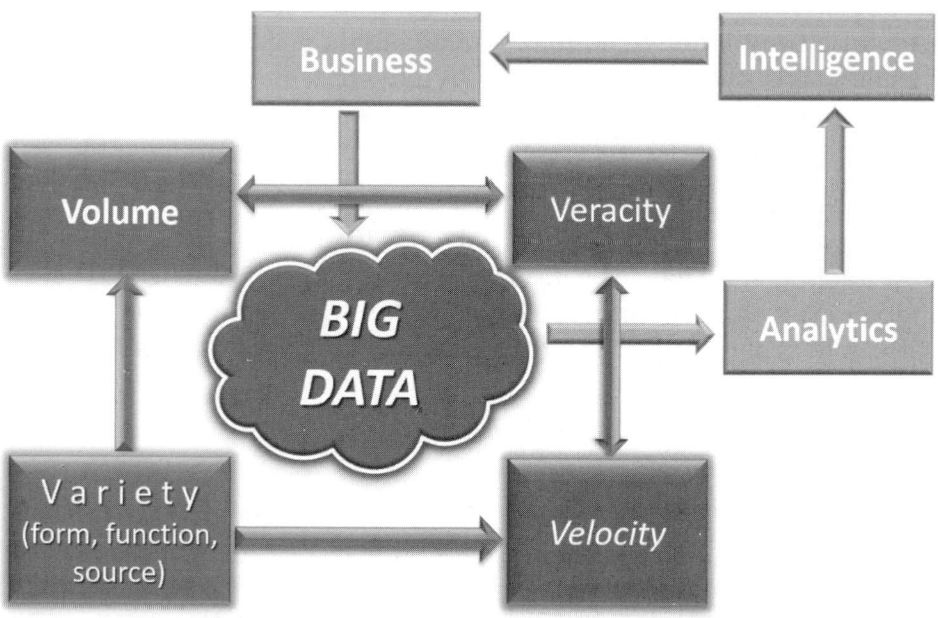

Figure 16.1 Big Data Context

This chapter will provide a complete overview of big data for the executive and the data scientist. It will cover the key challenges and benefits of big data, and the essential tools and technologies for organizing and benefitting from big data. For more on big data, check out my associated book on big data Made Accessible.

UNDERSTANDING BIG DATA

Big data can be examined on two levels (Figure 16.1). At a fundamental level, it is just another collection of data that can be analyzed and utilized for the benefit of the business. On another level, it is a special kind of data that poses unique challenges and offers unique benefits. This is the level that this chapter will focus on.

At the level of business, data generated by business operations can be analyzed to generate insights that can help the business make better decisions. This makes the business grow bigger, and generate even more data, and the cycle continues. This is represented by the cycle on the top-right of Figure 16.1.

On another level, big data is different from traditional data in every way: space, time, and function. The quantity of big data is 1000s of times greater than that of traditional data. The speed of data generation and transmission is 1000 times faster. The forms and functions of big data are 10 times more diverse: from numbers to text, pictures, audio, videos, web logs, machine data, and more. There are many more sources of data, from individuals to organizations to governments, using a range of devices from mobile phones to computers to industrial machines. Not all of big data is of equal quality and value. Big data is represented by the part of the picture on the bottom left of Figure 16.1. This aspect of big data, and its new technologies, is the main focus of this book.

Big data is mostly, over 90%, unstructured data. Every type of big data is structured differently, and therefore has to be dealt with its own appropriate way. There are huge opportunities for technology providers to innovate and manage the entire life cycle of big data ... to generate, gather, store, organize, analyze, and visualize this data.

CASELET

IBM Watson: A Big Data system

IBM created the Watson system as a way of pushing the boundaries of Artificial Intelligence and natural language understanding technologies. Watson beat the world champion human players of Jeopardy (quiz style TV show) in February 2011. Watson reads up data about everything on the web including the entire Wikipedia. It digests and absorbs the data based on simple generic rules such as books have authors; stories have heroes; and drugs treat ailments. A Jeopardy clue, received in the form of a cryptic phrase, is broken down into many possible potential sub-clues of the correct answer. Each sub-clue is examined to see the likeliness of its answer being the correct answer for the main problem. Watson calculates the confidence level of each possible answer. If the confidence level reaches more than a desirable threshold level, Watson decides to offer the answer to the clue. It manages to do all this in a mere 3 seconds.

Watson is now being applied to many important applications such as diagnosing diseases, especially cancer. Watson can read all the new research published in the medical journals to update its knowledge base. It can diagnose the probability of various diseases, by applying factors such as patient's current symptoms, health history, genetic history, medication records, and other factors to recommend a particular diagnosis.

Q1: *What kinds of big data knowledge, technologies, and skills are required to build a system like Watson? What other resources are needed?*

Q2: *Will doctors be able to compete with Watson in diagnosing diseases and prescribing medications? Who else could benefit from a system like Watson?*

CAPTURING BIG DATA

If data was only growing in size, OR only moving at greater speeds, OR only becoming too diverse, it would have been relatively easy. However, when three Vs (Volume, Velocity, Variety) arrive together in an interactive manner, it creates a perfect storm. While the Volume and Velocity of data drive the major technological concerns and the costs of managing big data, these two Vs are themselves driven by the 3rd V, the Variety of forms and functions and sources of data. The varying accuracy (veracity) and value of data complicate the situation further.

Volume of Data

The quantity of data generated in the world has been relentlessly doubling every 12--18 months. Traditional data is measured in Gigabytes (GB) and Terabytes (TB), but big data is measured in Petabytes (PB) and Exabytes (1 Exabyte = 1 million TB). This data is so huge that it is almost a miracle that one can find any specific thing in it, in a reasonable period of time. Searching the world-wide web was the first true big data application. Google perfected the art of this application, and developed many of the path-breaking big data technologies we see in use today.

The primary reason for the growth of data is the dramatic reduction in the cost of storing data. The costs of storing data have decreased by 30--40% every year. Therefore, there is an incentive to record everything that can be observed. It is called "datafication" of the world. The costs of computation and communication of data have also been coming down. Another reason for the growth of data is the increase in the number of forms and functions of data. That will be discussed further in the Variety section.

Velocity of Data

If traditional data is like a calm warehouse, big data is like a fast and furious river. Big data is being generated by billions of devices, and communicated at the speed of the internet. Ingesting all this data is like drinking from a fire hose. One does not have any control over how fast the data will come. A huge unpredictable data-stream is the new metaphor for thinking about big data.

The primary reason for the increased velocity of data is the increase in internet speed. Internet speeds available to homes and offices are now increasing from 10MB/s to 1 GB/s (100 times faster). More people are getting access to high-speed internet around the world. Another important reason is the increased variety of sources, such as mobile devices, that can generate and communicate data from anywhere, at any time.

Variety of Data

Big data is inclusive of all forms of data, for all kinds of functions, from all sources and devices. If traditional data from invoices and ledgers were like a small room full of data, big data is like the biggest imaginable shopping mall that offers unlimited variety. There are three major kinds of variety of data.

1. The first aspect of variety is the **Form** of data. Data types range from numbers to text, graph, map, audio, video, and others. Some of these types of data are simple while others are very complex. There are also composite data types that include many elements in a single file. For example, text documents include graphs and pictures embedded in them. Video movies include audio songs embedded in them. Audio and video have different and more complex storage formats than numbers and text. Numbers and text can be more easily analyzed than an audio or video file.
2. The second aspect of variety is the **Function** of data. There is data from human conversations, songs and movies, business transaction records, machine and operations performance data, new product design data, old archived data, etc. Human communication data would need to be processed very differently from operational performance data, with totally different expectations and objectives. Big data technologies could be used to recognize people's faces in pictures, and compare voices to identify the speaker; and compare handwriting to identify the writer.
3. The third aspect of variety is the **Source** of data. Broadly speaking, there are three types of sources of data: Human-human communications; human-machine communications; and machine-to-machine communications. Mobile phone and tablet devices enable a wide series of applications (or apps) to access data. They also generate data from anytime anywhere. Web access and search logs are another

new and huge source of data. Business systems generate massive amounts of structured business transactional information. Temperature and pressure sensors on machines, and Radio Frequency (RFID) tags on assets, generate incessant, and repetitive data. The sources of big data, and their business applications, will be discussed in the next chapter.

Veracity of Data

Veracity relates to the truthfulness, believability, and quality of data. Big data is messy. There is a lot of misinformation and disinformation out there. The reasons for the poor quality of data can range from technical error, to human error, to malicious intent.

1. The source of information may not be authoritative. For example, all websites are not equally trustworthy. Any information from whitehouse.gov or from nytimes.com is more likely to be authentic and complete. Wikipedia is useful, but not all pages are equally reliable. In each case, the communicator may have an agenda or a point of view.
2. The data may not be communicated and received correctly because of human or technical failure. Sensors and machines for gathering and communicating data may malfunction and may record and transmit incorrect data. Urgency may require the transmission of the best data available at a point in time. Such data makes reconciliation with later, accurate, records more problematic.
3. The data provided and received may however also be intentionally wrong, for competitive or security reasons. There could be disinformation and malicious information spread for strategic reasons.

Big data needs to be sifted and organized by quality, for it to be put to any great use.

BENEFITTING FROM BIG DATA

Data is the new natural resource. Data is the new oil, and Artificial Intelligence is the new electricity. Organizations cannot afford to ignore big data. They may choose to gather and store this data for later analysis, or to sell it to other organizations, that might benefit from it. They may also legitimately choose to discard parts of their data for privacy or legal reasons. However, organizations that do not learn to engage with big data could find themselves left far behind their competition, landing in the dustbin of history. Innovative and nimble small organizations can use big data to quickly scale up and beat larger and more mature organizations.

Traditionally, data usually belongs to the organization that generates it. There are other types of data, such as social media data, that are freely accessible under an open general license. Organizations can use this data to learn about their consumers, improve their service delivery, and design new products to delight their customers and gain a competitive advantage. Data is also being used to create new digital products, such as on-demand entertainment and learning.

Big data is used to train Artificial Intelligence systems. Such applications exist in all industries and aspects of life. There are three major types of big data applications: Monitoring and Tracking, Analysis and Insight, and Digital Product Development.

Monitoring and Tracking Applications: Consumer goods producers use monitoring and tracking applications to understand the sentiments and needs of their customers. Industrial organizations use big data to track inventory in massive interlinked global supply chains. Factory owners use it to monitor machine performance and do preventive maintenance. Utility companies use it to predict energy consumption, and manage demand and supply. Information Technology companies use it to track website performance and improve its usefulness. Financial organizations use it to project trends better and make more effective and profitable bets, etc.

Analysis and Insight: Political organizations use big data to micro-target voters and win elections. Police use big data to predict and prevent crime. Hospitals use it to better diagnose diseases and make medicine prescriptions. Advertisement agencies use it to design more targeted marketing campaigns more quickly. Fashion designers use it to track trends and create more innovative products.

New Product Development: Incoming data could be used to design new products such as reality TV entertainment. Stock market feeds could be a digital product. Imagination is the limit on how new products and services can be developed and delivered at the speed of thought.

MANAGEMENT OF BIG DATA

Big data is a new phase representing a digital world. Business and society are not immune from its impacts. Many organizations have started initiatives around the use of big data. However, most organizations do not necessarily have a good grip on it. Here are some emerging insights into making better use of big data.

1. Across all industries, the business case for big data is strongly focused on addressing customer-centric objectives. The first focus of deploying big data initiatives is to protect and enhance customer relationships and customer experience.
2. Big data should be used to solve a real pain-point. It should be deployed for specific business objectives in order to have management avoid being overwhelmed by the enormity of big data.

3. Organizations are beginning their pilot implementations by using existing and newly accessible internal sources of data. It is better to begin with data under one's control and where one has a superior understanding of the data. One should use more diverse data, and not just more data. This would permit tuning into a broader perspective of reality, leading to better insights.
4. Putting humans and data together leads to the most insights. Combining data-based analysis with human intuition and perspectives is better than going just one way. Most organizations lack the advanced analytical capabilities required to get the most value from big data. There is a growing awareness of building or hiring those skills and capabilities.
5. The faster one analyzes the data, the more will be its predictive value. The value of data depreciates rapidly with time. Many kinds of data need to be processed within seconds, or else the immediate competitive advantage is lost.
6. One should not throw away data if no immediate use can be seen for it. Data usually has value beyond what one initially anticipates. Data can add perspective to other data later in a multiplicative manner. One should maintain just one copy of your data, not multiple. This would help avoid confusion and increase efficiency.
7. Big data is growing exponentially, so one should plan for exponential growth. Storage costs continue to fall, data generation continues to grow, and data-based applications continue to grow in capability and functionality.
8. Big data builds upon a resilient, secure, efficient, flexible, and real-time information processing environment. Big data is transforming business, just like IT did.

ORGANIZING BIG DATA

Good organization depends upon the purpose for which the data is being organized. Given huge quantities of data, it would be desirable to organize the data to speed up the search process for finding a specific desired thing in the entire data. The cost of storing and processing the data, too, would be a major driver for the choice of an organizing pattern.

Given fast and variable speed of data, it would be desirable to create a scalable number of ingest points. It will also be desirable to create at least some element of control over the data by maintaining count and averages over time, unique values received, etc.

Given a wide variety of form factors, data will need to be stored and analyzed differently. Videos need to be stored separately and used for serving in a streaming mode. Text data may be stored separately, so it can be combined, cleaned, and analyzed for themes and sentiments.

Given the different quality of data, various data sources may need to be ranked and prioritized before serving them to the audience. For example, the quality of a webpage and its data may be evaluated using its PageRank value.

ANALYZING BIG DATA

Big data can be analyzed in two ways. Big data can be utilized to visualize a flowing or a static situation. These are called analyzing big data in motion or big data at rest. The first way is to process the incoming stream of data in real time for quick and effective statistics about the data. The second way is to store and structure batches of data and apply standard analytical techniques for generating insights. This could then be visualized using real-time dashboards. The nature of processing this huge, diverse, and largely unstructured data, can be limited only by one's imagination.

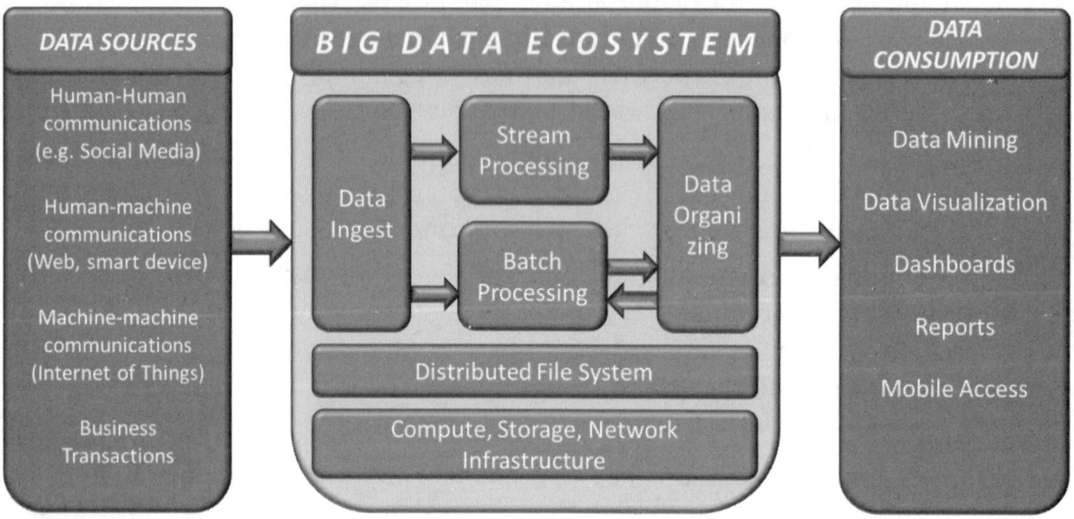

Figure 16.2 Big Data Architecture

A million points of data can be plotted in a graph and offer a view of the density of data. However, plotting a million points on the graph may produce a blurred image which may hide, rather than highlight the distinctions. In such a case, binning the data would help, or selecting the top few frequent categories may deliver greater insights. Streaming data can also be visualized by simple counts and averages over time. For example, below is a dynamically updated chart that shows up-to-date statistics of visitor traffic to the author's blogsite, anilmah.com. The bar shows the number of page views, and the inner darker bar shows the number of unique visitors. The dashboard could show the view by days, weeks, or years also.

Figure 16.3 Real-time Dashboard for Website Performance for the Author's Blog

Text Data could be combined, filtered, cleaned, thematically analyzed, and visualized in a wordcloud. Here is wordcloud from a recent stream of tweets (i.e., Twitter messages) from 2016 US Presidential candidates Hillary Clinton and Donald Trump. The larger size of words implies a greater frequency of occurrence in the tweets. This can help understand the major topics of discussion between the two.

TECHNOLOGY CHALLENGES FOR BIG DATA

There are four major technological challenges in managing big data. There are four matching layers of technologies to overcome those challenges.

Storing Huge Volumes

The first challenge relates to storing huge quantities of data. No storage machine is big enough to store the relentlessly growing quantity of data. Therefore, data needs to be stored in a large number of smaller inexpensive machines. However, with a large number of machines, there is the inevitable challenge of machine failure. Each of these commodity machines will fail at some point or another. Failure of a machine could entail a loss of data stored on it.

The first layer of big data technology thus helps store huge volumes of data, at an affordable cost, while avoiding the risk of data loss. It distributes data across a large cluster of inexpensive commodity machines. It ensures that every piece of data is systematically replicated on multiple machines to guarantee that at least one copy is always available.

Apache Hadoop is the most well-known clustering technology for big data. Its data storage system is called Hadoop Distributed File System (HDFS). This system is built on the patterns of Google's Big File system, designed to store billions of pages and sort them to answer user search queries.

Ingesting Streams at an Extremely Fast Pace

The second challenge relates to the Velocity of data, that is, handling unpredictable and torrential streams of data. Some of the data streams may be too large to store, but must still be monitored. The solution lies in creating scalable ingesting systems that can open an unlimited number of channels for receiving data. These systems can hold data in queues, from which business applications can read and process data at their own pace and convenience.

The second layer of big data technology manages this velocity challenge. It uses a special stream-processing engine, where all incoming data is fed into a central queueing system. From there, a fork-shaped system sends data to batch storage as well as to stream processing directions. The stream processing engine can do its work while the batch processing does its work. Apache Spark is the most popular system for streaming applications.

Handling a Variety of forms and Functions of Data

The third challenge relates to the structuring and access of all varieties of data that comprise big data. Storing them in traditional flat or relational structures would be too impractical, wasteful, and slow. Accessing and analyzing them requires different capabilities.

The third layer of big data technology solves this problem by storing the data in non-relational systems that relax many of the stringent conditions of the relational model. These are called NoSQL (Not Only SQL) databases. These databases are optimized for certain tasks such as query processing, or graph processing, document processing, etc.

HBase and Cassandra are two of the better known NoSQL databases systems. HBase, for example, stores each data element separately along with its key identifying information. This is called a key-value pair format. Cassandra stores data in a columnar format. There are many other variants of NoSQL databases. NoSQL languages, such as Pig and Hive, are used to access this data.

Processing Data at Huge Speeds

The fourth challenge relates to moving large amounts of data from storage to the processor, as this would consume enormous network capacity and choke the network.

The alternative and innovative mode would be to do just the opposite, that is, to move the processing to where the data is stored.

The fourth layer of big data technology avoids the choking of the network. It distributes the task logic throughout the cluster of machines where the data is stored. Those machines work, in parallel, on the data assigned to them, respectively. A follow-up process consolidates the outputs of all the small tasks and delivers the final results. MapReduce, also invented by Google, is the best-known technology for parallel processing of distributed big data.

Challenge	Description	Solution	Technology
Volume	Avoid risk of data loss from machine failure in clusters of commodity machines	Replicate segments of data in multiple machines; master node keeps track of segment location	HDFS
Volume & Velocity	Avoid choking of network bandwidth by moving large volumes of data	Move processing logic to where the data is stored; manage using parallel processing algorithms	Map-Reduce
Variety	Efficient storage of large and small data objects	Columnar databases using key-pair values format	HBase, Cassandra
Velocity	Monitoring streams too large to store	Fork-shaped architecture to process data as stream and as batch	Spark

Table 16.1 Technological Challenges and Solutions for Big Data

Once these major technological challenges arising from the 4 Vs of data are met, all traditional analytical and presentation tools, such as machine learning and statistics, can be reliably applied to big data. There are many additional technologies to make the task of managing big data easier. For example, there are technologies to monitor the resource usage and load balancing of the machines in the cluster.

SUMMARY AND CONCLUSION

Big data is a major social and technological phenomenon that impacts everyone. It also provides an opportunity to create new ways of knowing and working. Big data is extremely large, complex, fast, and not always clean, as it is data that comes from many sources such as people, web, and machine communications. Big data needs to be gathered, organized, and processed in a cost-effective way that manages the volume, velocity, variety, and veracity of big data. Hadoop, MapReduce, NoSQL, and Spark systems are popular technological platforms for this purpose.

To summarize, Table 16.2 shows the many differences between traditional and big data.

Feature	Traditional Data	Big Data
Representative Structure	Warehouses	Lakehouses
Primary Purpose	Manage business activities	Communicate, Monitor
Source of data	Business transactions, documents	Social media, Web access logs, machine generated
Volume of data	Gigabytes, Terabytes	Petabytes, Exabytes
Velocity of data	Ingest level is controlled	Real-time unpredictable ingest
Variety of data	Alphanumeric	Audio, Video, Graphs, Text
Veracity of data	Clean, more trustworthy	Varies depending on source
Structure of data	Well-Structured	Semi- or Un-structured
Physical Storage of Data	In a Storage Area Network	Distributed clusters of commodity computers
Database organization	Relational databases	NoSQL databases
Data Access	SQL	NoSQL such as Pig
Data Manipulation	Conventional data processing	Parallel processing
Data Visualization	Variety of tools	Dynamic dashboards with simple measures
Database Tools	Commercial systems	Open-source - Hadoop, Spark
Total Cost of System	Medium to High	high

Table 16.2 Comparing Big Data with Traditional Data

REVIEW QUESTIONS

1. What is big data? Why should anyone care?
2. Describe the 4V model of big data.
3. What are the major technological challenges in managing big data?
4. What are the technologies available to manage big data?
5. What kind of analyses can be done on big data?
6. Why did people pay attention to Hadoop/MapReduce when it was introduced?

TRUE/FALSE

1. Big data is the new oil, and Artificial Intelligence is the new electricity.
2. Big data is an all-inclusive term that refers to large, fast, and complex data that cannot be managed and owned by the big tech companies.

3. Big data can be examined through 4 Vs – Volume, Velocity, Variety, and Veracity.
4. The opposite of big data is Private data.
5. Big data is mostly structured data.
6. The reason for the growth of data is the reduction in the cost of storing data.
7. The reason for the increased velocity of data is the increase in the number of computers.
8. The variety of big data is driven by numerous forms, functions, and sources of data.
9. There are seven major types of big data applications.
10. Big data can be analyzed in two ways: in motion or at rest.
11. Big data is big, fast, and homogeneous.
12. Social media is a primary driver of big data.
13. Big data will disrupt mostly knowledge-based businesses.
14. The business case for big data is focused on addressing speed-centric objectives.
15. Cloud-based storage makes data sharing instantaneous.
16. The value of data appreciates with time.
17. *Map-Reduce* algorithm was originally generated at Google for doing web searches faster.
18. Spark is a new way of processing big data that is 10x faster than the Hadoop system.

CASELET

MAALA STORES Case Exercise: Step 10

Maala Stores Ltd. is a specialized global retail chain that sells organic food, organic clothing, wellness products, and education products to enlighten LOHAS (Lifestyles of the Healthy and Sustainable) citizens worldwide. The company is 20 years old, and is growing rapidly. It now operates in 5 continents, 50 countries, 150 cities, and has 500 stores. It sells 20,000 products and has 10,000 employees. The company has revenues of over Rs. 5000 crores and has a profit of about 5% of its revenue. The company pays special attention to the conditions under which the products are grown and produced. It donates about one-fifth (20%) from its pre-tax profits from global local charitable causes.

1: *Suggest a comprehensive big data strategy for the CEO of the company.*

2: *How can an AI system such as IBM Watson help this company?*

CHAPTER

17 Artificial Intelligence Primer

Learning Objectives

LO 1 Appreciate the era of Artificial Intelligence

LO 2 Describe the technologies to create AI

LO 3 Understand the impact of society and work

LO 4 Describe the ethical issues in development and use of AI systems

Artificial Intelligence (AI) is the way of abstracting intelligence capabilities out of the human mind, and embedding them into non-sentient objects. Ideally, AI will be able to express intelligent behavior surpassing human intelligence in every way. This is achieved by modeling human intelligence through the whole spectrum of perspectives from genetic, to neurological, to cognitive, to behavioral, and physical. AI ultimately models and implements the universal laws of nature.

Human beings have sought to improve their quality of life by building better tools. These have been revolutions in human life from hunter-gatherer caveman, to agricultural societies, to industrial cities, to information society. At every stage, human beings have tried to understand the phenomena in and around themselves and made tools to make their life easier and simpler. AI can be seen as the latest link in a series of innovations over the last many centuries that helped improve lives.

CASELET

ChatGPT: A Large Language Model

ChatGPT is an artificial intelligence system developed by OpenAI. It is an interactive conversational chatbot built using GPT-3.5 architecture. GPT 3.5, and the subsequent GPT 4 version, process vast amounts of natural language data from the internet and other sources, to generate human-like responses to a wide range of queries and prompts. ChatGPT describes itself as designed to engage in natural language conversations with users and provide relevant information and insights. ChatGPT has the ability to retain the past history of the conversations and respond within that context. ChatGPT can sometimes struggle with complex or ambiguous prompts and may generate responses that are inaccurate or inappropriate.

Here is a brief overview of some of the key steps involved in its operation:

Training: GPT is a Generative Pretrained Transformer model, which digests vast amounts of natural language data using unsupervised learning techniques. During this process, the model extracts patterns and relationships from the data. This creates the overall system that engages with the users. ChatGPT is the natural language interface atop GPT 3.5.

Input encoding: When a user inputs a question or prompt, ChatGPT converts the text into a sequence of numerical values called tokens, that the model can understand and process.

Contextual representation: GPT generates a contextual representation of the tokens, taking into account the surrounding context so that the model can interpret the tokens more accurately.

Language modeling: This is the art of generating a probability distribution over all possible words in the response, to probabilistically predict the most likely word to follow the input.

Sampling: It introduces some randomness to encourage creativity and avoid repeating the same responses.

Output decoding: Finally, ChatGPT decodes the numerical values generated by the model back into natural language text, which is presented to the user as the model's response.

ChatGPT has been used for a wide range of applications, from customer service and support to language translation and content creation. However, like all AI models, it is important to use ChatGPT and other AI models with care and ensure that they are trained on diverse and representative datasets.

Q1: *What are some of the benefits of ChapGPT?*

Q2: *How does big data support ChatGPT?*

AI, MACHINE LEARNING AND DEEP LEARNING

Artificial intelligence is a broad term that includes all manner of intelligent machines. Patrick Whinston of MIT describes AI as representations that support models targeted at thinking, perception, and action. AI includes Machine Learning, Natural Language Understanding, Expert Systems, Computer vision, Robotics, and other capabilities (Figure 17.1). Machine learning systems are those that help learn patterns from data using Neural Networks, Genetic Algorithms, and more. Deep Learning systems are prediction systems based on Neural Networks. They have been used for playing games like chess, Go, Pac-man, and others at a great level of expertise.

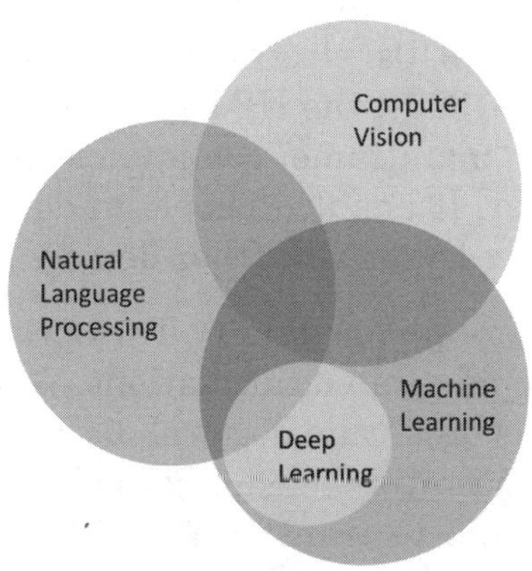

Figure 17.1 Categories of Artificial Intelligence

To understand the impact of AI on life and work, it may help to understand the revolutionary technologies that have come before it. The industrial revolution came about 200 years ago, and the information revolution came about 100 years ago. The AI idea started about 50 years ago and has come into full bloom in recent years.

THE INDUSTRIAL REVOLUTION

A few hundred years ago, work mostly meant physical work such as lifting, pushing, carrying, or otherwise manipulating physical stuff. The invention of the steam engine in the 18th century was the result of human creativity. At first, people did not recognize or appreciate it. Human and horse muscle was prided. Gradually, the steam engine began to be deployed in a variety of uses. This launched the industrial revolution, which made Britain an industrial power and a global empire. The creation of trans-continental railway transport systems in the 19th century was possible because of the steam engine. The invention of the internal combustion engine helped harness the physical motion in machines. The invention of flying machines began to further revolutionize transportation. This was the beginning of the end of the value of brute force work by human muscle. The power of horses was also being surpassed. Horse riders and whip makers worried about their profession. Science fiction imagined tele-portation as a possible way to travel instantly, and of traveling into space. The steam and internal-combustion engines, however, created new industries in the 20th century, such as steel and rubber and fuel and machine maintenance and highways and tourism and fast-food and motel industries. Millions of new jobs were created.

THE INFORMATION REVOLUTION

In the 1850s, the tele-graph enabled writing at a distance. In the late 1890s, the telephone made voice possible at a distance. In 1930, the tele-vision enabled seeing a picture at a distance. In about 1910s, electric light created the ability to work all day and improve public safety. In 1950s, the IBM corporation invented the computer. In the 1960s, the powerful IBM "mainframe" computer was launched. In 1976, Apple-II launched a personal computer. It enabled people to do their own writing and printing. In 1981, the launch of the IBM PC further democratized personal computing.

The spreadsheet was the killer-app for the PC. The spreadsheet enabled an ordinary person to do many kinds of sophisticated calculations. Word processing software made typing long documents such as books and doctoral dissertations easy. The combination of the PC and the internet democratized email. Powerful software called the Enterprise Resource Planning suites began to transform how businesses were run, providing up-to-date information to every manager. Business processes were re-engineered and people feared a massive loss of well-paying jobs.

In the 1960s, the US Defense Advanced Projects Agency funded the creation of a distributed computer network that would survive a nuclear attack. This evolved into the internet. Soon the internet was used for personal communications and email became the killer-app for the internet. In 1990s, the world-wide web was born as an internet application. It used a system of hyperlinks to link all information. In 1993, e-commerce, or the trading of goods and services on the web, emerged as a new industry. Amazon began selling books online in 1993. In 1998, Google began as a platform to "organize the world's information", and soon became a verb to search the web. In 2004, Facebook helped people communicate across distances and launched the social media.

In 2007, Apple launched the iPhone as a smart phone; it launched the mobile web browsing experience. Millions of software applications (or apps) now run on billions of smart phones of many types to fetch any information anywhere and anytime. Access to information has become democratized and cheap. Siri system on the iPhone represents an advanced AI-based voice assisted tool for easy user interaction.

THE COGNITIVE (OR AI) REVOLUTION

In 1950, a British mathematician Alan Turing, who worked to computationally crack communication codes in the second World War, expressed hope that computers someday will be able to work like a human being. Turing's test for a computer was to engage in a conversation with a human being, such that the human being could not decipher whether he was conversing with a machine or a human being. Turing's implicit aim was to extract intelligence, and place it into the disembodied device such as a computer. In 1956, a small seminar was held at Dartmouth college in New Hampshire, with the aim of developing AI. Many successful projects spawned from this academic gathering. These include natural language processing, Artificial Neural Networks, and Expert systems.

Expert systems captured human knowledge as logical if-then statements. Expert systems developed well to do some routine complex tasks with great efficiency and accuracy. Expert systems were also sought for playing games such as chess. In 1997, IBM's Deep Blue computer, an expert system with enormous computing power behind it, beat world chess champion Gary Kasparov decisively in a six-game match. Many of these systems worked on deterministic hard-coded logic. However, as the world's store of information kept growing, hard-coding deterministic logic became tenuous. Another class of techniques called stochastic or probabilistic systems came in handy. Genetic Algorithms are a class of probabilistic computational techniques that mimic genetic evolution systems. Genes mutate randomly, as they evolve into their next generation. Useful mutations, that enhance survival, get passed on to the next generation, while the unhelpful mutations die out. Natural language understanding systems also use a probabilistic approach to interpret a voice signal.

Deep learning systems: These are based on highly layered neural networks, which have demonstrated enormous predictive powers. Deep neural networks were first invented by Geoff Hinton in about 2003. In 2011, IBM's Watson system beat the world champion in the Jeopardy quiz challenge. In 2012, deep neural network based systems were demonstrated to accurately classify images in various categories. In 2017, Google's AlphaGo system (advanced neural networks) beat the world's Go champion. Some companies and countries have developed face recognition systems to identify the pictures on their system and associate them with the right people.

IBM Watson and Google TensorFlow and such systems are called Cognitive systems. These systems have capability to use relatively simple but clever algorithms in a recursive manner to achieve their objective functions. They can also learn from new instances of activities and can add that learning to their repertoire. These systems can easily engage in relatively intelligent and humorous conversations with human beings, in many languages. Voice-based interaction systems such as Apple's Siri and Amazon's Alexa have been deployed in smart phones and other devices. These systems understand human language commands and respond appropriately such as playing music, switching on lights, checking on weather and directions, and more.

Transformer systems: These are a neural network architecture designed for natural language processing (NLP) tasks, such as language understanding, translation, classification, and generation. The key difference in the transformer architecture is the self-attention mechanism, which is a way to assign different likelihood values on long-range dependencies and relationships between sets of words. This makes it concise and efficient in an otherwise infinite and sparse relational matrix between all possible combinations of words. Google deployed the BERT (Bidirectional Encoder Representations from Transformers) model in 2018. GPT is a Generative Pretrained Transformer. There are dozens of other such transformer models available.

Alan Turing set the ultimate test for AI, that it would be indistinguishable from human intelligence. By 2029, Ray Kurzweil has predicted, machines will be able to achieve the intelligence of human beings and pass the Turing Test.

AI AND JOBS LOSSES

There is a genuine fear that AI will take away the jobs of even white-collar professionals. However, the concept of a job is a relatively new concept in the last century or two. The advent of the industrial revolution created the concept of "jobs" to work with machines. Jobs developed into careers as people advanced from lower-level job to higher level. Industrial and information societies also created the concept of lifestyles as we know ourselves, with our clean and prosperous life, with resources for engaging in leisure and self-development activities.

What will be the future of work in the age of pervasive AI? No one can tell for sure. Workers may need to become Problem-solvers who are Adaptive, Creative, and Entrepreneurial (PACE) (Bolles, 2021). One can differentiate between labor, work, and action. Labor is for meeting one's personal needs. Work is for producing artifices and services for others. Action is creative and fulfilling for oneself and simultaneously evolutionary for the world. Creative actions are driven by intrinsic motivation. Universities would need to ensure that students are equipped with the skills and knowledge that employers need in the evolving workplace, while also ensuring that the students retain a strong sense of personal creative agency. Universities may build relationships with local and global organizations and create programs that allow students to take on real-world projects in a safe and creative learning environment.

There is also a psychological shift needed. One does know that human ingenuity knows no limitations, and creates new possibilities. One lesson is to stop leaning too much on our jobs for our self-esteem. Today, a job is considered as not only a source of income, but also a source of meaning and social status. If the income element could be taken care of, through Universal Basic Income, how important would a job be? The human need for challenge and status leads to many kinds of competitions to challenge ourselves, extend our perceived capabilities, and achieve recognition.

The media is full of stories about AI and its socio-political and economic impact. Many conferences are being devoted to AI. What kinds of challenges will remain in a world where machines would be able to do almost all the work, and be able to learn almost everything about our likes and desires and fears? What would we want to do? Ask a super-rich kid today what would he want to do. Perhaps he would want to engage in the hedonism of the pleasures-seeking type. That approach could lead to an aristocratic society that peaked just prior to the French Revolution. Or perhaps she would want to become more self-aware of her own divine nature and enjoy continuous bliss. That approach could lead to Ram Rajya where no one would need to worry about survival or being taken advantage of. Or she could want to become a creative person, engaged in creating art or knowledge or joyful environments for others.

AI AS EXISTENTIAL THREAT

A very important perspective on AI is existential; whether an AI that is superior to human intelligence will ignore its human creators and masters. Will it honor its principles and not harm human beings? Will it even need human beings? Could superior AI do to human beings what human beings did to the apes and to elephants? The Future of Life Institute has been holding very informative conferences on this area with participation from scientists and entrepreneurs. Many suggest that AI poses an existential threat to the human race. Others have expressed confidence in humanity's ability to master AI. And finally, it is said that whoever is able to master AI will be the world's first trillionaire!

CONCLUSION

Artificial Intelligence is a way of understanding intelligence and embedding it in software and devices. AI is able to do much routine knowledge work. It poses a threat to the jobs we see today. However, the industrial revolution before it created many new industries even as it destroyed old jobs. AI has the potential to match and exceed human intelligence in the next few years. It has the potential to pose an existential threat to humanity.

REVIEW QUESTIONS

1. What is Artificial Intelligence? Why should we care?
2. Compare Neural Networks with Genetic Algorithms, listing two similarities and two differences. How does big data relate to these techniques?
3. What are the lessons from the Industrial revolution that help us understand the Cognitive or AI revolution? How is the AI revolution different?
4. Imagine and list four new types of jobs that will be commonplace in the next 5--7 years. Does any of them appeal to you?
5. What are the ethical issues involved in the widespread deployment of Face Recognition systems?

TRUE/FALSE

1. Artificial Intelligence (AI) is the way of abstracting intelligence capabilities out of the human mind and embedding them into non-sentient objects.
2. Artificial Intelligence is a broad term that includes all manner of intelligent machines such as Machine Learning, Natural Language Understanding, Expert Systems, Computer vision, and Robotics.
3. In 1950 a British mathematician Alan Turing designed the first artificial intelligence system.
4. Cognitive systems have capabilities to use relatively simple but clever algorithms in a recursive manner to achieve sophisticated objective functions.
5. Expert systems captured human knowledge as logical if-then statements.

6. Deep Learning systems are based on highly layered neural networks have demonstrated enormous predictive powers.
7. Voice recognition systems are a neural network architecture designed for natural language processing (NLP) tasks, such as language understanding, translation, classification, and generation.
8. In the age of AI, workers may need to become Problem-solvers who are Adaptive, Creative, and Entrepreneurial (PACE).
9. AI poses an existential threat; however, AI can be programmed to not harm its human creators.
10. Whoever is able to master AI will be the world's first trillionaire.

CHAPTER 18

Data Ownership and Privacy

Learning Objectives

LO 1 Understand the value of data and its privacy

LO 2 Grasp the issues in data ownership and sharing

LO 3 Describe the three models of privacy

LO 4 Describe the features of GDPR model of privacy

Data is a digital resource that can be generated and shared by and with many entities simultaneously. The data revolution is so recent that most countries have had little time to develop ownership and privacy regimes for data. Data privacy begins with the expectation that data belongs to the subject of the activity that generated the data. The field of data privacy includes all the legal frameworks and technological tools related to gathering and using data. Recent cases such as Cambridge Analytics, and the pervasive use of Facial Recognition systems, have brought the issue of Data Privacy and ethics a hot issue.

CASELET

Cambridge Analytica

Cambridge Analytica, a consulting company based in the UK, misused data of more than 50 million Facebook users for political marketing, without the consent of those individuals. The initial activity was to collect data from a few hundred thousand Facebook users for academic purposes only, through a Facebook app by a researcher at Cambridge University. However, the app was able to collect data from the entire personal networks of these individuals. That data was somehow shared with Cambridge Analytica, which used this data on tens of millions of individuals for political marketing in the USA. There were public hearings in the UK parliament, and Facebook was called a "digital gangster" for its role in these activities. Facebook was also fined by the UK regulator for its failure to safeguard people's information. In July 2019, the US Federal Trade Commission FaceBook around $5 billion for failing to act on the improper data gathering methods of Cambridge Analytica.

Q1: *Is this a case of an illegal "data breach"? Who is responsible? What would be the downside to the companies involved?*

Q2: *Would Europe's GDPR have stopped this activity?*

DATA OWNERSHIP

Data is generated by human beings as well as by machines. Many devices and technologies are involved in the creation and dissemination of data. The question arises whether every entity involved in the data production and communication chain can make a copy of the data and own it. Here are some instances:

- First, the person or entity about whom the data is generated should have the right to control its dissemination and use. It may even be covered by copyright law. For example, a video of a dance should give the dancer the right over the ultimate use of the video. The performer of the activity may have commissioned the recording in the first place.
- Second, the owner of the data generating device, such as a video or audio recording device, may have used skill and presence of mind to generate that data, and would have some ownership of that data. However, if a mobile device such as a smart phone is used for making recording the dance above, and uploaded to a public cloud account, the ownership should not belong to the maker of the device or the owner of the cloud service.
- Third, if the data is posted on a social media application such as Facebook or Twitter, then the social media company would like to use that data for its own benefit. If the dance video is posted on a social media account, it becomes publicly available. However, it should be available for certain uses and not for other uses without the consent of the owner.
- Fourth, a collection of such data may be needed to develop and train an Artificial Intelligence application that may be developed by a national agency, and they may claim mandatory access to that data for training purposes.

Data ownership rights will almost necessarily work on top of copyright laws. Thus, anyone who can demonstrate clear copyright ownership of a video, or image, or graph, etc., will naturally own that data. However, the terms and conditions of the use of a social media site such as Facebook are such that the data may be jointly below to the social media site itself, in return for free sharing service.

DATA PRIVACY

Europe introduced GDPR (General Data Protection Rights) to provide the first comprehensive law about data protection and privacy. Many countries are still developing their data privacy regimes. The United States, in particular, is far behind Europe in guaranteeing data privacy rights to its citizens. India is developing a data privacy policy that essentially imitates GDPR.

Data Privacy Models

There are three different models of data privacy. On one end is the Chinese model where there is not much privacy. At the other end, there is the US model, which is commerce-driven where the consumer has essentially no inherent data rights, and vendor organizations are responsible for managing privacy through consent agreements. Then, there is the European model where the state takes cognizance of data privacy and enshrines certain rights for the consumer. Many other countries are taking this middle of the road approach to balance the rights of the individuals and the support for continuous innovation. All three models will be discussed next.

Chinese Model

There is little or no expectation or provision of data privacy. Most young people in China express no interest or expectation of data privacy. Why fear anything, if one has done nothing wrong, say these people. There has been an intense movement of the society toward using the digital platforms, most notably WeChat. This mobile platform enables a wide range of activities and payments whereby all data is captured in a digital form. Face-based recognition by the government and other organizations deployed to monitor individuals for security purposes. Only time will tell if this is the right approach to take.

USA Model

Privacy is very important to the average U.S. citizen. However, data privacy has been difficult to enforce. Financial data is used for the credit scoring of individuals, and such data is regulated by a few organizations. Financial organizations take great pains to protect the identity and financial details of all individuals. Whenever data breaches happen, there is a big hue and cry, and the organizations lose their reputation and market value. The Big Technology companies such as Google and Facebook collect extremely large amounts of data about individuals and their online activity. This data becomes the platform to generate new and profitable customized services for individuals. Mobile apps collect huge amounts of data without telling the users, or that consent is buried in the small print of the terms and conditions of use.

European Model–GDPR

Europe has taken great cognizance to need to protect individual privacy and codified certain rights as GDPR. This law came into force in May 2018, and it applies to all entities operating in any or all parts of Europe. It provides stiff penalties for companies violating those data privacy rights. Thus, it is important to understand the approach and the specifics of this law.

The key principles relate to (a) what data can be collected and stored, and (b) how that data might be processed and used.

Data should be collected and stored only for explicit, specific, and legitimate reasons. It should be collected with the consent of an individual. The individual has the right to withdraw consent for the storage of data. Data owners (about whom the data was) have the right to be forgotten, that is, data about them must be deleted after a certain time, if they so demand. The individual has the right to see that the data is accurate, and if needed the data should be corrected. The data should be stored in the geography of the individual. The data should be retained only for the duration of the specific purpose and then discarded.

Data should be processed in a lawful and transparent manner. It should be processed to meet specific purposes such as to meet legal or contractual obligations. It may be processed when certain vital public interest is involved. It should serve the transparent and legitimate interests of the individual of the organization.

GDPR prescribes a penalty of US$20 million or 4% of the global revenue of the company, whichever is greater. This amount should be proven to be a good deterrent, and the regulators have shown the propensity to enforce these laws. No major such penalty has been issued under GDPR so far though. There is a growing stream of data privacy professionals who advise organizations on being on the right side of the law, to protect themselves from financial and reputational loss.

India Model

Data Privacy regime is rapidly evolving in India. However, a standalone and comprehensive privacy law does not exist in India. There has been rapid adoption of technology in India, powered by enormous data sharing networks created by private and public entities. For example, the Aadhar system stores a huge set of personally identifying data about the entire population of India. In 2017, the Supreme Court of India declared the right to privacy as a fundamental right under the framework of the right to life as per our Constitution.

The emerging privacy policy's main tenets are likely to include individual consent, data breach notification, transparency, purpose-based processing, technical security, and rights of individuals who part with their personal data. Individuals would have more control over the processing of their data, as they would be able to remove, correct, and access their data easily. Exemptions will likely be extended to government agencies with respect to data processing for state security and other reasons.

DATA SHARING CONUNDRUM

Artificial intelligence holds an enormous promise, but to be effective, it must learn from massive sets of data -- and the more diverse the data the better. By learning patterns, AI tools can uncover insights and help decision-making in technology, hospitals, manufacturing, and more. However, data can't always be safely shared -- whether it's personally identifiable, holds proprietary information, or to do so would be a security concern. However, the world is shifting slowly from one with centralized data to one where one has to be comfortable with data being everywhere. One estimate has the number of connected devices at the edge increasing to 50 billion by 2022. There are more peer-to-peer communications, more peer-to-peer collaboration, more peer-to-peer learning. The center of gravity shifts from centralized to decentralized data. The challenge is to keep all data collected from these devices secure, and yet be able to share learnings from the data, which, in turn, helps teach AI to be smarter.

For example, suppose a hospital trains its machine learning models on chest X-rays. At this hospital, they see a lot of tuberculosis cases, but very few pneumonia cases. So therefore, their neural network model, when trained, will be very sensitive to detecting tuberculosis and less sensitive towards detecting pneumonia. Now, suppose one gets the opposite type of case in another hospital. Conceivably, it will help both hospitals to share their data so that their respective neural network models can predict both situations better. Without sharing data, one cannot reduce the bias of both hospitals.

To totally prevent the sharing of data, there may occur a model where one only shares the insights and the learnings. That would be fundamentally more secure. Suppose an industry blockchain comes in and collects all the learnings. It can combine them with learnings from other hospitals in other regions and countries, average them, and then send back down to all the hospitals, the updated globally combined averaged learnings. This may be the evolution of data sharing for the common good.

SUMMARY

Data can be put together, using software tools, to identify and target individuals without their consent. This requires a new data privacy regime to protect individuals against giant organizations. Different countries and regions follow different regimes in keeping with their cultures and political philosophies. Europe's GDPR system is the new gold standard in striking a good balance between individual privacy and economic innovation. Data privacy professionals are in increasing demand to guide organizations to be ready for the future.

REVIEW QUESTIONS

1. What are the complexities in determining ownership of data?
2. Why is data privacy important? How can it be ensured?
3. Describe the three models of privacy.
4. How would a retail organization like Maala (see Chapter 1) protect itself from GDPR violations?

TRUE/FALSE

1. Data privacy begins with the expectation that data belongs to the one that generated the data.
2. USA introduced GDPR (General Data Protection Rights) as a comprehensive law about data protection and privacy.
3. Data can be put together, using software tools, to identify and target individuals without their consent.
4. Every entity involved in the data production and communication chain can make a copy of the data and own it.
5. The data privacy regime aims to protect giant organizations from lawsuits by individuals.
6. Data ownership rights will almost necessarily work on top of copyright laws.
7. Data should be collected and stored only for explicit, specific, and legitimate reasons.
8. Data should be processed in a lawful and transparent manner.
9. Organizations are allowed to pool their customer data so that they can train their Artificial intelligence models to predict better results.
10. An industry blockchain and collect all the healthy data and secure its privacy.

CHAPTER 19 Data Science Careers

Learning Objectives

LO 1 Describe the nature of data science careers

LO 2 Describe the different data science roles

LO 3 Understand the data skills requirements

Data Science is a rapidly growing and maturing field of work. A useful parallel is to compare its rise with the rise of Computer science. Just like Computer Science took a couple of decades before it became mainstream, so also Data Science is becoming mainstream now. Computer Science had its first course offerings in the early 1960s. At this moment, every university is already offering, or developing, a Data Science curriculum.

A data science major takes on a wide range of jobs such as Data Engineer, Data Analyst, Data visualizer, Data Warehousing specialist, Machine learning specialist, and so on. Data scientists are earning high salaries. Fortunately, many online data science courses are available for just in time learning. This field evolves very rapidly, so one should continue to enhance one's skills.

DATA SCIENTIST

Everyone can become a data scientist. A data scientist works through the entire BIDM cycle (see Figure 1.1) to help grow the business. A good data scientist knows how to identify and focus on high-priority problems. He/she finds the right angle to approach the problem, dives into the data, and seeks new insights and models that the data may throw up, which can solve the problem.

The data scientist works through the entire data processing chain from gathering, preparing, modeling, warehousing, analyzing, and visualizing the data for easy consumption by business experts. The ideal data scientist is a multi-disciplinary person, persistent in pursuing the solution, and well-versed in business management, databases, statistics, artificial intelligence, and communication skills. The data scientist finds bliss in immersing in the data, and finding patterns that ultimately align with the unified field of all the laws of nature.

DATA ENGINEER

A Data Engineer focuses on ownership of data. It includes continuously gathering data from many data pipelines, organizing it to suit business needs, and then manipulating it to make it ready for analytics. A Data Engineer works with business analysts, software engineers, and data scientists to modify the database design and performance as needed. The Data Engineer may also work as a Data Warehouse engineer and work with ETL scripts to keep the data warehouse up to date. The Data Engineer defines and builds new data pipelines for faster, better, data-informed decision-making within the business.

DATA SCIENCE APTITUDE

There is no one really defining skill for a data scientist. The real test is how strongly you want to do data science. Are you willing to put your heart and effort into becoming good at it?

The first self-test is your relationship with data. Reflect upon yourself and see how much do you love working with data to solve problems or develop insights. What have you done with data lately? Collect a small dataset and start playing with it.

Analyze and visualize a new dataset. See what kind of insights you can generate out of the data. Can you visualize and communicate those insights? Does that process excite you? Visit kaggle.com to see free data sets, and find out the kind of data science challenges that are being offered for prize money.

Data preparation takes about 70–80% of the time of a data science project. It can be tedious work but very critical. Without good data, one gets GIGO (garbage in, garbage out). It requires patience and attention to detail.

Executives will not trust the data-based insights immediately. They will ask for the data to be looked at in many more ways before they will accept the results. Curiosity, persistence, and creativity are needed in any work, and more so in data science.

Download R and RStudio. Use it to complete the exercises from the tutorial in the Appendix. Does that process look easy and joyful to you? Do you enjoy programming in R?

POPULAR SKILLS

Data Science is a truly multidisciplinary discipline. The popular programming languages for data analytics are open-source languages such as R, Python, and Scala. There are many commercial GUI platforms from major providers such as IBM SPSS, SAS, and others. There are also open-source GUI-based platforms such as Weka.

There are many good sources on the web for advice on data science careers, and education opportunities. Here is a good one: www.mastersindatascience.org/careers/data-scientist/

CHAPTER

20 Data Wrangling and Dimensionality Reduction

Learning Objectives

LO 1 Appreciate the importance of data wrangling in performing data analytics

LO 2 Describe data preparation tools and techniques

LO 3 Describe data dimensionality reduction tools and techniques

Data wrangling is the preparation of data for a purpose. It helps make the analysis faster and easier and more accurate. It is achieved by improving the quality of the dataset to match the needs of the analysis, through adding, modifying, and removing certain data elements into a given dataset. Ultimately, a good clean valuable dataset will help provide good valuable insights.

DATA WRANGLING

Data wrangling is the act of gathering, cleaning up, and generally preparing the data in a format that is useful for certain analysis. Without clean and relevant data, the analysis may not be useful, and even misleading. Compare it with the preparation of a patient for surgery. The prep work such as initial examination, lab work, food fasting, washing and disinfecting the patient and the instruments, and so on could take a lot of time, even if lower skilled work. The surgery will become easier and will be more likely to be successful. Data preparation or wrangling can take up as much as 80–90% of the time in a data analytics project. Without clean data, it will be GIGO (Garbage In Garbage Out). With valuable clean data, it will be VIVO (Value In Value Out).

Wrangling can include adding, modifying, or removing parts of the data. It includes:

- Constructing a desired dataset by merging variables and rows from multiple data sources into a single dataset at the desired level of granularity. This may also involve a reduction in the granularity of data, and also potentially a reduction in the dimensionality of data.
- Cleaning up and improving the quality of the dataset by plugging in any holes such as missing values in certain cells, or missing certain rows altogether, with suitable values. Since one does not know whether a blank cell means a zero value, or a Not Applicable value, or simply missing, value, that judgment needs to be done heuristically.

- Rightsizing the data by deleting any irrelevant data that is outside the scope of a particular analysis. Very often the analytics toolset will allow filters to unselect unneeded data.
- Moderating the dataset by deleting outlier cases that could distort and bias a particular analysis. The extent of outlying the nature of a point will depend upon the analysis. Very often, the analytics toolset will allow filters to unselect outlier values, such as points that are three SD away from the mean value on any particular dimension.

Wrangling is required depending upon the extent of pre-existing structure in the dataset.

Structured data produced by internal business operation systems such as SAP is likely to be cleaner and need less handling. Textual data or social media data or other external data would likely be unstructured or semi-structured, incomplete, and inconsistent. Remember that the external data is created by other parties to suit their own purpose, and one has to pick and choose and transform it to get some information value out of it. Structured data comes in a clear rectangularized format, where the columns are well understood and easily usable. Tabular CSV worksheets with financial or other statistical data points are a case in point. Geolocation or network data too could be structured in its own ways. Pivot Tables in Excel are one of the easiest ways to manipulate and clean up numeric data.

Unstructured data comes with limited metadata, or limited definition of its columns and rows, if those are even there. An image database may contain just the name and size of the file, without any indication of what it is about. Video files are similarly difficult to structure beyond the identifier, size, date, and general category. All other audio and text files similarly may come with more or less metadata. The data is more structured if it has richer metadata. Web log files and RFID files may be structured but will need to be structured of de-duped to make a meaningful dataset out of them. Email archives are often managed through discovery systems for legal and other searchability needs. Similarly, there exist tools to deal with every kind of unstructured data, such as PDF files, XML files, etc. There are data mapping and migration tools to help prepare specialized forms of data.

This data could be binned and analyzed in batch mode, after the fact, or it could be done to streams of data. In general, because of the unpredictability of the size and velocity of streams, very limited data preparation can be done in real time. When the data files get very large, the datasets may need to be broken into smaller components according to different logics of those components of data for more suitable analysis by subsets.

Example 1: Wrangling for T-shirt Sizes

Suppose one were to analyze the physical sizes of a certain group of people to order T-shirts for them. When one collects data manually, there could be many difficulties.

- Some people may not give the data, or give it late, or give it incorrect (inadvertently). So, the completeness of the data will be varying. Some data such as age could be picked upon personnel systems, while the weight may change over time. Data from different sources will need to be merged on some common indicator.
- Some values could be missing, because someone was in a hurry. Someone may mistakenly enter weight data in the height column and vice versa. Similarly, some data may be entered in inches and some in centimeters, some in pounds and some in kg. They will need to be converted assuming one can figure out that the value was in a different unit.
- Depending upon analysis one may want to remove some outliers. Or one may look for outliers.

Once the clean data about the height, weight, and girth of folks have been collected, it becomes possible to do a cluster analysis to figure out how many distinct sizes of T-shirts would be required.

Example 2: Wrangling Rental Transaction Data

Support a dataset is available for bike rental company's rental transactions.

The CSV file will have a date field for the start and a date field for the end of the transaction. From the date field, one can extract the Hour of Day, Day of Week, and Month of the transaction. One can subtract the two values to compute the length of the rental in second, and can convert it into minutes. Thus, one can extract many fields of relevance from the given basic data.

The transactional data may be too large for a visualization, and may need to be binned into hours of the day. A pivot table is an easy way to bin the transactions with a count of transactions and average duration of transactions during that hour. Or it may need to be binned by the day.

One may want to bin by Station pairs of where the rental originated and where it was terminated. One may be interested only in transactions related to the busiest rental stations, and thus, the remaining data could be deleted. Further, other variables such as weather (such as rain or wind or sunniness) at every station could help enrich the data for analysis.

For example, the raw data may look like this:

trip_id	start_time	end_time	bikeid	tripduratio	from_stati	from_stati	to_station	to_station	usertype	gender	birthyear
18000527	4/1/2018 0:04	4/1/2018 0:13	3819	499	22	May St & T	171	May St & C	Subscriber	Male	1994
18000528	4/1/2018 0:06	4/1/2018 0:27	5000	1,225.00	157	Lake Shore	190	Southport	Subscriber	Male	1965
18000529	4/1/2018 0:07	4/1/2018 0:23	5165	960	106	State St &	106	State St &	Customer		
18000530	4/1/2018 0:07	4/1/2018 0:14	3851	434	241	Morgan St	171	May St & C	Subscriber	Male	1998
18000531	4/1/2018 0:10	4/1/2018 0:22	5065	709	228	Damen Av	219	Damen Av	Subscriber	Male	1983
18000532	4/1/2018 0:11	4/1/2018 0:22	5962	659	244	Ravenswo	325	Clark St &	Subscriber	Male	1991
18000533	4/1/2018 0:15	4/1/2018 0:19	4570	238	128	Damen Av	130	Damen Av	Subscriber	Male	1978
18000534	4/1/2018 0:17	4/1/2018 0:22	1323	353	130	Damen Av	69	Damen Av	Subscriber	Male	1991
18000535	4/1/2018 0:18	4/1/2018 0:23	1977	282	130	Damen Av	69	Damen Av	Subscriber	Male	1990
18000536	4/1/2018 0:20	4/1/2018 0:26	2602	382	121	Blackstone	351	Cottage Gr	Subscriber	Female	1992
18000537	4/1/2018 0:20	4/1/2018 0:26	3869	367	121	Blackstone	351	Cottage Gr	Subscriber	Female	1992
18000538	4/1/2018 0:23	4/1/2018 0:35	4213	702	31	Franklin St	180	Ritchie Ct	Subscriber	Male	1985
18000539	4/1/2018 0:23	4/1/2018 0:35	2028	741	31	Franklin St	180	Ritchie Ct	Subscriber	Male	1986
18000540	4/1/2018 0:24	4/1/2018 0:44	6401	1,177.00	596	Benson Av	517	Clark St &	Subscriber	Male	1974
18000541	4/1/2018 0:26	4/1/2018 0:31	6333	301	145	Mies van d	24	Fairbanks	Subscriber	Male	1984

The prepared data uses the start time to extract the hour, weekday, day, and month of each transaction, and discards the start_time field. It converts the trip duration into minutes by dividing it by 60. It retains the start and end station ids. It converts the user type into a binary numeric field. It also converts the gender similarly into a binary numeric field. All other fields are deleted.

TripID	Hour	Weekday	Day	Month	Duration	from_stati	to_station	Sub1Cust2	Male1Fem2
18000527	0	1	1	4	8	22	171	1	1
18000528	0	1	1	4	20	157	190	1	1
18000529	0	1	1	4	16	106	106	2	2
18000530	0	1	1	4	7	241	171	1	1
18000531	0	1	1	4	12	228	219	1	1
18000532	0	1	1	4	11	244	325	1	1
18000533	0	1	1	4	4	128	130	1	1
18000534	0	1	1	4	6	130	69	1	1
18000535	0	1	1	4	5	130	69	1	1
18000536	0	1	1	4	6	121	351	1	2
18000537	0	1	1	4	6	121	351	1	2
18000538	0	1	1	4	12	31	180	1	1
18000539	0	1	1	4	12	31	180	1	1
18000540	0	1	1	4	20	596	517	1	1
18000541	0	1	1	4	5	145	24	1	1

All the data has been extracted and transformed into a numeric value, which makes it much more friendly to do analysis by Weekday, Month, customer type, and gender.

Some variables have been deleted, and some new variables have been created. Further, the number of fields has been reduced from 12 to 10.

DIMENSIONALITY REDUCTION

It has become easier than ever to capture as many aspects of activity as one wishes. Each measure is a dimension. For example, for a sales transaction, one could gather demographic and psychographic variables about a customer. One can gather details about the specific transaction such as sales agent, sales counter, payment mode, the waiting time in line, time spent on the website in the store, the composition of the basket of goods purchased, the type of smart phone used (in case of m-commerce), and so on. The relevance of variables will depend on the nature of the analysis. Multiple variables may be indicators of some basic underlying latent parameter such as the customer's satisfaction with the transaction. One can reduce the number of dimensions for analysis purposes by preparing the data such as to extract the signal from various measures into a single measure. That makes for a clearer analysis that relates to a business purpose.

There are many statistical techniques to reduce the number of dimensions. The most popular is called Factor Analysis. In other words, one wants to find out what are the few key factors that are being represented by a host of detailed indicators. A version of factor analysis is Principal Component Analysis, where a PC is equivalent to a factor. There are other feature selection methods too.

Example 3: Employee Survey

Suppose an employee survey was done to measure their well-being. The survey contained the following 11 questions:

1. Energy – This is about vibrant mental energy to engage with the world.
2. Health – This connotes *overall health, including physical, mental, and spiritual.*
3. Enthusiasm – It is about having a positive outlook and mental energy.
4. Mental Clarity – This is the feeling of lightness and lack of confusion.
5. Happiness – This is about having a deeply positive perception of the self.
6. Peacefulness – This is a state of deep rest that relates to joyfulness.
7. Creativity – This is a measure of being able to generate original and useful ideas.
8. Focus – This is being able to concentrate and apply one's energies to work-related tasks.
9. Teamwork – This is being able to work with colleagues and other stakeholders in a friendly and collaborative manner.

10. Productivity – This is being able to complete tasks and contribute.
11. Success – This is a feeling of a sense of accomplishment of one's important goals.

Factor Analysis was done using an Excel Add-on for two factors. Ten out of 11 items loaded over 0.7 on Factor 1. The Health item loaded over 0.7 on Factor 2. (The negative loading sign for health does not mean much as the scoring can be reversed. It is only the magnitude that matters.) This shows that all the items loading high on F1 can be combined as a single variable called Well-Being, while item W2 alone is an indicator of health.

	F1	F2
W1	0.736	-0.257
W2	0.507	-0.764
W3	0.850	0.012
W4	0.775	0.139
W5	0.829	-0.138
W6	0.870	-0.087
W7	0.813	-0.113
W8	0.849	0.233
W9	0.767	0.406
W10	0.871	0.299
W11	0.823	-0.036

BEST PRACTICES FOR DATA WRANGLING AND DIMENSIONAL REDUCTION

There are many ways to improve productivity in data wrangling.

1. Understand the business purpose for which data is being prepared. Preparing medical domain data, for example, will require an understanding of the nature of numeric and non-numeric data expected, and the privacy requirements, etc. It will also enable the selection of the relevant datasets.
2. Understand the data and its metadata. It then helps understand what part of the data needs to be kept and what are reasonable values so that the missing values can be suitably plugged.
3. Automate the process by a writing series of scripts for each data transformation, to reduce human error and also increase efficiency. Add metadata to every transformation so the data can be understood and be useful for a long time for a variety of purposes.
4. Reduce dimensions as needed to make it easier for the analysts to deal with fewer but more meaningful dimensions in the data.

CONCLUSION

Data Wrangling is a necessary task to structure the data for analytics. The more structured is the data, the less effort will be required. Dimensionality reduction helps deal with high dimensional data especially that which is directly captured by electronic devices.

REVIEW QUESTIONS

1. What is the difference between data wrangling and data analytics?
2. What proportion of time is taken up by data wrangling and why?
3. What is dimensionality, and why should it be reduced?

TRUE/FALSE

1. Data wrangling is the act of gathering, cleaning up, and preparing the data for a certain analysis.
2. Wrangling can include adding, modifying, or removing parts of the data for constructing a desired dataset.
3. Unstructured data is produced by internal business operation systems such as SAP.
4. Data may need to be binned to create fewer interesting categories.
5. Multiple measured variables may be indicators of some basic underlying latent parameter such the customers satisfaction.
6. There are many statistical techniques such as Factor Analysis and Principal Component Analysis to increase the number of dimensions in the data.
7. Understanding and defining metadata is not related to data preparation.
8. A pivot table is an easy way to bin transactions into fewer categories.
9. Cleaning up the dataset by plugging requires average values in place of blank cells.
10. Moderating the dataset by deleting outlier cases that could distort and bias a particular analysis.

APPENDIX

A Data Modeling and SQL

Learning Objectives

LO 1 Know the qualities of good data

LO 2 Understand modeling of data for effective organization

LO 3 Learn about relational data model

LO 4 Understand the Structured Query Language

Data needs to be efficiently structured and stored so that it includes all the information needed for decision making, without duplication and loss of integrity. Here are the top 10 qualities of good data.

Data should be:

1. **Accurate**: Data should retain consistent values across data stores, users, and applications. This is the most important aspect of data. Any use of inaccurate or corrupted data to do any analysis is known as the garbage-in-garbage-out (GIGO) condition.
2. **Persistent**: Data should be available at all times, now and later. It should thus be nonvolatile, stored, and managed for later access.
3. **Available**: Data should be made available to authorized users, when, where, and how they want to access it, within policy constraints.
4. **Accessible**: Not only should data be available to the user, but it should also be easy to use. Thus, data should be made available in desired formats, with easy tools. MS Excel is a popular medium to access numeric data, and then transferred to other formats.
5. **Comprehensive**: Data should be gathered from all relevant sources to provide a complete and holistic view of the situation. New dimensions should be added to data as and when they become available.
6. **Analyzable**: Data should be available for analysis, for historical and predictive purposes. Thus, data should be organized such that it can be used by analytical tools, such as OLAP, data cube, or data mining.
7. **Flexible**: Data is growing in a variety of types. Thus, data stores should be able to store a variety of data types: small/large, text/video, and so on.

8. **Scalable**: Data is growing in volume. Data storage should be organized to meet emergent demands.
9. **Secure**: Data should be doubly and triply backed up, and protected against loss and damage. There is no bigger IT nightmare than corrupted data. Inconsistent data has to be manually sorted out, which leads to loss of face, loss of business, downtime, and sometimes the business never recovers.
10. **Cost-effective**: The cost of collecting data and storing it is coming down rapidly. However, still the total cost of gathering, organizing, and storing a type of data should be proportional to the estimated value from its use.

EVOLUTION OF DATA MANAGEMENT SYSTEMS

Data management has evolved from manual filing systems to the most advanced online systems capable of handling millions of data processing and access requests every second.

The first data management systems were called file systems. These mimicked paper files and folders. Everything was stored chronologically. Access to this data was sequential.

The next step in data modeling was to find ways to access any random record quickly. Thus, hierarchical database systems appeared. They were able to connect all items for an order, given an order number.

The next step was to traverse the linkages both ways, from the top of the hierarchy to the bottom, and from the bottom to the top. Given an item sold, one should be able to find its order number, and list all the other items sold in that order. Thus, there were networks of links established in the data to track those relationships.

The major leap came when the relationship between data elements itself became the center of attention. The relationship between data values was the key element of storage. Relationships were established through matching values of common attributes, rather than by location of the record in a file. This led to data modeling using relational algebra. Relations could be joined and subtracted, with set operations like union and intersection. Searching the data became an easier task by declaring the values of a variable of interest.

The relational model was enhanced to include variables with non-comparable values like binary objects (such as pictures), which had to be processed differently. Thus emerged the idea of encapsulating the procedures along with the data elements they worked on. The data and its methods were encapsulated into an *object*. Those objects could be further specialized. For example, a vehicle is an object with certain attributes. A car and a truck are more specialized versions of a vehicle. They inherited the data structure of the vehicle, but had their own additional attributes. Similarly, the specialized object inherited all the procedures and programs associated with the more general entity. This became the object-oriented model.

RELATIONAL DATA MODEL

The first mathematical theory driven model for data management was designed by Ed Codd of IBM in 1970.

1. A relational database is composed of a set of relations (data tables), which can be joined using shared attributes. A "data table" is a collection of instances (or records), with a key attribute to uniquely identify each instance.
2. Data tables can be JOINed using the shared "key" attributes to create larger temporary tables, which can be queried to fetch information across tables. Joins can be simple ones as between two tables. Joins can also be complex with AND, OR, UNION or INTERSECTION, and more operations.
3. High-level commands in Structured Query Language (SQL) can be used to perform joins, selection, and organizing of records.

Relational data models flow from conceptual models, to logical models to physical implementations. Data can be conceived of as being about entities, and relationships among entities. A relationship between entities may be a hierarchy between entities, or transactions involving multiple entities. These can be graphically represented as an entity–relationship diagram (ERD).

In Figure A.1, the rectangle reflects the entities for Students and Courses. The relationship is enrolment. In the example below, the rectangle reflects the entities Students and Courses. The diamond shows the Enrolment relationship.

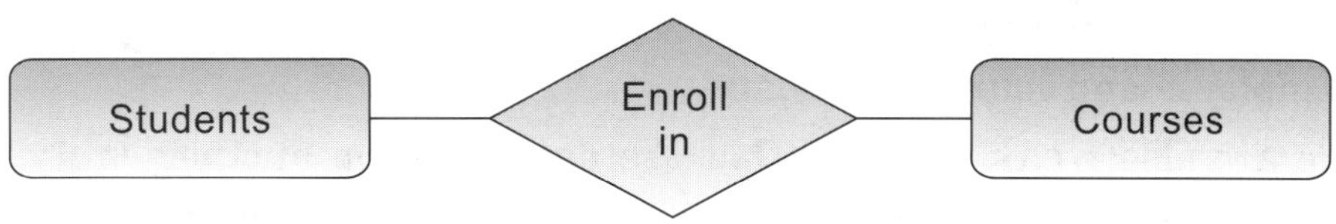

Figure A.1 Simple Relationship Between two Entities

Here are some fundamental concepts on ERD:

1. An **entity** is any object or event about which someone chooses to collect data, which may be a person, place, or thing (e.g., sales person, city, product, vehicle, employee).

2. Entities have **attributes**. Attributes are data items that have something in common with the entity. For example, student id, student name, and student address represent details for a student entity. Attributes can be single-valued (e.g., student name) or multi-valued (list of past addresses for the student). Attribute can be simple (e.g., student name) or composite (e.g., student address, composed of street, city, and state).
3. Every entity must have a **key attribute**(s) that can be used to identify an instance. For example, Student ID can identify a student. A primary key is a unique attribute value for the instance (e.g., Student ID). Any attribute that can serve as a primary key (e.g. Student Address) is a candidate key. A secondary key, a key that may not be unique, may be used to select a group of records (Student city). Some entities will have a composite key – a combination of two or more attributes that together uniquely represent the key (e.g., Flight number and Flight date). A **foreign key** is useful in representing a one-to-many relationship. The primary key of the file at the one end of the relationship should be contained as a foreign key on the file at the many ends of the relationship.
4. **Relationships** have many characteristics: degree, cardinality, and participation.
5. **Degree of relationship** depends upon the number of entities participating in a relationship. Relationships can be unary (e.g., employee and manager-as-employee), binary (e.g., student and course), and ternary (e.g., vendor, part, warehouse).
6. **Cardinality** represents the extent of participation of each entity in a relationship.
    a. One-to-one (e.g., employee and parking space)
    b. One-to-many (e.g., customer and orders)
    c. Many-to-many (e.g., student and course)
7. **Participation** indicates the optional or mandatory nature of the relationship.
    a. Customer and order (mandatory)
    b. Employee and course (optional)
8. There are also **weak entities** that are dependent on another entity for their existence (e.g., employees and dependents). If an employee data is removed, then the dependent data must also be removed.
9. There are **associative entities** used to represent **many-to-many relationship** (e.g., student-course enrolment). There are two ways to implement a many-many relationship. It could be converted into two one-to-many relationships with an associative entity in the middle. Alternatively, the combination of the primary keys of the entities participating in the relationship will form the primary key for the associative entity.

10. There are also **super sub type entities**. These help represent additional attributes, on a subset of the records. For example, vehicle is a supertype and passenger car is its subtype.

IMPLEMENTING THE RELATIONAL DATA MODEL

Once the logical data model has been created, it is easy to translate it into a physical data model, which can then be implemented using any publicly available DBMS. Every entity should be implemented by creating a database table. Every table will be a specific data field (key) that would uniquely identify each relation (or row) in that table. Each master table or database relation should have programs to create, read, update, and delete the records.

The databases should follow three Integrity Constraints.

1. *Entity integrity* ensures that the entity or a table is healthy. The primary key cannot have a null value. Every row must have a unique value. Or else that row should be deleted. As a corollary, if the primary key is a composite key, none of the fields participating in the key can contain a null value. Every key must be unique.
2. *Domain integrity* is enforced by using rules to validate the data as being of the appropriate range and type.
3. *Referential integrity* governs the nature of records in a one-to-many relationship. This ensures that the value of a foreign key should have a matching value in the primary keys of the table referred to by the foreign key.

DATABASE MANAGEMENT SYSTEMS (DBMS)

These are many database management software systems that help manage the activities related to storing the data model, the data itself, and doing the operations on the data and relations. The data in the DBMS grows, and it serves many users of the data concurrently. The DBMS typically runs on a computer called a database server – in an n-tier application architecture. Thus, in an airline reservation system, millions of transactions might simultaneously try to access the same set of data. The database is constantly monitored and managed to provide data access to all authorized users, securely and speedily, while keeping the database consistent and useful. Content management systems are special purpose DBMS, or just features within standard DBMS, that help people manage their own data on a website. There are object-oriented and other more complex ways of managing data.

STRUCTURED QUERY LANGUAGE (SQL)

SQL is a very easy and powerful language to access relational databases. There are two essential components of SQL: the Data Definition Language (DDL) and Data Manipulation Language.

DDL provides instructions to create a new database, and to create new tables within a database. Further, it provides instructions to delete a database, or just a few tables within a database. There are other ancillary commands to define indexes, etc., for efficient access to the database.

DML is the heart of SQL. It provides instructions to add, read, modify, and delete data from the database and any of its tables. The data can selectively be accessed, and then formatted, to answer a specific question. For example, to find the sales of movies by quarter, the SQL query would be:

```
SELECT Product-Name, SUM(Amount)
FROM Movies-Transactions
GROUP BY Product-Name
```

CONCLUSION

Data should be modeled to achieve the business objectives. Good data should be accurate and accessible, so that it can be used for business operations. Relational data model is the most popular way of managing data today.

REVIEW QUESTIONS

1. Who invented relational model and when?
2. How does relational model mark a clear break from previous database models?
3. What is an Entity-Relationship diagram?
4. What kinds of attributes can an entity have?
5. What are the different kinds of relationships?

APPENDIX

B Statistics Tutorial

Learning Objectives

LO 1 Understand the purpose of statistics

LO 2 Explain descriptive statistics and its methods

LO 3 Know the various measures of central tendency and spread in data

LO 4 Learn about histograms

LO 5 Learn about normal distribution and its usefulness

LO 6 Show how to draw inferences from a random sample

Statistics is a mathematically elegant and efficient way of understanding the characteristics of a whole population by projecting from the understanding of a sample of the population. Ideally, the statistical analysis would give a completely accurate and parsimonious description of the whole population with the least amount of effort. This is achieved by accessing a truly random representative sample of the population, gathering data on sample observations, analyzing the data to discover patterns, and projecting the results to the whole with a certain high minimum level of confidence. Statistical analyses ultimately lead to a deeper understanding of the Totality, the unified field of all the laws of nature.

There are many prominent applications of statistics. It is mostly useful in understanding human populations. Politicians conduct polling surveys to understand the needs of voters. Marketers use statistics to understand the needs and wants of consumers. Statistics is also useful in assessing quality in production processes, by measuring the quality of a sample of products.

There are two main types of Statistics: Descriptive and Inferential. Descriptive statistics describes the characteristics of the data at hand. Inferential statistics seeks to describe a larger population using the dataset at hand as a representative sample of the overall population.

DESCRIPTIVE STATISTICS

These are tools and techniques to describe a collection of data. Data is often described by its central tendency and its spread. The primary central tendency is the mean, or the average, of the values. There are other central tendencies such as the median and mode. The spread within the data is called variance, and is often described by "standard deviation".

Example Data Set

For example, use this data set of people as shown below.

Gender	Age	Height	Weight
M	24	71	165
M	29	68	165
M	34	72	180
F	21	67	113
M	32	72	178
F	25	62	101
M	26	70	150
M	34	69	172
M	31	72	185
F	49	63	149
M	30	69	132
M	34	69	140
F	28	61	115
M	30	71	140

A person might be described by their gender, age, height, and weight, for example. Those are the attributes of a person. A collection of persons can be described by their total count, and their average age, height, and weight. The averages could be computed separately for different values of gender.

Averages need to be complemented by the spread, or variance in the values of the attributes. For example, two groups may have the same average age. However, in one group, all members have the same exact age. While in the other group, the age ranges from low values to high values. In the first group, the variability, or spread, is zero. In the other group, there is a non-zero spread.

Computing Mean, Median and Mode

The count of instances in this data set is 14. The average age is 30.5 years. (It can be computed by using the function "Average" in MS Excel). The average height is 68.3 inches. The average weight is 149.9 lbs.

To appreciate the concept of spread, it helps to sort the data by one of the attributes. This data is sorted by Age and is shown below.

Gender	Age	Height	Weight
F	21	67	113
M	24	71	165
F	25	62	101
M	26	70	150
F	28	61	115
M	29	68	165
M	30	69	132
M	30	71	140
M	31	72	185
M	32	72	178
M	34	72	180
M	34	69	172
M	34	69	140
F	49	63	149

The age of the members in this group ranges from 21 to 49 years. The average may not tell the full story about the group. Thus, another way to describe the central tendency of the age of this group is to describe the age of the person in the middle of this group. The age of the middle member in this group of 14 people is 30 years. That is called the median value of the age of the group. (It can be computed by using the function "Median" in MS Excel). Median is particularly useful when the distribution of values is highly skewed. Thus, the median height of the group is 69 inches. And the median weight is 149.5 lbs.

Another way of describing central tendency is of particular relevance when the values are non-numeric, such as their gender, native language, etc. It is not possible to average out the non-numeric data. Thus, the concept of "mode" becomes important. A mode is the value that shows the highest frequency of occurrence in the data. In this data, the age value of 34 occurs three times, the age value of 30 occurs two times, and all the other values occur just one time each. Thus, the mode value of the age of this group is 34 years. (It can be computed by using the function "Mode" in MS Excel). Similarly, the modal height of the group is 69 inches and 72 inches as both occur three times each. In such cases, it is called a bi-modal data. The modal value of weight is 140 lbs.

The concept of mode can be useful in describing the dominant gender of this group. The M value occurs 10 times, and the F value occurs four times. Thus, one can say that the modal value of the gender for the group is M.

Computing the Range and Variance

The spread of the data can be defined in two primary ways. One is the range, the other is variance.

The range is simply defined by the minimum and maximum values of the variable. Thus, the range of values of age in this dataset is from 21 to 49. Similarly, the range of height is from 61 to 72 inches, and the range of weight is from 101 to 185 lbs. The greater is the range, the more is the variation in the data. The lower is the range, the greater is the homogeneity in the data. The limitation of the range measure is that it depends upon only the extreme values on either side, and ignores the distribution of the rest of the data in the middle.

The variance is a more inclusive measure of the spread of the data. Variance is defined as the sum of squares of the distance from the mean. Thus, to compute the variance for the age variable for this group, first calculate for each instance the difference between the age and the average value for the group (which is 30.5). Make a square of those difference values by multiplying each value with itself. Summing up those squared values leads to the total variance. Dividing the total variance by the number of instances leads to the average variance of the data. The standard deviation is defined as the square root of the average variance. Mathematically speaking, here is the formula for standard deviation:

$$s = \sqrt{\frac{\Sigma(x - \bar{x})^2}{n - 1}}$$

where S is the standard deviation, $\sum$ means the sum of all the values, X is the value of the variable for an instance in the dataset, $\bar{X}$ is mean for that variable in the data set, and N is the number of instances in the dataset.

Thus, computing the average variance for age in this group will lead to a value of 6.64 years. (It can be computed with the function "Stdev" in MS Excel). Similarly, the standard deviation can be computed for all the other numeric variables. The standard deviation for height is 3.75 years, and the standard deviation for weight is 26.8 lbs.

Thus, any dataset can be defined quite meaningfully in terms of its mean and standard deviation.

Histograms

Histograms are a particularly useful way of visually describing the distribution of data. Below are histograms for each of the variables. (Figures B.1, B.2. B.3)

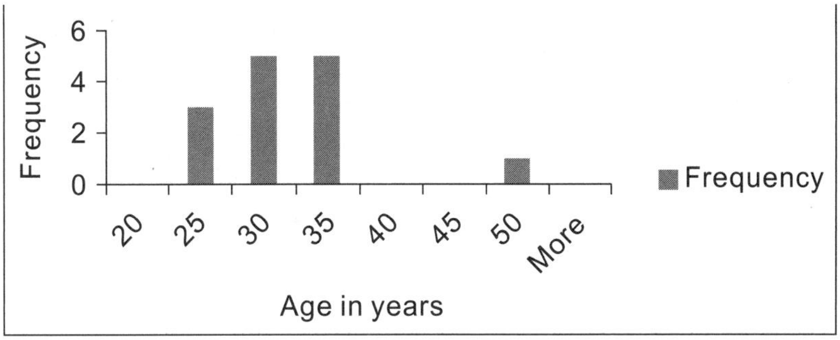

Figure B.1 Histogram of Age

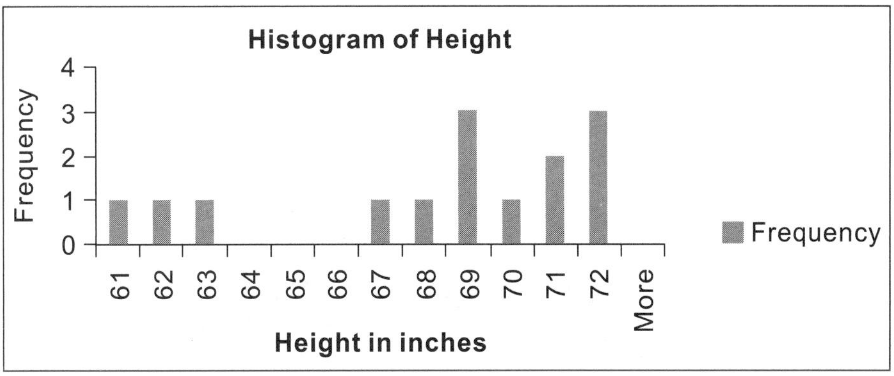

Figure B.2 Histogram of Height

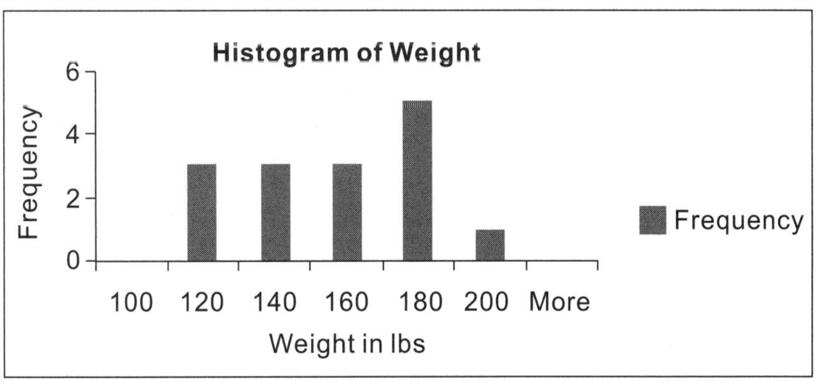

Figure B.3 Histogram of Weight

Histograms are usually developed for numeric variables, though in principle they can also be developed for non-numeric variables such as Gender.

These histograms show a wide range of data values, with major gaps in the middle. Therefore, the range of each variable should be specified in addition to the mean value to give a more accurate picture of the data. And more importantly, the gaps suggest that there are probably different subgroups within the data. In this case, it is likely that the values vary significantly based on the value of Gender. The Analysis of Variance (ANOVA) technique helps determine the impact of such variables.

Normal Distribution and Bell Curve

The data is normally distributed if the data values are evenly distributed like a symmetric bell-shaped curve (see Figure B.4).

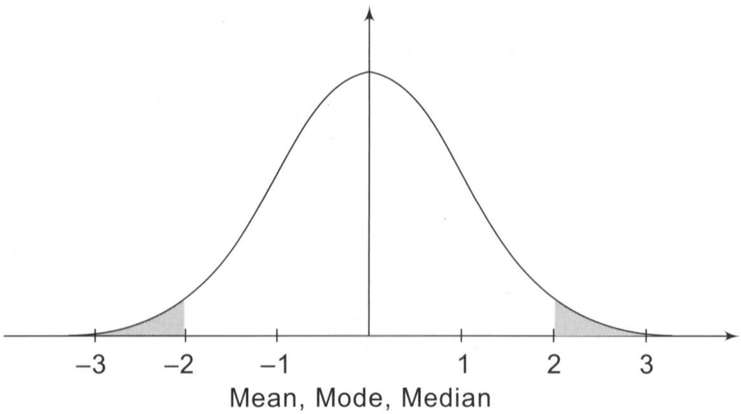

Figure B.4 Bell Curve of Normal Distribution

The central tendency is the middle point of the distribution in data. The perfect symmetry ensures that this central point is the mean, as well as the median, and the mode for the data distribution. The frequency of the values decreases on either side of the central value. The numbers on the x-axis represent the number of standard deviations away from the central tendency, or the mean. Approximately 95% of the data values, the area under the curve, fall within 2 standard deviations (s.d.) on each side.

If the data set were normally distributed, 95% of the age values in the data set will fall within Mean ± 2* s.d. Assuming the age is normally distributed, 95% of the data values would fall within that 2 s.d. range, that is, $(30.5 - 2 \times 6.64)$ to $(30.5 + 2 \times 6.64)$. Or from about 17 to 44 years. This adequately reflects this data set.

A normal distribution assumes a natural clustering of values around the central value. It is considered a naturally occurring pattern in most situations. In most data sets, data is assumed to be normally distributed unless otherwise specified. As the dataset gets larger, it would more and more begin to resemble the bell curve.

The normal distribution can be mathematically modeled in terms of two parameters, that is, mean and standard deviation. Parametric curves have many properties and benefits. For example, normal curves can be instantly compared. Also, the area under the normal curve can be used using calculus functions, and will follow another symmetric curve called the S-curve. That can be used in further computations. A normal distribution of data helps infer the properties of the population from a randomized sample, with a certain high degree of confidence.

INFERENTIAL STATISTICS

The primary purpose of statistics is to infer the properties of the population without having to reach out to and measure the entire population. If a suitably randomized sample is selected, such that it can reasonably be assumed to be representative of the overall population, then the properties of the population can be inferred from it, with a certain high degree of confidence. The larger the sample size is, the greater would be the confidence.

Random Sampling

A random sample is a mathematically rigorous technique of selecting a sample that is representative of the population. It should be contrasted with other forms of sampling, such as convenience sampling, which finds the easiest way to gather data without caring much about its representativeness of the entire population. The random sampling process uses a random number generating mechanism to select a random a certain number of instances from the total population, such that every instance has an equal chance of being selected. An example of random selection would be how lottery winners are selected from the entire pool of lottery tickets sold. The size of the random sample is chosen by the statistician based on the accuracy needs, and the time and resources available.

The random sample can be analyzed using any of the descriptive techniques described above. And even analytical techniques such as Analysis of Variance.

Confidence Interval

Unless the entire population has been measured, a completely true value of the variable for the population cannot be provided. The random sampling method can provide an estimate of the true mean of the population, with a certain degree of confidence. The true population mean will fall within a range centered about the sample. This is called the confidence interval. The larger the sample size, the narrower will be the confidence interval. The greater the sample size, the greater will be the confidence in the projection from the sample mean.

Suppose that the data set used above was actually representative of the people in a certain community. How confidently can one claim that the average age of the population of the community is 30.5 years (the average age of the sample)?

The range, around the sample mean, within which the true population mean (P) is likely to fall, is called the confidence interval. The higher the confidence level that is desired, the wider will be the confidence interval.

Based on the normal distribution of data, the confidence interval of 95% translates into 2 standard deviations worth of distance on either side of the mean. It means that if such randomized sampling and analysis were done often, then 95% of the time, the confidence interval of mean +- 2 s.d. will bracket (i.e., include) the true population mean. The confidence level is usually specified by its inverse, the chance or error, that is, $1 - \alpha$, where α is called the significance level, or simply the *p*-value. For a 95% confidence level, the *p*-value should be less than or equal to 0.05.

PREDICTIVE STATISTICS

Statistical techniques such as regression analysis can be used for predicting the values of variables of interest. Correlations among variables show which variables might influence the values of others. There are many variations of regression, such as linear, non-linear, and logit regression. Time series analysis is a special case of regression analysis where the key independent variable is time. These are described in full detail in Chapter 7.

SUMMARY

Statistical tools are time-tested ways of understanding large populations using small randomized samples. Data is described using central tendencies such as mean, median, and mode, and its distribution using range and variance. Predictive statistical methods like regression and others are prominent tools in data analytics. These are fully covered in the chapter on Regression.

REVIEW QUESTIONS

1. What is statistics? What are its different types?
2. What is a histogram? How does it help?
3. What is the difference between central tendency and spread?
4. What is the difference between mean, mode, and median?

5. What is the standard deviation? How is it computed? How does it help?
6. What is random sampling? How does it help?
7. What is the difference between confidence level and confidence interval?

CASELET

Introductory Statistics Exercise

This exercise will help understand what kind of analysis can be done with numbers, pairs of numbers, and sets of numbers.

Exercise 1a: Here are some numbers:

11	20.5	888	388
100	544	62.9	981.87
1000	5393	6000	1234

Action: Please count the numbers, sequence them in increasing order, calculate the mean and standard deviation. Count odd, even, prime numbers, and fractions. Can you cluster them into three groups?

Exercise 1b: Here are numbers in two dimensions

11, 22	20, 80	888, 1111	388, 1000
100,200	544, 997	62, 154	981, 2345
1000, 4000	5393, 11111	6000, 17066	1234, 5432

Action: What else can one do with these numbers? Calculate the center point (or mean value of all these numbers). Compute the standard deviation between the points. Compute the correlation between the two variables. Can you fit a line between the two variables?

Exercise 1c: Here are numbers in three dimensions

11, 22, 33	544, 997, 3000	6000, 17066, 30500
100,200, 400	5393, 11111, 27000	388, 1000, 8000
1000, 4000, 7000	888, 1111, 2300	981, 2345, 9666
20, 80, 450	62, 154, 700	1234, 5432, 7000

Action: What else can you do with these sets of numbers? Organize the data as a matrix. Compute the center point, and the standard deviation. Sort the matrix by each of the variables. Compute the correlations among the three variables. Can you predict the third variable using the first two variables? Any other ways to grasp these numbers?

APPENDIX

C Main Points of the Book – A Summary

Learning Objectives

LO 1 Quick summary for revision of the entire book

LO 2 Key answers for job interview questions

This is a conclusion chapter to summarize the main points of Business Intelligence and Data Mining covered in this book.

FRAMEWORKS AND APPLICATIONS

1. **BIDM cycle**: Business is the act of doing something productive to serve someone's needs. Business activities are recorded on paper or using electronic media, and then these records become data. Data can be analyzed and mined using special tools and techniques to generate patterns and intelligence. These ideas can then be fed back into the business so it can evolve to become more effective and efficient.
2. **Data processing chain**: Data can be modeled and stored in a database. Relevant data can be extracted for reporting and analyzing purposes, and it can be stored in a Data Warehouse. The data from the warehouse can be mined to generate new insights. Executive dashboards are designed to provide information on a select few variables for every executive. The insights need to be visualized and communicated to the right audience.
3. **Business intelligence**: It includes tools and techniques for data gathering, analysis, and visualization. These include data warehousing, online analytical processing, social media analytics, reporting, dashboards, querying and data mining. The specific designs of BI systems will match the information delivered with the key performance areas (KPIs) of the executive's needs.
4. **Decision-making**: The speed of action has risen exponentially with the growth of the Internet. In a hyper-competitive world, the speed of a decision and the consequent action can be a key advantage. Decision Types: There are two main kinds of decisions: strategic decisions and operational decisions. BI can help with what-if analysis of many possible strategic scenarios. BI can help automate operations-level decision-making and improve efficiency.

5. **BI applications**: BI tools are required in almost all industries and functions to help the manager have up-to-date metrics about business performance. BI applications include best practices identification, fraud detection, segmentation, logical decision-making models, etc. BI systems help calculate risks, and make decisions based on a broad set of facts and insights. Reliable knowledge about the future can help managers make the right decisions with lower levels of risk.
6. **Patterns**: A pattern is a design or a model that helps grasp something. All patterns are essentially about what hangs together and what is separate. A perfect pattern or model is one that (a) accurately describes a situation, (b) is broadly applicable, and (c) can be described in a simple manner. The value of the insight depends upon the problem being solved.
7. **Types of patterns**: Patterns can be temporal, which is something that regularly occurs over time. Patterns can also be spatial, such as things being organized in a certain way. Patterns can be functional, in that doing certain things lead to certain effects. Long-established patterns can also be broken. The past cannot always predict the future.
8. **Data mining**: Data Mining is the art and science of discovering useful innovative patterns from data. It is the act of digging into large amounts of raw data to extract unique nontrivial useful patterns. Data mining can even be done by end users without much knowledge of algorithms, and with limited data. It is a multi-disciplinary field that borrows techniques from a variety of fields, including databases, statistics, artificial intelligence, and business decision-making. Data mining can lead to interesting insights and be a source of new ideas and initiatives. Data Scientist has been called the hottest job of this decade.
9. **Data mining projects**: Data Mining should be done to solve high-priority, high-value problems. Selecting the right data mining problem is an important skill. The problem should be valuable enough that solving it would be worth the time and expense. The problem needs to be looked at from a wider perspective to consider many imaginative solutions. Knowledge of the business domain helps select the right streams of data for pursuing new insights. Data that suits the nature of the problem being solved should be gathered.

DATA PROCESSING CHAIN

10. **Data**: Anything that is recorded is data. Data can come in many ways. The data could come from any number of sources. Data can be nominal, ordinal, interval, or ratio types. There is also data about data.
11. **Datafication**: It means that almost every phenomenon is now being observed and stored. The density and capability of hard drive storage media will double

every 18 months. Unstructured data can come from databases, blogs, images, videos, chats, social media, machine-generated, RFID tags, and so on.

12. **Data preparation**: Data should be cleaned up and organized, and then special tools and techniques can be applied to search for patterns. Gathering and curating data take time and effort. Data cleansing and preparation is a labor-intensive or semi-automated activity that can take up to 80--90% of the time needed for a data mining project. It includes removing de-duping, removing missing values and outliers, binning, and transforming values.
13. **Clean data**: The data should be put in rectangular data shapes with clear columns and rows before submitting it to data mining. The quality of data is critical to the success and value of the data mining project, and avoids garbage in and garbage out (GIGO). Diving into clean and nicely organized data from the right perspectives can increase the chances of making the right discoveries.
14. **Database**: A database is a modeled collection of data that is accessible in many ways. It is often used for transaction processing systems to store comprehensive, detailed, accurate data persistently to support business activities.
15. **Data warehouse**: A Data warehouse (DW) is an organized collection of integrated, subject-oriented databases specifically designed to support decision support functions. The DW is organized at the right level of granularity to provide clean enterprise-wide data in a standardized format for reports, queries, and analysis. DW supports business reporting and data mining activities.
16. **Developing DW**: There are two fundamentally different approaches to developing a data warehouse: Top down and Bottom up. The top-down design develops an integrated enterprise-wide data warehouse to support the entire organization. It takes more time, cost, and coordination to develop and maintain. The bottom-up approach develops data marts for specific departments or functions. It is easier and faster to develop. However, integrating data marts can pose challenges for the organization.
17. **Maintaining DW**: A data warehouse has four key elements: data sources, data extraction and transformation, data loading into the DW, and data access and analysis. The heart of a useful data warehouse is the Extract-Transform-Load (ETL) process to populate the DW with good quality data. DWs uses Star schema as the preferred data architecture. There is a central fact table that provides most of the information of interest.

DATA MINING PROCESS AND TECHNIQUES

18. **Data mining process**: The Data Mining industry has proposed a Cross-Industry Standard Process for Data Mining (CRISP-DM). It has six essential steps:

business understanding, proposing imaginative hypotheses, gathering clean and relevant data, modeling, testing the solution, and deploying.

19. **Data mining systems**: There are a variety of tools for BI and DM. These include industrial strength systems such as IBM SPSS Modeler, and end-user systems such as MS Excel. Open-source systems include such as GUI-oriented Weka and programming languages such as R and Python.
20. **Data mining techniques**: This includes statistical and machine learning techniques to build decision-making models from raw data. The more important Data mining techniques are covered in this book: These include Decision Trees, Regression, Artificial Neural Networks, Cluster analysis, and more. The output of data mining can be in the forms of decision trees, regression equations, cluster centroids, association rules, discriminant functions, etc.
21. **Types of learning**: There are two kinds of patterns or learning: Supervised learning and unsupervised learning. Supervised learning used labeled data to develop models for future decisions. Unsupervised learning looks for patterns within unlabeled data to help create some structure to divide and conquer large amounts of data.
22. **Supervised learning**: It is also called a classification system. Classification techniques are called supervised learning as there is a way to supervise whether the model is right or wrong. It creates models using the data of past instances to develop a good model of the domain. About 80% of the data is used to create a model. The remaining data is used to test the model for its accuracy. A common metric for all of classification techniques is predictive accuracy, defined as Correct Predictions/Total Predictions.
23. **Unsupervised learning**: These are ways to divide and conquer data to look for patterns such as clusters within the data, or some associations between different values of data.
24. **Decision trees**: They are hierarchical tree structures to help classify populations into classes. Decision trees (DT) are the most popular data mining technique, as they are easy to understand, easy to use, and show a high predictive accuracy. Using DTs one can come to a decision based on asking certain questions in a particular sequence. A good DT should ask just a few questions and help come to a good decision.
25. **DT algorithms**: There are many algorithms to implement DTs. They may produce different trees for the same data. They select the most relevant variables automatically, are tolerant of data quality issues, and do not require much data preparation from the users. The algorithms vary in their splitting criteria, as well as stop and pruning criteria. In building DTs trees, one should ask the more important questions first, which would lead to maximum information gain. One

can keep building the sub-trees in a recursive manner till leaf nodes are reached or a stopping criterion is reached.

26. **Cluster analysis**: It is an unsupervised or exploratory learning technique that helps in automatic identification of natural groupings of things. In cluster analysis, there is no output or dependent variable for which a right or wrong answer can be computed. There is no ideal way to determine how many good clusters exist in the data. The right number of cluster depends upon business needs.

27. **Cluster analysis algorithms**: Cluster analysis is a machine-learning technique. The quality of a clustering result depends on the *algorithm*, the *distance* function, and the application. Inter-clusters distance Þ maximized; and Intra-clusters distance Þ minimized. The K-means technique is a popular technique. K-Means algorithm is simple, easy to understand, easy to implement, and computationally efficient. It uses a recursive algorithm to create a user-specified K number of clusters from the data. Other cluster algorithms include K-Modes, and others.

28. **Regression**: Regression helps find the best fitting curve in data; to predict a dependent variable in a multi-dimensional space. The quality of fit is measured by the amount of variance explained by the curve. It is expressed by the correlation coefficient, which is the square root of the variance explained.

29. **Regression process**: Scatter plots can help visually determine the best fitting curve among a few variables. The key steps for regression include establishing a Dependent Variable (DV), and other independent variables, and finding a way to predict DV using the other variables.

30. **Artificial Neural Networks**: Artificial Neural Networks (ANN) are versatile systems inspired by the information processing model of the mind/brain. ANNs are multi-layer, non-linear information processing models that learn from past data and predict future values.

31. **ANN learning process**: Learning in ANN occurs when the various processing elements in the neural network adjust the underlying relationship (weights, transfer function, etc.) between input and outputs, in response to the feedback on their predictions. Their intermediate synaptic parameter values evolve, as the system obtains feedback on its predictions, and thus, an ANN learns from more training data. One big limitation is that ANNs are like a black box trained into solving a particular type of problem and they can develop high predictive powers.

32. Association rule mining is also known as market basket analysis. It is an unsupervised learning technique that looks for associations between data values. It is used in business to find interesting relationships (affinities) between variables (items or events) to cross-sell related items and increase the size of a sale.

33. **ARM algorithms**: In Association rule mining, the goal is to find all rules that satisfy the user-specified *minimum support* and *minimum confidence* in a transaction data set T. The set of association rules existing in T is uniquely determined irrespective of the algorithm used. The Apriori algorithm is the most popular algorithm and it used a bottom-up approach. ECLAT and FP-growth are other algorithms.

BIG DATA MINING

34. **Big data**: This is an umbrella term for a collection of data sets so large and complex that it becomes difficult to process it using traditional data management tools. It can be characterized by the exponentially growing volume, variety, and velocity of data.
35. **Big data impact**: It is disrupting every industry. Any industry that produces information-based products is most likely to be disrupted. Using big data, the IT platform can be strengthened to enable a 'Digital Business Strategy' around digital assets and capabilities.
36. **Big data ecosystem**: Speed and scale are important in managing big data. The big data ecosystem includes technological systems for scalable data ingest systems, distributed file systems, stream processing systems. massively parallel computing processes, non-relational databases, and all often hosted on cloud computing infrastructure.
37. **Text mining**: It is the art and science of discovering knowledge, insights, and patterns from an organized collection of textual databases. The source of the text can be social media, legal cases, academic publications, or any other.
38. **Text mining process**: It is a semi-automated process. Text data is gathered, structured, and then mined, in a three-step process: gathering the text into a corpus; analyzing the corpus to create a Term-Document Matrix; and analyzing the TDM using Data mining techniques.
39. **Web mining**: It is the art and science of discovering patterns and insights from the world-wide web, which is an enormously large and fast growing entity. The web could be analyzed for its structure as well as content, and usage pattern. Three types of web mining are web usage mining, web content mining, and web structure mining.
40. **Web content mining**: It evaluates websites for quantity and quality of content on webpages.
41. **Web structure mining**: Web is a hyperlinked structure. Web structure looks for patterns of relationships between websites. It looks for sub-networks of dense

relationships. It also looks for key websites such as Hubs and Authorities. Hubs are considered as a portal to surf the web. The authorities are terminal nodes for authoritative or truthful knowledge about specific domains.

42. **Web structure mining algorithms**: Hyperlink-Induced Topic Search (HITS) is a link analysis algorithm that rates web pages as being hubs or authorities. PageRank is the version of HITS algorithm that Google uses to determine the order of pages listed upon a Search query.
43. **Web usage mining**: This is a way to extract usage activity by consumers of information from data logs generated through click streams of web page visits and transactions. The clickstreams are often packaged into usage sessions to identify user interests to better design the user experience.

ARTIFICIAL INTELLIGENCE AND DATA PRIVACY

44. **Artificial Intelligence (AI)**: These are fast-evolving very powerful systems that use big data to generate insights in real time. AI technologies include Machine Learning, Natural Language Processing, Expert Systems, Computer vision, Robotics, and other capabilities. Machine learning systems are those that help learn patterns from data using Neural Networks, Genetic Algorithms, and more. AI systems include robots and drones, and voice systems such as Alexa and Siri, and many more.
45. **AI and the future of work and life**: The growing power and penetration of AI-based systems in the workplace have produced a genuine fear that AI will take away the jobs of even white-collar professionals. By 2029, Ray Kurzweil has predicted that machines will be able to achieve the intelligence of human beings. A very important perspective on AI is whether an AI that is superior to human intelligence will ignore its human creators and masters.
46. **Data analytics careers**: There are four basic categories of careers, depending upon skill set. All of them require some love for data, though. A starter skill requirement category is called Data Engineering. This helps with data preparation, and building a data pipeline. An advanced skill set based role is called the Data Scientist. They help solve business problems using various data analytics techniques. An artistic skill set based role is the Data visualization role. These will help bring large data sets and insights to life, by making the insights accessible in interesting ways. A legal mindset would help bring attention to managing the data according to evolving privacy concerns and government policy. Data privacy professionals are in increasing demand to guide organizations to be ready for the future.

47. **Data privacy**: Data privacy begins with the expectation that data belongs to the subject of the activity that generated the data. The field of data privacy includes all the legal frameworks and technological tools related to gathering, storing, and using data.

48. **Data ownership**: Many devices and technologies are involved in the creation and dissemination of data. The question arises whether every entity involved in the data production and communication chain can make a copy of the data and own it. Data ownership rights will almost necessarily work on top of copyright laws. Thus, anyone who can demonstrate clear copyright ownership of a video, or image, or graph, etc., will naturally own that data.

49. **Data privacy models**: There are three different models of data privacy. At one end is the Chinese model where there is not much privacy. On the other end, there is the US model, which is commerce-driven where the consumer has essentially no inherent data rights, and vendor organizations are responsible for managing privacy through consent agreements. Then, there is the European model where the state takes cognizance of data privacy and enshrines certain rights for the consumer.

50. **Europe's GDPR system**: The General Data Protection Rights (GDPR) is the new gold standard in striking a good balance between individual privacy and economic innovation. The key principles relate to (a) what data can be collected and stored, and (b) how that data might be processed and used. Data should be collected and stored for legitimate reasons. It should be processed in a lawful and transparent manner. GDPR prescribes a penalty of US$20 million or 4% of the global revenue of the company, whichever is greater, for any violation.

APPENDIX

D Data Analytics Sample Projects

RESEARCH QUESTION: DOES EDUCATION AFFECT DIVORCE

EXECUTIVE SUMMARY

Background

Across societies, the prevailing viewpoint is that divorces in the society are on the rise due to an increase in education levels, as higher education enables individuals to subsequently achieve an increase in awareness, income levels, and independence.

Objectives and Methods

Using secondary data from various public domains, we aimed to explore the variables affecting divorce rates amongst different levels of education, income, and unemployment for 51 states in the USA from 1990 to 2009.

Findings

Our strongest finding is that contrary to popular belief, education has an inverse relationship with divorce with the bachelor's degree being the single variable with the most predictor importance, which remained strong even after controlling other variables. High school, on the other hand, shows a positive correlation with divorce.

Conclusion

Our results confirmed that divorce is inversely related to all variables studied in the USA, with the exception of high school. However, more contextual data analysis is required to prove the reasoning behind this.

INTRODUCTION

Divorce is the final termination of a marriage, canceling legal duties and responsibilities of the marriage and dissolving the bonds of marriage between husband and wife. In the past, people prolonged their suffering marriages to avoid divorce, especially women. However, it is not the case in today's world. The divorce rate is believed to increase at an alarming rate, and this has become a global trend. Many researches and studies were conducted that focused on the impacts divorce has on children and their education. Only few researches were performed to look at the factors affecting the divorce rate. In America, it is believed that the divorce rate is on the rise and it has become an unavoidable fact in today's American society. There are many factors affecting the divorce rate such as education, religion, ethnic groups, no-fault law, median income, women employment rate, poverty rate, unemployment rate, age, gender, etc.

In our research, we looked at education and divorce domain to see if education has any effect on divorce rate in 51 states of America. Our primary research question is "Does education influence divorce?" However, our research has been expanded to include other significant variables such as median income, unemployment rate, and different levels of education: high school graduate, bachelors and advanced degrees, which we believe have a substantial impact on divorce rate. And, our research question has changed to include those variables: "Within the factors investigated, which one has the strongest significance in determining divorce rate?" As part of our analysis, we collected data for all of these variables for 51 states in America, and we analyzed the effects they have on divorce rate over 20 years, that is, from 1990 to 2009. Our research objectives are:

(i) to find out whether education attainment really impacts the divorce rate;

(ii) to find out if divorce rate is influenced by other factors such as median income and unemployment rate and

(iii) to find out if those predictor variables are correlated.

Education is a primary need for every individual living in the society where marriage is universal to all continents and cultures. But divorce is also a co-existent feature, which displays human behavior. The trends in the rate of marriage dissolution have been a frequent topic of public discussion. In our research, we focused on the effects that education level has on divorce rate occurring in the society in 51 states of America in particular. Although the impact of education on the risk of divorce has been demonstrated in numerous studies. At the same time, there is no consensus about the strength and the direction of this effect: Do societies with a higher education have a higher or a lower risk of divorce? The UK has a literacy rate of 99 percent, and in 2010, it led the statistics being the country with the highest divorce rate of around 120,000 divorces every year as reported by the Telegraph. According to Torkild Hovde Lyngstad, a couple's divorce rate may be influenced by their own educational attainment, that of their parents, and whether they have taken further education after marriage, although predictions are ambiguous. However, these three variables have never been included simultaneously and few studies have included both partners' characteristics. Higher education of partners meant that as they earn more, the family experiences fewer economic problems and this factor lowers the divorce risk. This analysis uses the Sickle regression by Diekmann and Mitter (1984). The results show that family events, such as age at first marriage, type of the union, or presence of children in the family significantly affect the risk of divorce. These studies generated our interest to further explore this yonder.

LITERATURE REVIEW

The following articles highlight the importance of studying variables affecting divorce for the benefit of society due to its wide and extended effects for continuing generations:

1. **Epidemiology of Divorce**

   Author(s): Patricia H. Shiono and Linda Sandham Quinn

   Source: The Future of Children, Vol. 4, No. 1, Children and Divorce, 1994

   Published by: Princeton University

   The study analyzed the severe social consequences of divorce in American families. The children have been hard hit by the change in social structure brought on due to marriage, divorce, re-marriage, and live-in relationships in America. Each year since the 1970s, more than one million children have been affected by divorce, and it has been forecasted that nearly half of all the babies born today will spend some time in a one-parent family occurred as a result of single parenthood or divorce. Consequently, these children will have more adjustment and psychological issues depending on their living arrangements with the new family.

2. **Is Marriage Dissolution Linked to Differences in Mortality Risks for Men and Women? By Örjan Hemström**

   The two purposes of this research are to analyze the long-term effect of divorce on mortality risk and to examine whether or not this mortality risk is different for men and women. This study is based on 44,000 deaths in Sweden. The results showed that the gender mortality difference is lower than expected when employment and the number of children are considered. Unemployed individuals are more at risk of death due to divorce. In most countries, divorced individuals have the highest mortality rate, followed by the widowed, those who have never married, and finally the married (Goldman & Hu, 1993).

3. **Country Differences in the Effects of Divorce on Well-Being: The Role of Norms, Support, and Selectivity by Matthijs Kalmijn**

   This article uses data from the European and World Values Studies for 38 developed countries to check three premises about social variances. Results show that, in most countries, the divorced have a lower level of well-being than the married, but the magnitude of this difference varies significantly across countries. The results show that the effect of divorce is weaker in countries where the family is strong, in line with notions of support and when divorce is more common, which points to the role of declining selectivity as divorce rates go up. Mixed evidence was found for the role of norms. The divorce effect is stronger in countries that have stronger norms against divorce, but this was only found for religious persons. Together, these three factors explain more than half of the variances in the divorce effect.

4. **Making a Case for Premarital Education**

   Author(s): Scott M. Stanley

   Source: Family Relations, Vol. 50

   Published by: National Council on Family Relations

   Education in all forms helps reduce divorce. This article states that premarital education efforts can reduce marital distress and divorce. Here, four benefits of engaging in education have been discussed:

   1. It can slow couples down to foster deliberation.
   2. It can send a message that marriage matters.
   3. It can help couples learn of options if they need help later.
   4. It can lower the risk of subsequent marital distress or termination in some couples.

5. **The Effect of Divorce on Suicide in Denmark, 1951-1980**

   Author(s): Steven Stack

   Source: The Sociological Quarterly, Vol. 31, No. 3

   Published by: Wiley on behalf of the Midwest Sociological Society Stable

   The article studies Denmark on the effects of divorce on suicide. The results show that a 1% increase in divorce is associated with a 0.32% increase in suicide. Divorce trends also predict the frequency of youth suicide.

The following articles are directly related to our research hypothesis:

6. **Demographic Research: Volume 28, Article 6**

   Educational Differences in Divorce in Japan

   By James M. Raymo1 Setsuya Fukuda2 Miho Iwasawa3

   This study analyzed our primary research question in Japan based on data from 1980 to 2005. Results show that education is inversely related to divorce in Japan, and unlike previous studies, the negative relationship between women's education and divorce has not become stronger in recent years. Analyses of 14 years of panel survey data provided some support for theories that focused on the role of economic strain and on cultural values regarding repute, but they also showed that the negative relationship between education and divorce remained strong even after controlling these.

7. **The Effect of No-Fault Divorce Law on the Divorce Rate across the 50 States and Its Relation to Income, Education, and Religiosity**

   Author(s): Paul A. Nakonezny, Robert D. Shull and Joseph Lee Rodgers

   From the National Center for Health Statistics, the effect of no-fault divorce law on the divorce rate across the 50 US states was examined. Also, education and income data from the United States Bureau of the Census and religiosity data from the Glenmary Research Center were used to assess the relation of education, median family income, and religiosity to the post-no-fault divorce rate. Results revealed that no-fault divorce law had a significant positive effect on the divorce rate across the 50 states. Of the moderators that we considered, median family income was the only significant predictor of the change in divorce rate; the post-no-fault divorce rate increased as median family income increased.

8. **Wives' Part-time Employment and Marital Stability in Great Britain, West Germany, and the United States by Lynn Prince Cooke & Vanessa Gash**

   This paper looked at the widely popular theory that females who work after marriage lead to relationship instability based on panel data from GB, Germany, and US. Results showed that it varied across countries. In Germany, part-time working married females made relations more stable. Whereas in the US and Britain, no correlation was found between the two. In the United States, however, mothers working part time had significantly lower divorce risk. West German and British husbands' unemployment proved more detrimental to marital stability than wives' employment. This showed how important it was for both partners to be educated and working in the modern economy for a stable social structure.

9. **Female Education and Marriage Dissolution: Is it a Selection Effect?**

   Fabrizio Bernardi **and** Juan-Ignacio Martínez-Pastor

   This article aimed at testing our primary research question that whether education influences divorce in females as divorce rate has increased considerably in

Spain since 1970s. Multiple studies concluded that women with higher education are more likely to get divorced. However, when divorce becomes more common, the relationship between female education and divorce changes from being positive to being negative. It is, however, also well known that highly educated women tend to marry less frequently. Highly educated women who do marry have some overlooked characteristics like great belief in the institution of marriage, which makes them less likely to divorce later on. The study also looked at whether the negative correlation between education and divorce was caused by educated females choosing to marry in recent years. However, the results showed that the decline in the effect of education on divorce was a consistent finding; one that was not biased by the self-selection into marriage among highly educated women.

10. **Labor and Love: Wives' Employment and Divorce Risk in its Socio-Political Context**

    This study looks at how social policy affects marital stability regarding macro and micro effects of wives' employment on divorce risk in 11 Western countries. Statistical analysis on related data supports the hypotheses that divorce rates are higher where more wives are employed and where policies support that employment. However, there may be some natural mistakes in the data. As in the United States with its lack of policy support, a wife's employment still significantly increases the risk of divorce. A wife's employment has no significant effect on divorce risk in Australia, Flanders, France, Germany, Italy, the Netherlands, and the United Kingdom. In Finland, Norway, and Sweden, wives' employment predicts a significantly lower risk of divorce when compared with wives who are out of the labor force. The results indicate that greater policy support for equality reduces and may even reverse the relative divorce risk associated with a wife's employment.

11. **Women's Changing Attitudes toward Divorce, 1974-2002: Evidence for an Educational Crossover**

    Author(s): Steven P. Martin and Sangeeta Parashar

    This article looks at trends in divorce attitudes of women in the United States by educational attainment from 1974 to 2002. Women with 4-year college degrees, who previously had tolerant attitudes toward divorce, have become more restrictive in their attitudes toward divorce than high school graduates and women with some college education, whereas women with no high school diplomas had increasingly liberal attitudes toward divorce. The study also examined this educational limit in divorce attitudes against variables associated with women's educational attainment, including family attitudes and religion, income and occupational prestige, and family structure. It concluded that the educational crossover in divorce attitudes was associated most strongly with work and family structure variables.

12. **Population Studies, Vol. 61, No. 3, 2007**

    Explaining cross-national differences in marriage, cohabitation, and divorce in Europe, 1990-2000

    Matthijs Kalmijn, Tilburg University

    In Europe, we observed that rates of marriage and remarriage have fallen, rates of divorce and separation have increased, and age at marriage has risen. The study presented in this paper describes the differences in European countries' marriage patterns for the 1990s and attempts to explain them from a macro-level perspective. It found that various gauges of marriage (i.e., marriage rate, age at marriage, divorce rate, and prevalence of unmarried cohabitation) are not indicators of 'strength of marriage'. Women's employment, individualistic values, religion, men's socioeconomic prospects, higher education, and school enrolment are also important indicators for understanding differences among countries including historical continuity and societal disintegration.

13. **The Impact of Parents' and Spouses' Education on Divorce Rates in Norway by Torkild Hovde Lyngstad**

    http://www.demographic-research.org/Volumes/Vol10/5/10-5.pdf

    According to both economic and sociological theory, a couple's divorce rate may be influenced by their own educational attainment, that of their parents, and whether they have taken further education after marriage, although predictions are ambiguous. However, these three variables have never been included simultaneously and few studies have included both partners' characteristics.

14. **American Sociological Review, Vol. 51, No. 4 (Aug., 1986)**

    Contains: Determinants of Divorce over the Marital Life Course Scott J. South and Glenna Spitze

    High level of education for both husband and wife (which are highly correlated) has been found to be associated with more stable marriages. However, there is some evidence of nonlinearity in this effect.

15. **Journal of Marriage and Family, Vol. 50, No. 3 (Aug., 1988)**

    Contains: The Impact of Parental Divorce on Children's Educational Attainment, Marital Timing, and Likelihood of Divorce by Verna M. Keith and Barbara Finlay

    According to this research, parental divorce has diminished the economic and social resources available to children. Negative consequences for children's educational attainment, marital timing, and marital and divorce probability are other effects of parental divorce. Also, the research showed that parental divorce is associated with lower educational attainment and earlier age marriage for both sexes.

16. The Effect of Education on Divorce Risk in Estonia by Kadri Rootalu at the University of Tartu

This study showed that people with higher educational levels have lower divorce risk in Estonia. Although the economic theory of the family predicts that the educational level of the wife should increase the risk of divorce and people with higher education have more resources to handle divorce costs, the empirical evidence suggests otherwise. Higher education of partners means that as they earn more, the family experiences fewer economic problems and this factor lowers the divorce risk. This analysis used the Sickle regression by Diekmann and Mitter (1984). The results showed that family events, such as age at first marriage, type of the union, or presence of children in the family significantly affect the risk of divorce.

17. European Sociological Review, Volume 22, Number 5, December 2006: Stability and Change in the Educational Gradient of Divorce. A Comparison of Seventeen Countries by Juho Härkönen and Jaap Dronkers

http://www.diva-portal.org/smash/get/diva2:401478/FULLTEXT01.pdf

The study looked at the relationship between female educational attainment and the risk of divorce across marriage groups in 16 European countries and the United States. The study found that educational gradient of divorce was positive in France, Greece, Italy, Poland, and Spain, and negative in Austria, Flanders, Lithuania, and the United States. However, no significant statistical differences were found in other countries.

HYPOTHESES

In this section, we will try to find the determinants of the divorce rate in 51 states of America in five different times. As explanatory variables we used, income level, unemployment rates and education in each state. The models used for analyzing the data in this research are linear, regression, Neural Network, CART, K-means, and two-steps models.

Our dependent variable is the divorce rate in the USA in selected years (1990, 1995, 2000, 2006, and 2009). We have three independent variables: Education levels, Income levels, and unemployment rates.

Our hypothesis will be as follows:

1. Divorce rate is inversely affected by education levels.
2. Divorce rate is inversely affected by income levels.
3. Divorce rate is directly affected by unemployment rates.

However, in getting the results, it's possible that any relationship that appears in our data was produced by random chance. In order to back up our hypothesis we need to compare the results against the opposite situation: divorce rate is not affected by education. This will be our null hypothesis – the assertion that the things we are testing (i.e., rates of divorce and education) are not related and our results are the product of random chance events. When the null hypothesis is rejected in the significance level (90 or 95 or 99 percent), then we can conclude that the alternate hypothesis is not rejected and that the variables under test are related in a meaningful way (thus, the chance that results are generated by random events or chance will be as low as 10, 5, or 1 percent based on the confidence level we choose). In order to do so, we will use the following model to demonstrate the relationship between the variables:

$$DIV_t = (\alpha)EDU_t + (\beta)UNEM_t + (\gamma)INC_t + \varepsilon$$

Where:

DIV = Divorce rate in year t

EDU = Education rate in year t

UNEM = Unemployment rate in year t

INC = Average income level in year t

ε = Error term

We will hypothesize the relationships among variables as follows:

1. The global test to see if there is a relationship between any of the independent variables and the dependent variable.

$$\begin{cases} H_0 : \alpha = \beta = \gamma = 0 \\ H_1 : \alpha \neq \beta \neq \gamma \neq 0 \end{cases}$$

2. The relationship between education rate and divorce rate is significant and negative:

$$\begin{cases} H_0 : \alpha \geq 0 \\ H_1 : \alpha < 0 \end{cases}$$

3. The relationship between unemployment rate and divorce rate is significant and positive:

$$\begin{cases} H_0 : \beta \leq 0 \\ H_1 : \beta > 0 \end{cases}$$

4. The relationship between income level and divorce rate is significant and negative:

$$\begin{cases} H_0 : \gamma \geq 0 \\ H_1 : \gamma < 0 \end{cases}$$

DATA COLLECTION AND RESEARCH METHODOLOGY

An extensive search was conducted to look for data sources where related data could be found for our research analysis. Only secondary data was used and no primary data was collected for the purpose of our study to time limitation and scope. We collected data from various sources such as Center for Disease Control and Prevention, The United States Census Bureau of the US Department of Commerce, Bureau of Labor Statistics of the United States Department of Labor, and various sources including publications and journals.

The data was collected and organized to form a set of data we believed could be used for our analysis. The divorce rate data was extracted from National Vital Statistics Report issued by Center for Disease Control and Prevention. There is a number of information in the report; however, only divorce rate was extracted, and the data collected on divorce rate represented the divorce rate per 1000 population. The data with regard to median income and education attainment rates were extracted from the reports issued The United States Census Bureau of US Department of Commerce. Education attainment is divided into three different levels: high school graduate, bachelor's degree graduate, and advanced or more graduate. The education attainment is the percentage of the population of each state who is the high school graduates, bachelor's graduates, or advanced or more degrees graduates. The adjustment was done to remove the co-linearity of the data because the percentage of high school graduates also includes those of bachelor's graduates and advanced or more graduates so to arrive at the percentage of pure high school graduates, percentages of bachelor's graduates and advanced or more needed to be removed. In addition, data with regard to unemployment was extracted from the report issued by the Bureau of Labor Statistics of the U.S. Department of Labor.

All required data was extracted from those reports highlighted above and combined in Microsoft Excel format, and SPSS Modeler was used. Various classification and clustering business applications were used to find out the correlation between divorce rates or other variables, and what the most important predictor variables are. First of all, Microsoft Excel was used to find the trend of all the variables followed by SPSS Modeler. K-Means was used to identify clusters among the variables selected followed by Two-Step clustering technique. Linear, regression, neural network, CHAID, and C&R Tree were also used to predict the divorce rate and find out the correlation between divorce rate and selected variables.

FINDINGS AND INTERPRETATION

We conducted a series of analysis on the data collected using various analytical tools, including Microsoft Excel, Weka, and IBM SPSS Modeler.

Microsoft Excel data analysis results showed that there was an upward trend of all the independent variables (Figure D.1): education, median income, and unemployment, from 1990 to 2009. The graphs below depict that there was a significant increase in the level of average median income from 1990 of $29,410 to $49,8670 of 2009; however, there was a downward trend of divorce rate. This initial analysis explains that there is a negative correlation between divorce rate and the predictor variables. Further analysis using more advanced analytical tools is required to find out which variable has the closest correlation with divorce rate and to see whether it is the predictor of the divorce rate.

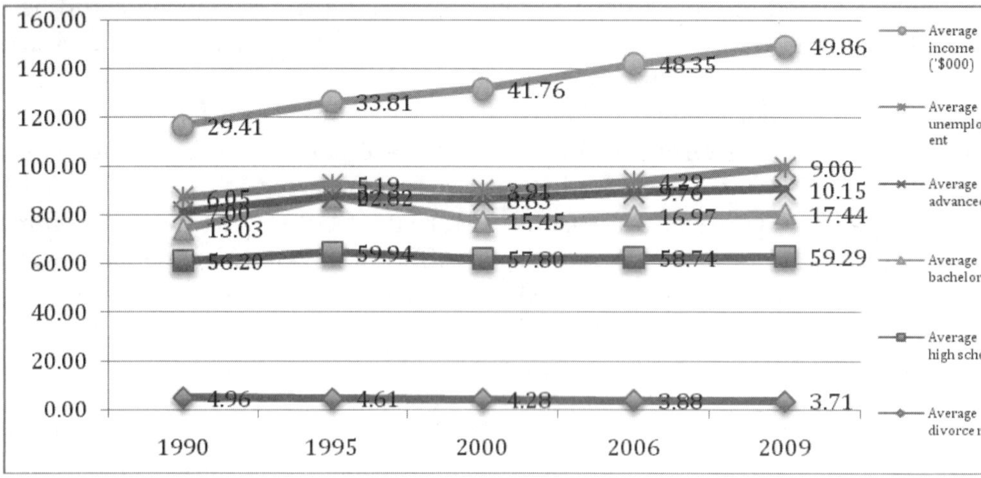

Figure D.1 Trend Analysis

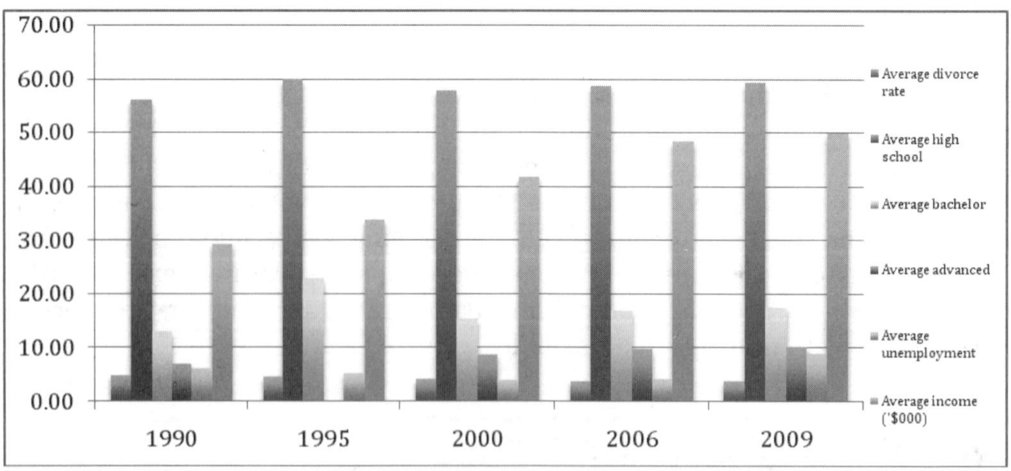

Figure D.2 Comparison of Variables from 1990 to 2009

SPSS Modeler was used to conduct further analysis and the following are the results of our analysis.

Clustering is done on the entire data sorted by years for 51 states to partition the entire dataset into homogenous group demonstrating more similar behavior or within which robustness of the results is higher. Through K-Means algorithm for value of K being equal to 3 and 4, we figured out that the quality of the clusters is higher when K = 3. K-Means showed that the most important predictor is the advanced education level. This indicated that those states with a higher percentage of advanced degrees have a lower rate of divorce. Figure D.3 shows that 56.1% of data population was clustered into one group, and 42% of the population was clustered into another group. The remaining 2% represented the outlier. K-Means clustering indicated that states with a higher rate of advanced degree or more of 9.99%, higher income of $47,000, higher percentage of bachelor's degree of 19% have a lower divorce rate of 3.72 per 1000 population. It is noted that the level of high school education and unemployment rate has minimal effect on divorce. However, those states with a lower advanced degree or more of 7%, lower income of $32,000 and bachelor's degree of 14% have a higher divorce rate of 5.16 per 1000 population. This could be summarized that education attainment and income influence the divorce rate. In addition, District of Columbus is the outlier state because it has got the highest education attainment level and income, but the lowest divorce rate of 3.14 per 1000 population. This indicated that the higher the education and income, the lower the divorce rate.

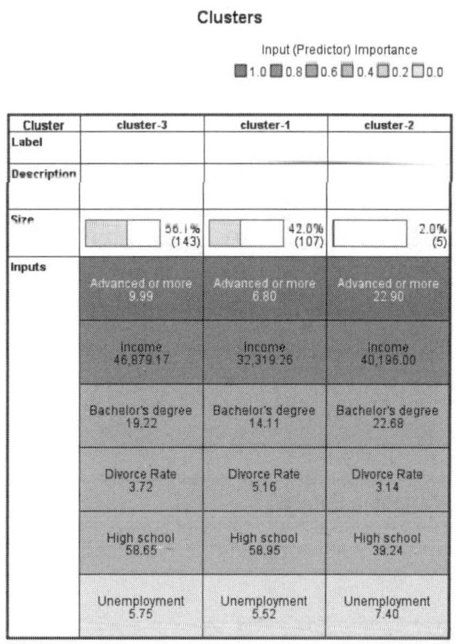

Figure D.3 K-Means Clustering

The result has been reinforced by further analysis using other models such as regression analysis and decision tree to confirm the results of the K-Means.

Regression analysis concludes that bachelor's degree is the most important predictor of divorce rate with predictor importance of 54% compared to other variables. This indicates that couples with higher bachelor's degree are less likely to divorce than those without. Unemployment was found to be the least important predictor with only 8% predictor importance, whereas high school and income have almost the same impact of 12% predictor importance on divorce.

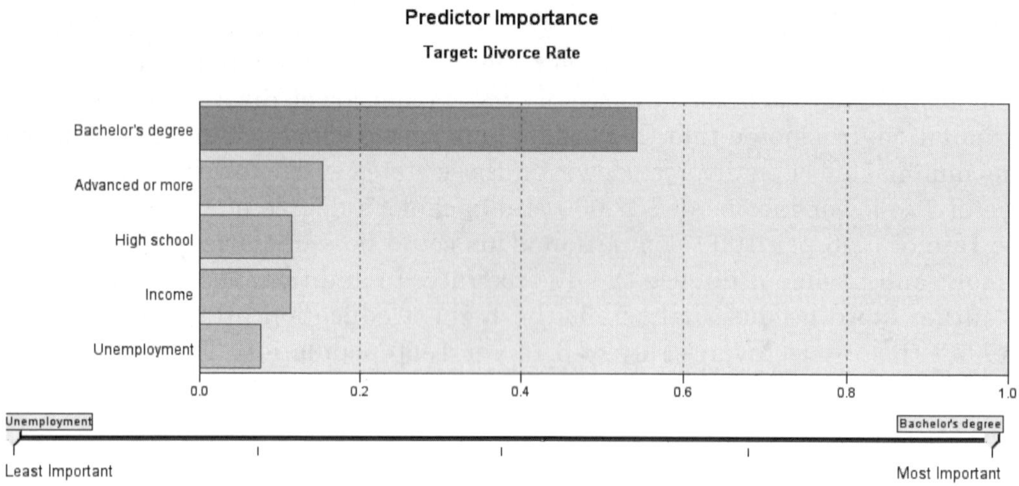

Figure D.4 Predictor Importance

The coefficients for each of the variables indicate the amount of change one could expect in divorce given a one-unit change in the value of that variable, given that all other variables in the model are held constant. For example, consider the variable bachelor's degree. We would expect a decrease of 0.36 in the divorce rate for every one-unit increase in bachelor's degree assuming that other variables in the model are constant.

Variables Entered/Removed(a)

Model	Variables Entered	Variables Removed	Method
1	Income, High school, Unemployment, Bachelor's degree , Advanced or more(b)	.	Enter
a. Dependent Variable: Divorce Rate			
b. All requested variables entered.			

Model Summary

Model	R	R Square	Adjusted R Square	Std. Error of the Estimate
1	.600(a)	.360	.342	1.028114

a. Predictors: (Constant), Income, High school, Unemployment, Bachelor's degree , Advanced or more

ANOVA(a)

Model		Sum of Squares	df	Mean Square	F	Sig.
1	Regression	107.098	5	21.420	20.264	.000(b)
	Residual	190.263	180	1.057		
	Total	297.361	185			

a. Dependent Variable: Divorce Rate

b. Predictors: (Constant), Income, High school, Unemployment, Bachelor's degree , Advanced or more

Coefficients(a)

Model		Unstandardized Coefficients		Standardized Coefficients	t	Sig.
		B	Std. Error	Beta		
1	(Constant)	6.696	1.447		4.626	.000
	High school	.021	.024	.087	.891	.374
	Bachelor's degree	-.190	.046	-.460	-4.130	.000
	Advanced or more	-.033	.050	-.087	-.667	.505
	Unemployment	-.016	.032	-.030	-.492	.623
	Income	-7.95E-006	.000	-.065	-.575	.566

a. Dependent Variable: Divorce Rate

Figure D.5 Regression Analysis

As per the results above, it indicated that bachelor's degree is the most important predictor of the divorce rate compared to other variables. T value of bachelor's degree is 4.130, which is the highest and with the lowest (.000) significance. This tells that divorce rate is influenced more by educational attainment than income and unemployment. We also used a neural network to confirm the results and we found that the neural network gave a similar result to that of regression. SPSS Decision Trees models were used for further analysis.

Decision Trees help better identify groups, discover relationships between them and predict future events. They show highly visual classification and decision trees enable to present categorical results in an intuitive manner, so clearer categorical analysis to non-technical audiences can be explained. The module provides specialized tree-building techniques for classification within the IBM SPSS Statistics environment. Some of the four tree-growing algorithms include:

- **CHAID**—a fast, statistical, multi-way tree algorithm that explores data quickly and efficiently, and builds segments and profiles with respect to the desired outcome.
- **Classification and regression trees (C&RT)**—a complete binary tree algorithm that partitions data and produces accurate homogeneous subsets.

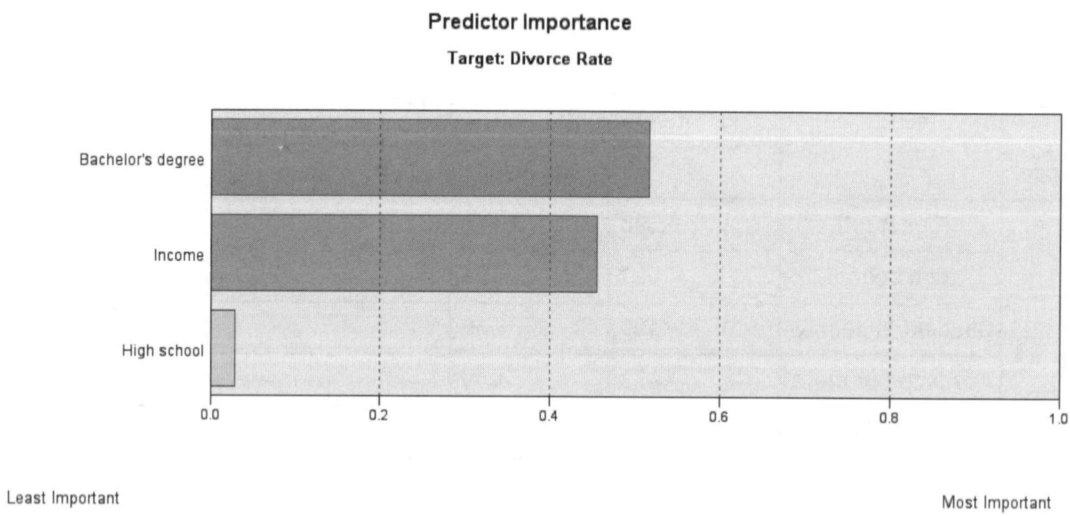

Figure D.6 Predictor Importance

We ran the CHAID (Chi-squared Automatic Interaction Detection) on the entire data and observed that bachelor's degree had the highest predictor importance which is consistent with the results observed over all other results with income as the next best. A three-level tree depth was observed with income as the first splitting variable that we pruned to two levels for simplicity and understanding.

First Split	Second Split	Results
Income	Education	
1. More than 40,000	Bachelor's Degree is divided into 1. High 2. Medium 3. Low	Negative Correlation between bachelor's education and divorce.
2. Between 28,000 and 40,000	High School is divided into 1. High 2. Medium 3. Low	Positive Correlation between high school education and divorce
3. Less than 28,000	Highest Predicted Divorce Rate (No further split)	

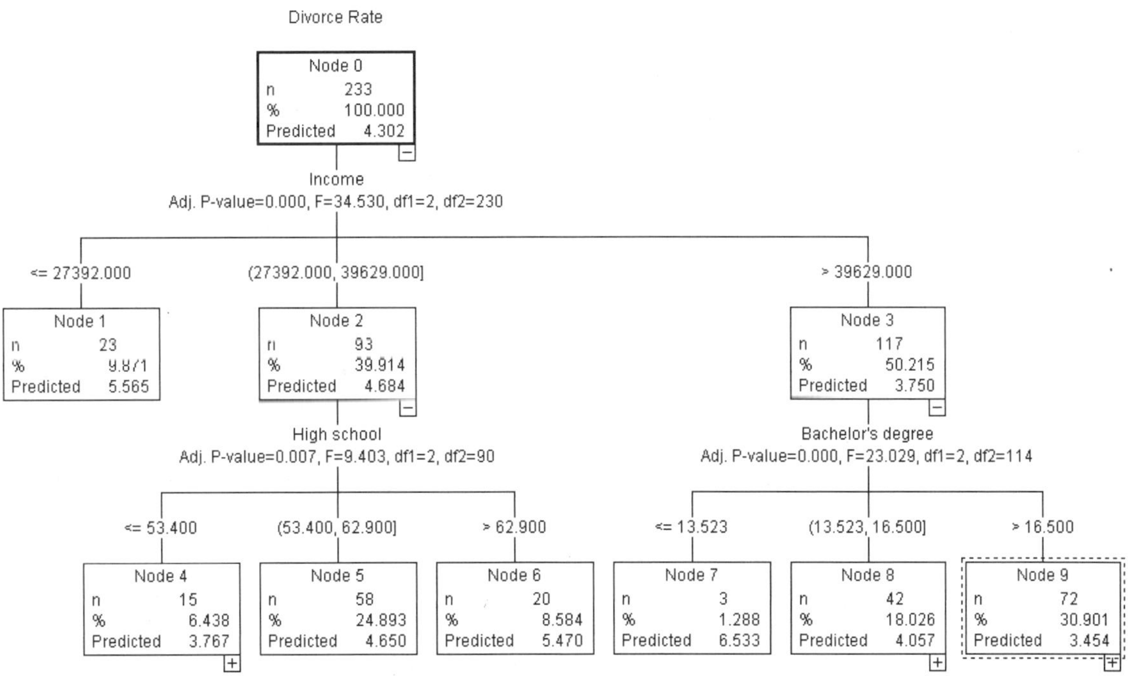

Figure D.7 CHAID Decision Tree

This is a very interesting observation that within varying education levels it is the difference between a bachelor's and a high school education that splits whether ultimately predicted divorce would be high or not. This is proven when we run regression analysis on the same data proves this as the equation comes out to be:

High school * 0.02134 +

Bachelor's degree * −0.19 +

Advanced or more * −0.03344 +

Unemployment * −0.01579 +

Income * −0.000007946 + 6.696

It shows that divorce has a negative relation with all variables but high school. If the level of high school graduates only is high in certain states as observed in 20 US states with middle levels of income, then divorce rates will be high. (Figure D.8)

Running CHAID is better for our kind of analysis in comparison to CART as we are trying to interpret results here rather than predict. CHAID uses multi-way splits by default, which leads to better segments and easier interpretation. However, CART does binary splits by default. CHAID uses a pre-pruning idea. A node is only split if a significant criterion is fulfilled. CART, on the other hand, grows a large tree and then post-prunes the tree back to a smaller version.

Thus, CHAID tries to prevent over-fitting right from the start (only split is there is significant association), whereas CART may easily over-fit unless the tree is pruned back. On the other hand this allows CART to perform better than CHAID in and out-of-sample (for a given tuning parameter combination). The most important difference is that split variable and split point selection in CHAID is less strongly confounded as in CART. This is largely irrelevant when the trees are used for prediction but is an important issue when trees are used for interpretation. Also, if we run CART, it gives a slightly inconsistent result with the rest of our data as it weighs advanced degrees as most important with 48%. However, the decision tree is simpler to understand and the final correlation still holds true, that is, higher education leads to lower divorce rates. We split between high and low advanced degrees at the first split. On the second level, for a high percentage of advanced degrees, we split between high and medium-income levels. We conclude that if state has a higher percentage of advanced degrees and higher income, divorce percentage would be very low. But for medium-income levels a little higher divorce rate is observed in comparison. On the other hand, for a lower percentage of advanced degrees, we split on high and low percentages of bachelor's level education. Our results are re-affirmed again, that with a higher level of education, divorce rate is low.

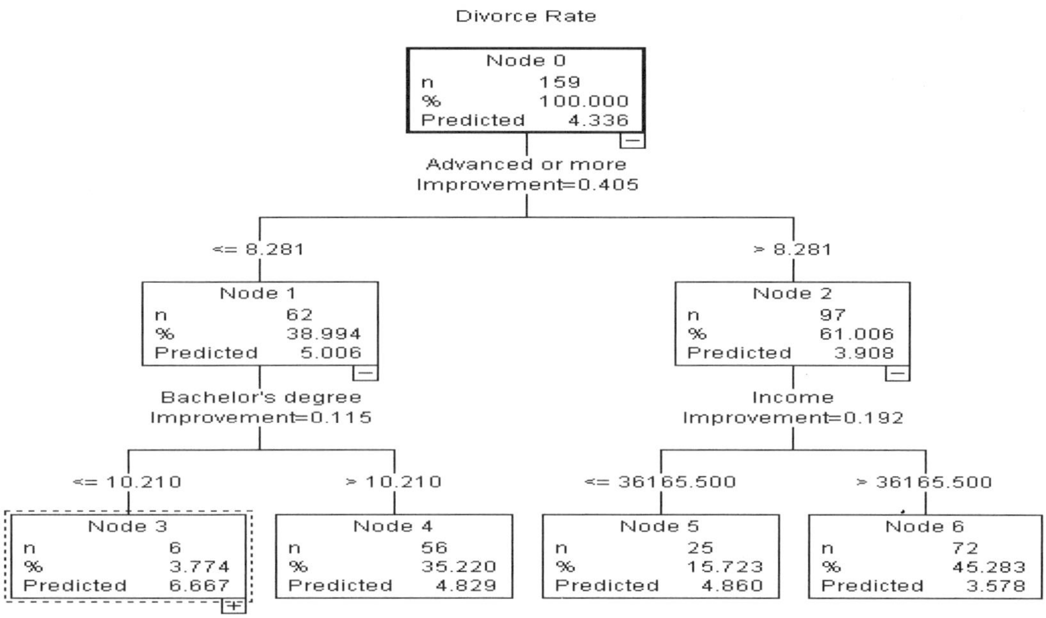

Figure D.8 CART Decision Tree

CONCLUSION

In conclusion, our research has found a strong negative educational gradient in the risk of divorce. Our data confirms that states with better social economic conditions like higher education, higher income, and low unemployment ultimately lead to lower divorce rates. More than any other variable, it is the level of education in the USA, which ultimately influences the divorce rate. States where individuals completed a four-year college degree or more are less likely than high school graduates to divorce. States where individuals only completed high school and did not study further have a much higher likelihood of divorce.

Subsequent efforts to understand the unexpected relationship between education and divorce in the USA should be encouraged as gaining a better understanding of the conditions that contribute to clusters of lower end states together. Further reasons for divorce between races and countries could have important implications for the evaluation of linkages between family change and processes of stratification.

Thus, it is imperative for the current governments to understand these phenomena and discourage the increasing number of dropouts from the university. These drop-outs ultimately lead to a social disequilibrium when they step out of marriages with low-income jobs, being single parents and pass on to the next generation so the cycle continues.

"Education is the most powerful weapon, which you can use to change the world" Nelson Mandela.

LIMITATION AND OPTION FOR FUTURE RESEARCH

Limitations of Research

- The categories that are used might not reflect local constituencies' understandings
- The theories that are used might not reflect local constituencies' understandings
- Knowledge produced might be too abstract for direct application to specific local situations, contexts, and individuals.
- The correlations produced (e.g., between costs and benefits, gender, and access to services or benefits) may mask or ignore underlying causes or realities.
- Research is often carried out in an unnatural, artificial environment so that a level of control can be applied to the exercise. This level of control might not normally be in place in the real world yielding laboratory results as opposed to real-world results
- Preset answers will not necessarily reflect how people really feel about a subject and in some cases might just be the closest match.
- Development of standard questions often leads to 'structural' bias and false representation, where the data actually reflects the view of group instead of the participating subject.
- Many kinds of information are difficult to obtain through structured data collection instruments, particularly on sensitive topics such as domestic violence or relationships outside marriage.
- There is often no information on contextual factors to help interpret the results or to explain variations in behavior between households with similar economic and demographic characteristics.
- Errors in the hypotheses tested may yield misimpressions of program quality or influential factors.

Options for Future Research

- Variables to be further divided in terms of races, for example, Hispanic, white, Asian, and trends analyzed.
- Variables to be divided based on continent specific or country-specific information and comparison made.
- Reasons behind the underlying trends to be explored.

RELATIONSHIP WITH PRINCIPLES OF DEVELOPMENT OF THE SELF

As we found from our research, people with bachelor's and higher degrees have less divorce rate than those without. This finding relates to the development of consciousness. Actions established in higher level of consciousness will yield greater rewards effortlessly. The more knowledge and consciousness we have, the higher the level of creative capability and happiness we experience. This helps us to make better decisions in our marriage and life in general.

Using the right and appropriate data mining tools and techniques for our specific problem was important. Starting from the beginning, we have to search for the right data, clean it and use tools that are easy to use, understand and are powerful, like IBM's SPSS Modeler. Without those steps or directions, we wouldn't have been able to get the results we got. The principle of diving coincides with this. It states that diving into the data at the right angle gives the right results.

APPENDIX

P

Python Tutorial for Data Mining

ABOUT THIS TUTORIAL

This tutorial was created for Dr. Anil K. Maheshwari to complement the R Tutorial in his book "Data Analytics Made Accessible." One of the differences between the Python and the R Tutorials is that there is a considerable amount of code, so all codes will not be printed in the tutorial. I will put in the tutorial the first major code segment Data Visualization and explain what needs to be changed in subsequent code segments to make the code work. All the rest of the codes will be available for download so that you can execute it, modify it, and try different things as I feel that it is the best way to learn.

The tutorial will start out by showing you how to download and install Anaconda, which utilizes Python and numerous scientific and statistical libraries. The Anaconda environment is the ideal environment to perform Data Analytics/Data Science/Machine Learning with Python due to it installing the majority of necessary libraries to do what has to be done.

GETTING STARTED

As is the case with R, Python is a free and open-source language. "Python is a programming language that lets you work quickly and integrate systems more effectively." I will start off by saying that R is not better than Python and Python is not better than R. They both are very powerful and useful languages to accomplish the task that they were meant to do. In my research for completing this tutorial and learning Python and R, I came across many blogs where Data Analysts were using Python to munge and string process data to do analytics on in R. So, it is my opinion that it is best to learn both languages and utilize their individual strengths to accomplish.

The first step to understand how Python works is to go to https://www.continuum.io/downloads and download Anaconda, install it, set-up some shortcuts on your desktop to Idle (a quick and dirty editor for Python), Spyder (a full blown IDE for developing Analytics code in Python), and the help file for Python 2.7.12, as there are a number of tutorials on Python that can help you "get your feet wet."

INSTALLATION

Click on the official Anaconda site (https://www.continuum.io/downloads).

Click either the 64-BIT INSTALLER or the 32-BIT INSTALLER. Note: I installed and utilized the 64-BIT INSTALLER. Everything should work with the 32-BIT INSTALLER. However, being a developer and knowing how "Murphy" is everywhere, there could be problems. I developed and tested everything utilizing the 64-bit version as most developers have 64-bit OS's.

Go ahead and enter your email address as you will get a "cheat sheet" for Anaconda, which is most useful. I have included numerous "cheat sheets" in the directory "PythonCheatSheets" in the directory "PythonTutorial."

Double-click on "Anaconda2-4.2.0-Windows-x86_64 to start the installation and follow the prompts.

Go ahead and sign up for Anaconda Cloud if you want to or not – it is up to you!

Get into command prompt as Administrator and get to Anaconda2 directory as follows:

Update Anaconda2 package as follows by typing "conda update anaconda" at the command prompt.

Press "y"

The above packages will be updated. This is good to do, as maybe some packages have been updated since the installation was created for Anaconda 2.

Then proceed to update and install other necessary packages that will be needed/required to execute the tutorials.

Type the following commands in the command prompt:

conda update spyder

conda update pip

conda install nltk

For wordcloud – necessary for the WordCloud display

Anaconda2

https://blogs.msdn.microsoft.com/pythonengineering/2016/04/11/unable-to-find-vcvarsall-bat/

Download and *run VCForPython27.msi*

pip install wordcloud

pip install tweepy

pip install pydotplus

For Graphviz – necessary for the Decision Tree display

http://graphviz.org/Download..php

Download and install the graphviz-2.38.exe and it will install to your C:\Program Files (x86) directory. THEN ADD THE PATH TO YOUR WINDOWS PATH STATEMENT!!! On my machine, I added "C:\Program Files (x86)\Graphviz2.38\bin" to the path statement. NOTE: If you had Spyder running when you did this, you need to restart Spyder to be able to get the new path into the environment. If Spyder is running and you do NOT restart, you will get an error message "Graphviz executable not found." *It took me a while to get all this figured out!!!*

Make the command line window larger – mode con lines=50

Then, enter the command "conda list," as this will display ALL packages installed in the Anaconda environment and their version.

You can also do a conda list > e:\analytics\conda_pkgs.txt, which will create a text file that contains a list of all the packages installed in Anaconda. You can then print this out to keep a track of what you have installed in your Anaconda environment and see what version you have installed.

It is a good idea to do a "conda update conda" frequently, I do it every day, as it ensures that all your packages necessary for Anaconda are updated and current.

WORKING ON PYTHON

Note: this is based on Windows 10.

Right click on Spyder -> select "More" -> select "Open File Location"

Right click on "Spyder" -> select "Send to" -> select "Desktop (create shortcut)"

Go to Windows Explorer and select directory "C:\Program Files\Anaconda\Doc"

Go to Windows Explorer and select directory "C:\Program Files\Anaconda\Scripts"

Right click your mouse on Idle file "Send to" and then "Desktop." That will create a short-cut to the Python Idle editor, which is an ideal editor to go through the tutorials in the Python help file. Idle is an excellent editor to "get your feet wet" in Python and it is easy to use.

Python Help and Tutorial

Click on the help file on the desktop and select "The Python Tutorial" and you will get the following window:

A quick and dirty example of using Python as a calculator:

Click on the Idle icon on the desktop and you will see as follows (it may take a little while to come up the first time):

Type the following commands in to Idle and you are on your way to becoming a Pythonista!

Just type exit() to exit Idle.

Note: Python is case sensitive, so **Variable** is different from **variable**.

As for Spyder, the IDE that is included with Anaconda, here is a URL with some tutorials on how to get going with Spyder: http://datasciencesource.com/python with spyder-tutorial/. Spyder is a full-blown development environment for doing Data Analytics utilizing Python and it will take a while to get familiar with but will be well worth your effort.

Import a Dataset in Python

Before importing your dataset, you must convert your .xls or .xlsx file to .csv file and save it in the working directory. There are libraries for reading in .xls and/or .xlsx files, but for simplicity, I kept everything in .csv format.

Load the data to a variable using pd.read.csv command. For example, for the code below, we used the following code:

```
import os.path

import pandas as pd

import sys
```

```
DEBUG = True
DRIVE = "E:\\"
DATA_DIR_PATH = "PythonTutorial\\ADataVisualization"
IN_FILE_NAME = "HeightWeight2016.csv"

def get_data(drive, data_dir_path, in_file):
    file_path = os.path.join(drive + data_dir_path, in_file)
    try:
        return pd.read_csv(file_path, delimiter=",", names=None)
    except IOError:
        msg = "An error occured trying to read file: %s" % file_path
        print(msg)
        sys.exit()
```

and it is called as follows:

```
ht_wt_df = get_data(DRIVE + DATA_DIR_PATH, IN_FILE_NAME)
if DEBUG == True:
    print('*** ht_wt_df ***')
    print(ht_wt_df.head(n = DISPLAY_RECORDS))
    print(ht_wt_df.tail(n = DISPLAY_RECORDS))
```

Code displayed in IPython Console in Spyder as follows

```
*** ht_wt_df ***
  height age gender weight
0 71.0 24 M 165.0
1 68.0 29 M 165.0
2 72.0 34 M 180.0
3 67.0 21 F 113.0
4 72.0 32 M 178.0
```

```
   height age gender weight
175 65.0 31 M 120.0
176 70.0 33 M 178.2
177 68.0 34 M 140.0
178 71.0 26 M 130.0
179 69.0 27 M 170.0
```

A number of important items to note about the above code:

1. Import – imports a specific library which is important and has methods that are used throughout the code segment. It is always recommended to put these at the top of the module, then you can see ALL imports that are used in the code.
2. Constants – these are variables that are constants used in the program. I put the DEBUG constant in there as I am developing so as things go, I can see what the results of my code are and I can turn this off and on as need be.
3. Def defines a function in Python
4. Executing a function ht_wt_df = get_data(DRIVE + DATA_DIR_PATH, IN_FILE_NAME) creates a DataFrame variable named ht_wt_df from the results of the get_data function
5. If DEBUG == True: prints data that you want to see printed in the IPython Consold in Spyder

Data Visualization

See directory A Data Visualization and look at code modules DataVisualization.py and DataVisualizationOO.py. The first example used Python code and functions and the second example utilized a strictly object-oriented approach.

Plotting a Histogram

```
# function to create histogram
def histogram_it(df, color, title, xlabel, ylabel, img_name, orient=None):
   plt.clf()
   plt.figure()
      if orient == None:
      df.hist(color=color)
```

```
    else:
        df.hist(color=color, orientation=orient)
    plt.title(title)
    plt.xlabel(xlabel)
    plt.ylabel(ylabel)
    write_image(DRIVE, DATA_DIR_PATH, img_name)
    plt.show()

# Histogram of height – call the histogram_it function
histogram_it(ht_wt_df['height'],
    'yellow',
    "PEOPLE'S HEIGHTS",
    'Height',
    'Frequency',
    OUT_IMG_NAME + "_height_hist.png")
# Histogram of weight
histogram_it(ht_wt_df['weight'],
    'grey',
    "PEOPLE'S WEIGHTS",
    'Weight',
    'Frequency',
    OUT_IMG_NAME + "_weight_hist.png",
    'horizontal')
```

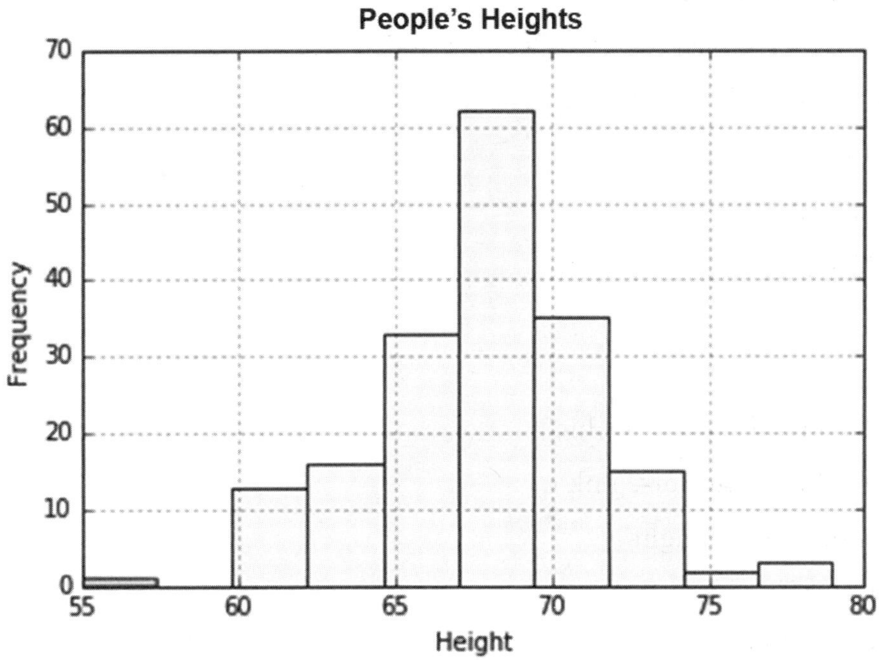
People's Heights
Frequency
Height
70
60
50
40
30
20
10
0
55
60
65
70
75
80

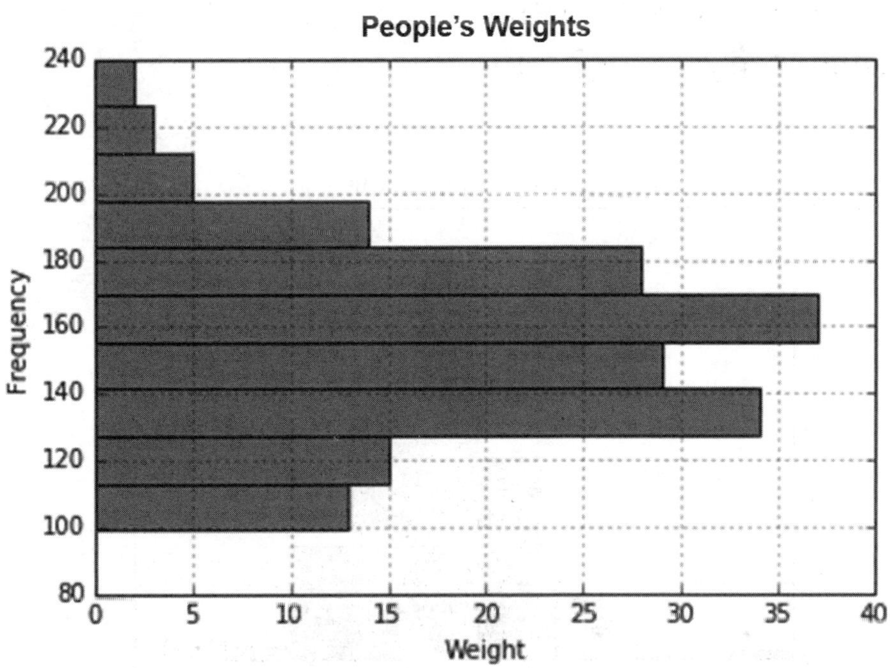
People's Weights
Frequency
Weight
240
220
200
180
160
140
120
100
80
0
5
10
15
20
25
30
35
40

```
#Histogram of height by gender
gend_m_df = ht_wt_df.loc[(ht_wt_df['gender']=="M")]
gend_f_df = ht_wt_df.loc[(ht_wt_df['gender']=="F")]
if DEBUG == True:
   print(gend_f_df)
   print(gend_m_df)
plt.clf()
plt.figure()
gend_m_df['height'].hist(color='blue')
gend_f_df['height'].hist(color='pink')
plt.title("Histogram of Height")
plt.xlabel("Height")
plt.ylabel("Frequency")
plt.legend(('Male', 'Female'), loc=0)
out_dir_file_image = OUT_IMG_NAME + "_ht_gend_hist.png"
write_image(DRIVE, DATA_DIR_PATH, out_dir_file_image)
plt.show()
```

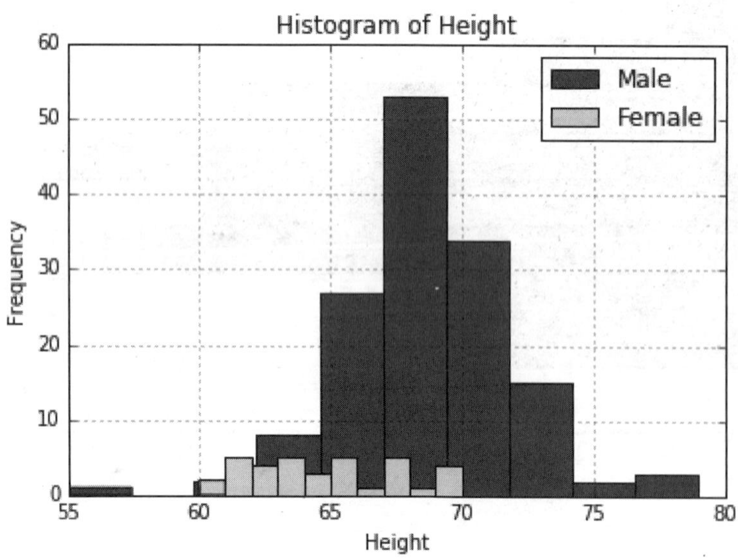

```
# Histogram of age by gender
plt.clf()
plt.figure()
gend_m_df['age'].hist(color='blue')
gend_f_df['age'].hist(color='pink')
plt.title("Histogram of Age")
plt.xlabel("Age")
plt.ylabel("Frequency")
plt.legend(('Male', 'Female'), loc=0)
out_dir_file_image = OUT_IMG_NAME + "_age_gend_hist.png"
write_image(DRIVE, DATA_DIR_PATH, out_dir_file_image)
plt.show()
```

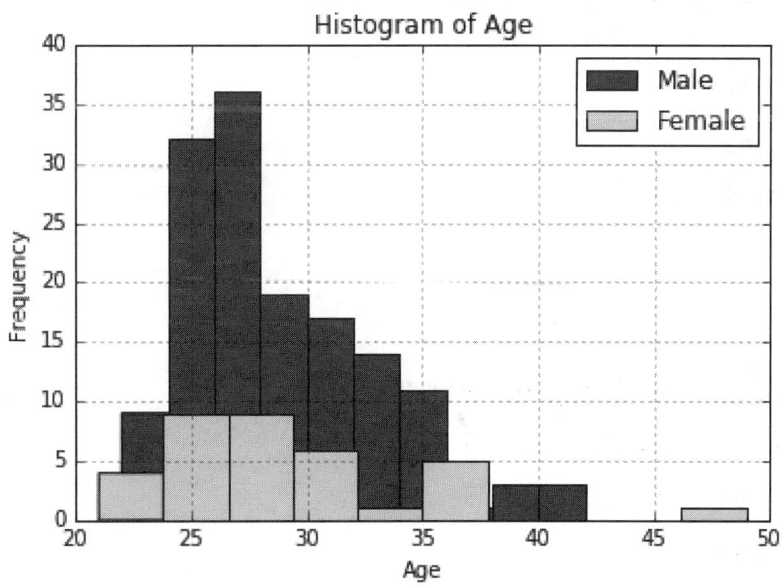

Plotting a Bar Chart

```
# Histogram of gender
# Convert 'F' and 'M' to 0 and 1 to create histogram
```

```
# (data has to be numeric so it is essential to convert F and M to 0 and 1)
female = []
for row in ht_wt_df['gender']:
    if row == 'F':
        female.append(0)
    else:
        female.append(1)

# Append female array to ht_wt_df dataframe
ht_wt_df['female'] = female

# Repurpose gend_ dataframes for this histogram
gend_m_df = ht_wt_df.loc[(ht_wt_df['female']==1)]
gend_f_df = ht_wt_df.loc[(ht_wt_df['female']==0)]

if DEBUG == True:
    print(gend_f_df)
    print(gend_m_df)

plt.clf()
plt.figure()
gend_f_df['female'].hist(color='pink', bins=2)
gend_m_df['female'].hist(color='blue', bins=2)
plt.title("Histogram of Gender")
plt.xlabel('Gender')
plt.ylabel('Frequency')
plt.legend(('Female', 'Male'), loc=0)
out_dir_file_image = OUT_IMG_NAME + "_gend.png"
write_image(DRIVE, DATA_DIR_PATH, out_dir_file_image)
plt.show()
```

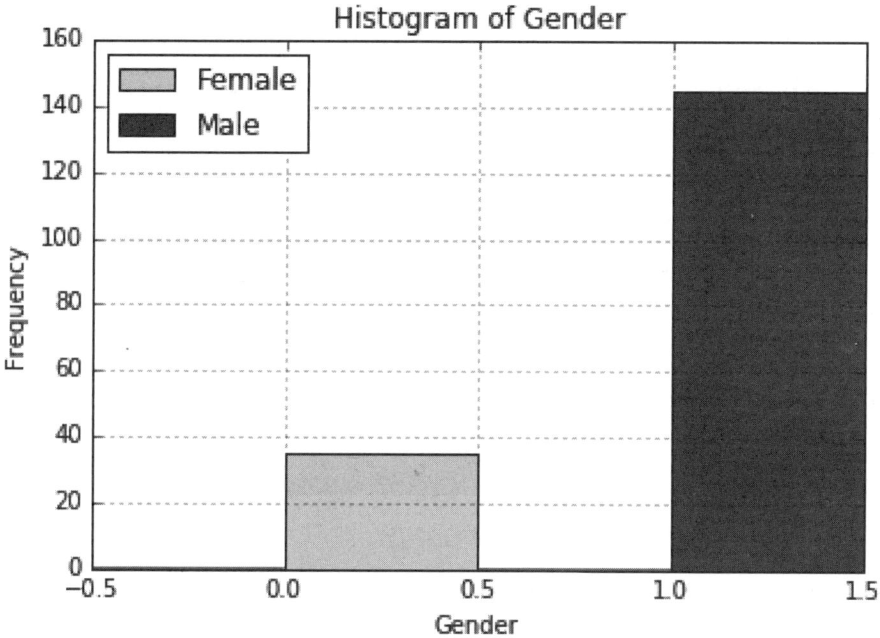

Plotting charts side by side

```
# Multiple Plots
# Set up for multiple plots 2 rows and 2 columns
fig, axes = plt.subplots(nrows=2, ncols=2)
ax0, ax1, ax2, ax3 = axes.flat

# Histogram of height
ax0.hist(ht_wt_df['height'], histtype='bar', color='yellow')
ax0.set_title("PEOPLE'S HEIGHTS")
ax0.set_xlabel('Height')
ax0.set_ylabel('Frequency')

# Histogram of weight
ax1.hist(ht_wt_df['weight'], histtype='bar',
   orientation='horizontal', color='grey')
```

```
ax1.set_title("PEOPLE'S WEIGHTS")
ax1.set_xlabel('Frequency')
ax1.set_ylabel('Weight')

# Histogram of age
ax2.hist(ht_wt_df['age'], histtype='bar', color='gray')
ax2.set_title("PEOPLE'S AGE")
ax0.set_xlabel('Age')
ax0.set_ylabel('Frequency')

# Histogram of gender
ax3.hist(gend_f_df['female'], color='pink', bins=2)
ax3.hist(gend_m_df['female'], color='blue', bins=2)
ax3.set_title("Histogram of Gender")
ax3.set_xlabel('Gender')
ax3.set_ylabel('Frequency')
ax3.legend(('Female', 'Male'), loc=0)

plt.tight_layout()
out_dir_file_image = OUT_IMG_NAME + "_multi.png"
write_image(DRIVE, DATA_DIR_PATH, out_dir_file_image)
plt.show()
```

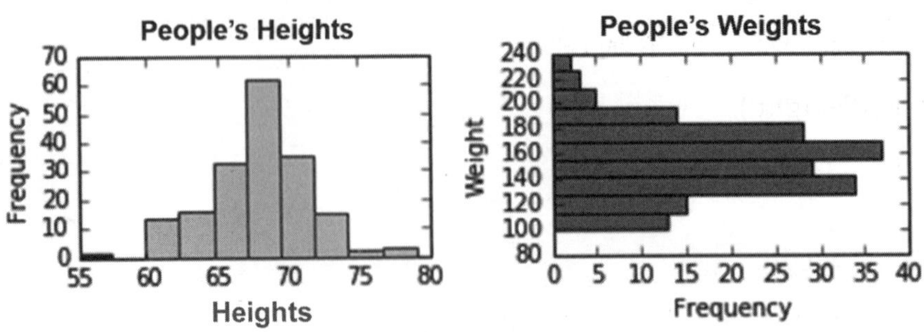

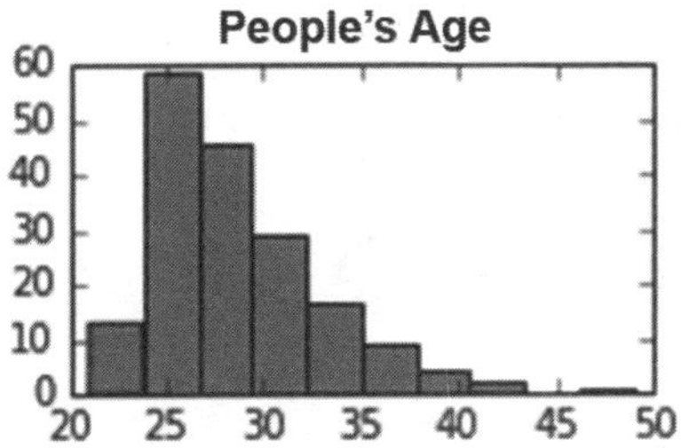

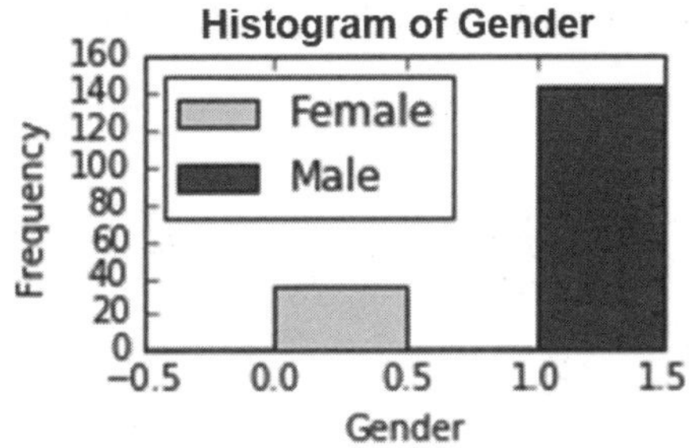

DATA MINING TECHNIQUES

Decision Tree (Supervised Learning)

```
# Important libraries
  from sklearn.externals.six import StringIO
  from sklearn.tree import DecisionTreeClassifier
  from sklearn import tree

  def visualize_tree(self, dec_tree_cls, feature_names):
    drive_file_path = os.path.join(self.drive + self.data_dir_path,
      self.out_image)
  dot_data – StringIO()
  try:
    tree.export_graphviz(dec_tree_cls, out_file=dot_data,
      filled=True, rounded=True,
      special_characters=True)
    graph = pydotplus.graph_from_dot_data(dot_data.getvalue())
    graph.write_pdf(drive_file_path)
  except:
    exit("Could not run dot, ie graphviz, to "
      "produce visualization")
```

Above code created .pdf file in the current working directory.

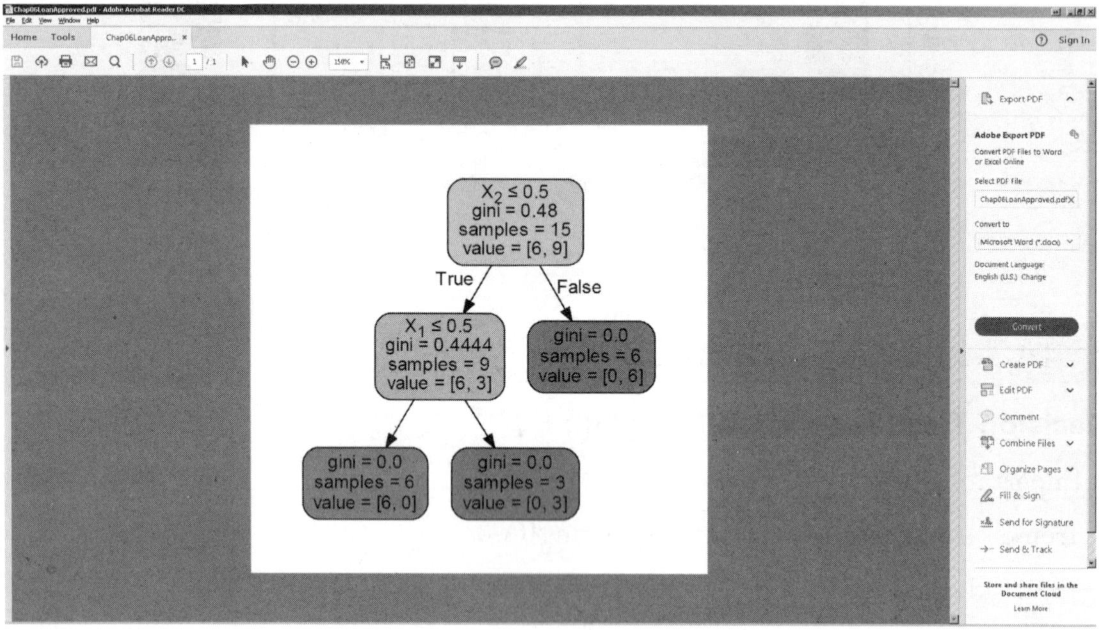


```
def get_code(self, dec_tree_cls, feature_names, target_names,
             spacer_base="    "):
    left      = dec_tree_cls.tree_.children_left
    right     = dec_tree_cls.tree_.children_right
    threshold = dec_tree_cls.tree_.threshold
    features  = [feature_names[i] for i in dec_tree_cls.tree_.feature]
    value = dec_tree_cls.tree_.value

    def recurse(left, right, threshold, features, node, depth):
        spacer = spacer_base * depth
        if (threshold[node] != -2):
            print(spacer + "if ( " + features[node] + " <= " + \
                  str(threshold[node]) + " ) {")
            if left[node] != -1:
                recurse(left, right, threshold, features,
```

```
                    left[node], depth+1)
            print(spacer + "}\n" + spacer +"else {")
            if right[node] != -1:
                recurse(left, right, threshold, features,
                    right[node], depth+1)
            print(spacer + "}")
        else:
            target = value[node]
            for i, v in zip(np.nonzero(target)[1],
                    target[np.nonzero(target)]):
                target_name = target_names[i]
                target_count = int(v)
                print(spacer + "return " + str(target_name) + \
                    " ( " + str(target_count) + " examples )")
    recurse(left, right, threshold, features, 0, 0)
```

The above code created this group of statements in the IPython Console.

```
if ( House <= 0.5 ) {
   if ( Job <= 0.5 ) {
      return 0 ( 6 examples )
   }
   else {
      return 1 ( 3 examples )
   }
}
else {
   return 1 ( 6 examples )
```

Regression (Supervised Learning)

With Python, it is possible to work with multiple linear regression.

```
self.ht_wt_df = self.get_data()


*** Formulas ***
*** ht_wt_df ***
   height  age gender  weight
0    71.0   24      M   165.0
1    68.0   29      M   165.0
2    72.0   34      M   180.0
3    67.0   21      F   113.0
4    72.0   32      M   178.0
     height  age gender  weight
175    65.0   31      M   120.0
176    70.0   33      M   178.2
177    68.0   34      M   140.0
178    71.0   26      M   130.0
179    69.0   27      M   170.0


*** OLS Regression Results Parameters (formulas) ***
Intercept     -58.703262
gender[T.M]    20.076624
height          2.734531
age             0.431700


*** OLS Regression Results Summary (formulas ***
OLS Regression Results
```

```
==============================================================================
Dep. Variable:          weight   R-squared:                     0.305
Model:                  OLS   Adj. R-squared:                   0.293
Method:                 Least Squares   F-statistic:            25.72
Date:                   Tue, 24 Jan 2017   Prob (F-statistic):  7.58e-14
Time:                   15:26:40   Log-Likelihood:              -819.88
No. Observations:       180   AIC:                              1648.
Df Residuals:           176   BIC:                              1661.
Df Model:               3
Covariance Type:        nonrobust
==============================================================================
               coef    std err      t      P>|t|     [95.0% Conf. Int.]
------------------------------------------------------------------------------
Intercept     -58.7033  36.826   -1.594   0.113   -131.380   13.973
gender[T.M]    20.0766   4.928    4.074   0.000     10.350   29.803
height          2.7345   0.542    5.050   0.000      1.666    3.803
age             0.4317   0.402    1.075   0.284     -0.361    1.224
==============================================================================
Omnibus:             8.771   Durbin-Watson:             1.961
Prob(Omnibus):       0.012   Jarque-Bera (JB):          9.235
Skew:                0.553   Prob(JB):                  0.00988
Kurtosis:            2.905   Cond. No.                  1.56e+03
==============================================================================
```

Warnings:

[1] Standard Errors assume that the covariance matrix of the errors is correctly specified.

[2] The condition number is large, 1.56e+03. This might indicate that there are strong multicollinearity or other numerical problems.

*** Rainbow test for linearity ***

(1.1947660651585406, 0.2034517105727254)

There are a number of other runs: categorization of variables (multiple regression) and contrast coding systems for categorical variables: (Patsy) in the code segment but I did not want to paste the tables and results in the Word Document as it does not format nicely as displayed above!

Correlation (Supervised Learning)

In the same way described in decision tree, you can install the necessary library and load the data.

Using self.ht_wt_df.cov() you can see relation. Ran with and without gender.

*** Covariance Data 1 ***

	height	age	weight	male
height	13.008211	-0.261263	48.528256	0.650990
age	-0.261263	18.820453	5.450666	-0.097610
weight	48.528256	5.450666	765.871420	4.900301
male	0.650990	-0.097610	4.900301	0.157511

*** Covariance Data 2 ***

	height	age	weight
height	13.008211	-0.261263	48.528256
age	-0.261263	18.820453	5.450666
weight	48.528256	5.450666	765.871420

Scatter plotting the data, you can see the regression

With gender:

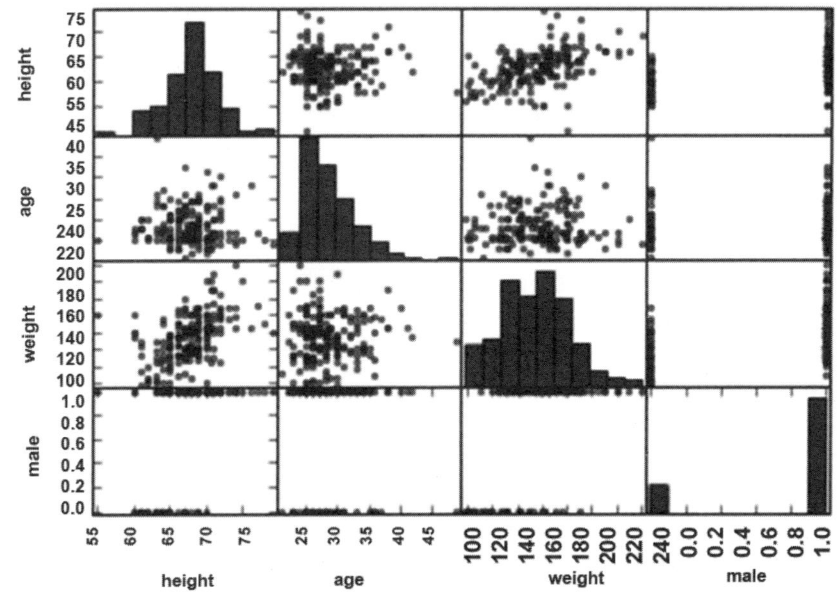

Without gender:

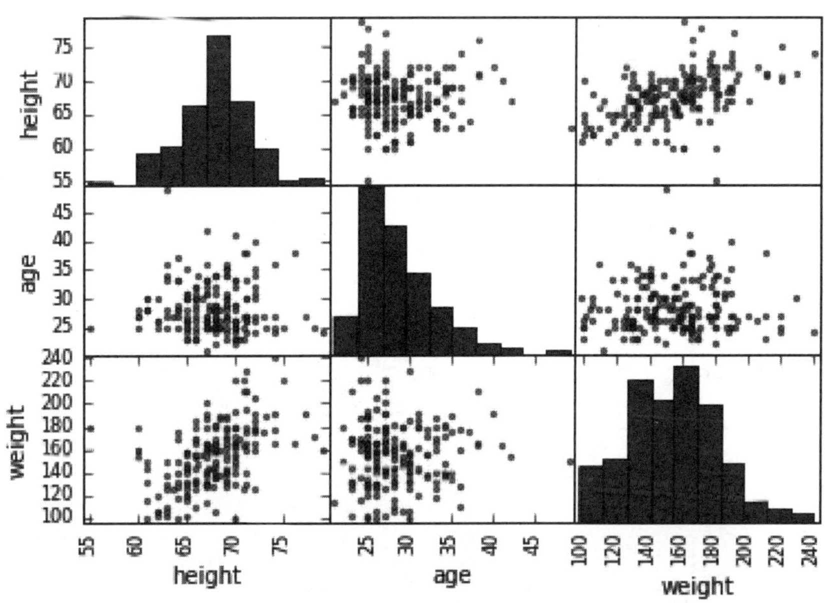

Clustering – Kmeans (Unsupervised Learning)

```
"""
The following two lines reduce the number of dimensions by applying
a dimensionality reduction algorithm that operates on four numbers
and outputs two new numbers so you can plot.
"""
self.pca = PCA(n_components=2).fit(self.iris.data)
self.pca_2d = self.pca.transform(self.iris.data)

if DEBUG == True:
    print(self.pca_2d)

self.title = 'Reference Plot'
pl.clf()
pl.figure(self.title)
pl.title(self.title)
pl.scatter(self.pca_2d[:, 0], self.pca_2d[:, 1], c=self.iris.target)
self.write_image(self.out_image + "_ref_plot.png")
pl.show()
```

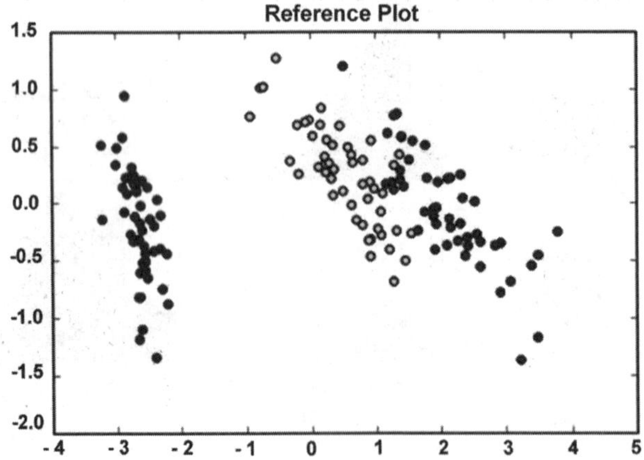

```
for self.idx in range(0, self.pca_2d.shape[0]):
    if self.iris.target[self.idx] == 0:
        self.c1 = pl.scatter(self.pca_2d[self.idx, 0],
                             self.pca_2d[self.idx, 1],
                             c='r',
                             marker='+')
    elif self.iris.target[self.idx] == 1:
        self.c2 = pl.scatter(self.pca_2d[self.idx, 0],
                             self.pca_2d[self.idx, 1],
                             c='g',
                             marker='o')
    elif self.iris.target[self.idx] == 2:
        self.c3 = pl.scatter(self.pca_2d[self.idx, 0],
                             self.pca_2d[self.idx, 1],
                             c='b',
                             marker='*')

self.title = 'Iris dataset with 3 clusters and known outcomes'
pl.legend([self.c1, self.c2, self.c3],
          ['Setosa', 'Versicolor', 'Virginica'])
pl.title(self.title)
self.write_image(self.out_image + "_3_clusters_known.png")
pl.show()
```

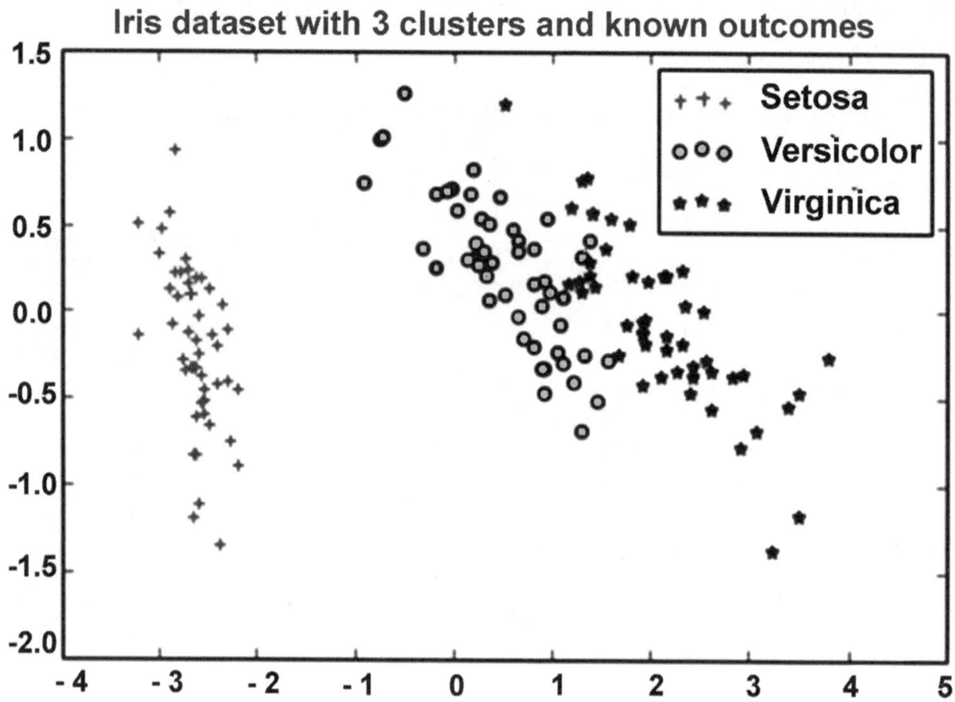

Scatter plots with a variety of k-means ranges

```
for self.k_range in range(self.start_k_range,
                                   self.end_k_range):
        if DEBUG == True:
    print('k = %d' % self.k_range)
            self.kmeans = KMeans(n_clusters=self.k_range, random_state=111)
  self.kmeans.fit(self.iris.data)

  self.title = 'K-means with ' + str(self.k_range) + ' clusters'
  pl.clf()
  pl.figure(self.title)
```

```
pl.title(self.title)


pl.scatter(self.pca_2d[:, 0],
           self.pca_2d[:, 1],
            c=self.kmeans.labels_)


self.write_image(self.out_image + "_" \
                         + str(self.k_range) \
                          + "_clusters.png")

pl.show()
```

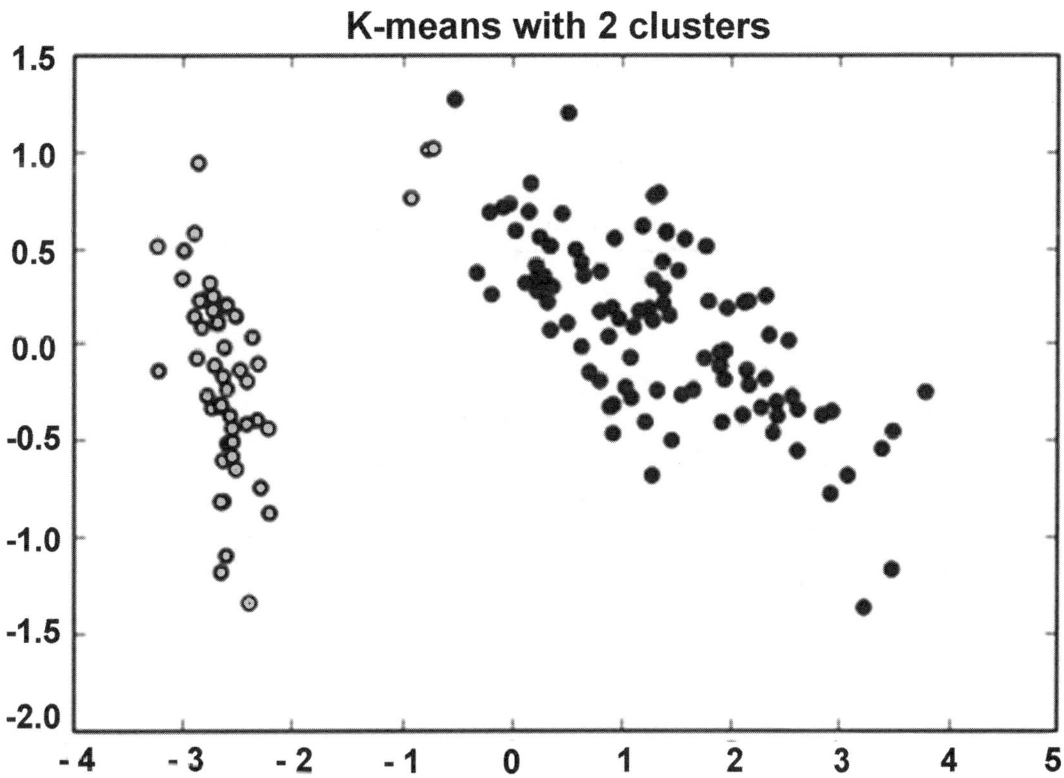

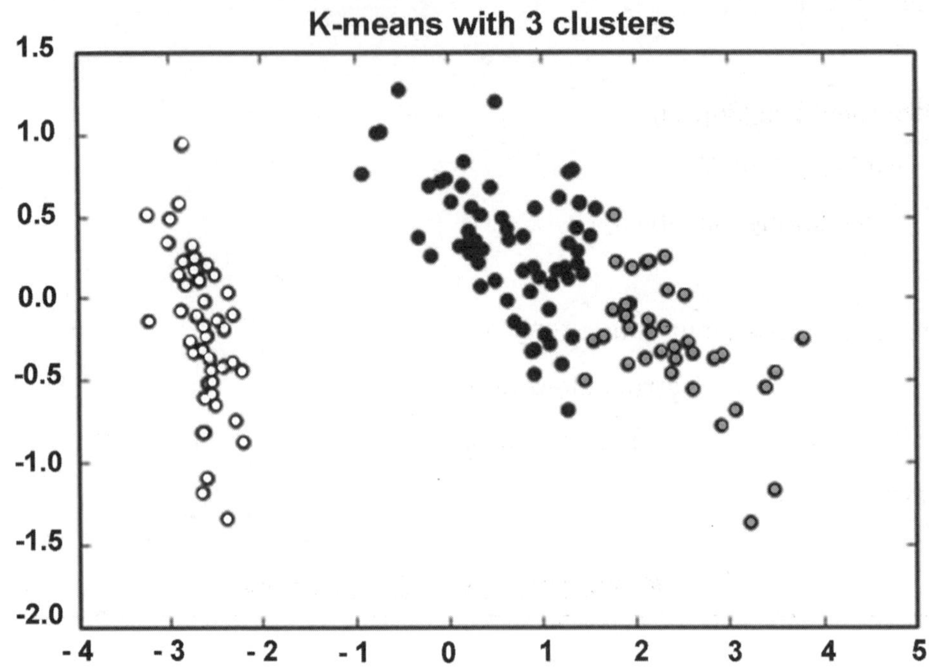
K-means with 3 clusters
1.5
1.0
0.5
0.0
-0.5
-1.0
-1.5
-2.0
-4
-3
-2
-1
0
1
2
3
4
5

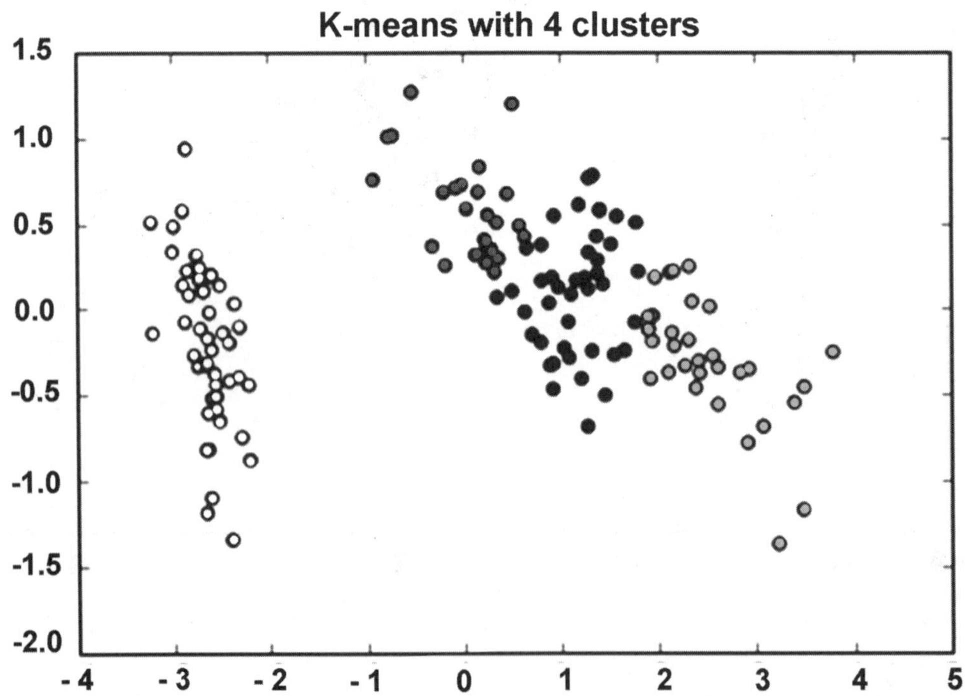
K-means with 4 clusters
1.5
1.0
0.5
0.0
-0.5
-1.0
-1.5
-2.0
-4
-3
-2
-1
0
1
2
3
4
5

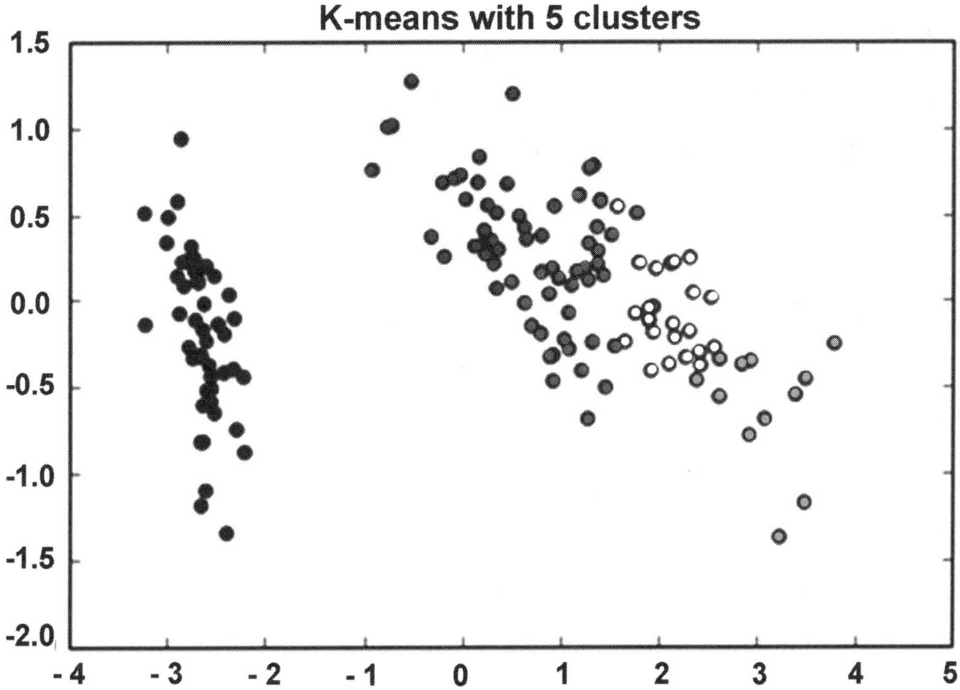

BIG DATA MINING

WordCloud – directory FWordCloud and look at code module WordCloud.py.

```
import string
def remove_punctuation(self, s):
    table = string.maketrans("","")
    return s.translate(table, string.punctuation)


self.text = self.get_data()
self.text = self.remove_punctuation(self.text)
self.word_cloud = WordCloud().generate(self.text)
```

```
plt.imshow(self.word_cloud)
plt.axis("off")
self.out_dir_file_image = self.out_image + "_1.png"
self.write_image(self.out_dir_file_image)
plt.show()

self.word_cloud = WordCloud(max_font_size=self.max_font_size) \
                                        .generate(self.text)
plt.figure()
plt.imshow(self.word_cloud)
plt.axis("off")
self.out_dir_file_image = self.out_image + "_2.png"
self.write_image(self.out_dir_file_image)
plt.show()
```

Page Rank

```
# Imports
import matplotlib.pyplot as plt
import networkx as nx
import os.path

DEBUG = True
DRIVE = "E:\\"
DATA_DIR_PATH = "PythonTutorial\\HPageRank"
OUT_IMG_NAME = "PageRank.png"

G = nx.DiGraph()
```

```
G.add_edges_from([("A", "B"), ("B", "A"), ("B", "B"), ("B", "C"), ("C", "A")])
G.add_node("D")
edge1=("A", "D")
G.add_edge(*edge1)
edge2=("D","C")
G.add_edge(*edge2)
edge3=("D","D")
G.add_edge(*edge3)

pr = nx.pagerank(G)

nx.draw(G, with_labels=True)
img = os.path.join(DRIVE + DATA_DIR_PATH, OUT_IMG_NAME)
plt.savefig(img)
plt.show()
```

```
*** Page Ranks ***
{'A': 0.28511854592348873, 'C': 0.21751453588898481, 'B': 0.22140856006497459, 'D':
0.27595835812168851}
```

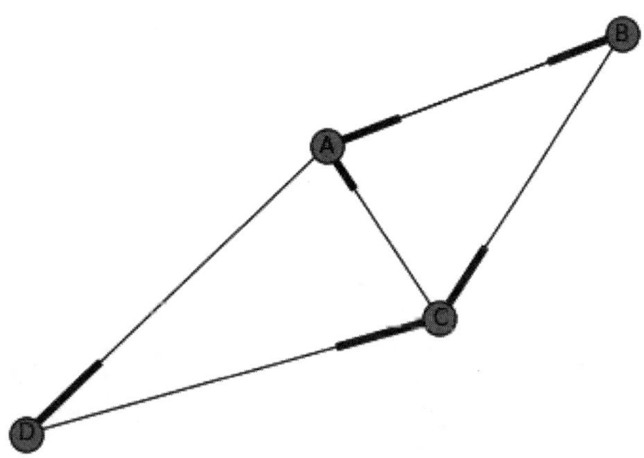

ADDITIONAL DOCUMENTATION

At the top of each .py file in all the tutorials are numerous references that I used in creating the appropriate tutorial for that section. Without the hard work of the people who created the code that I used for references, I would still be on the first tutorial – Data Visualization! As a developer, it is of the utmost importance that you are able to search all available resources and find an algorithm, and/or code that you can utilize. It is also of the utmost importance to give credit to the individual(s) that helped you along the way.

http://datasciencesource.com/python-with-spyder-tutorial/

https://pythontips.com/2013/07/30/20-python-libraries-you-cant-live-without/

http://programminghistorian.org/lessons/text-mining-with-extracted-features

http://www.nltk.org/

http://pandas.pydata.org/

http://scikit-learn.org/stable/index.html

http://matplotlib.org/

http://www.tweepy.org/

http://statsmodels.sourceforge.net/devel/contrasts.html

APPENDIX

R

R Tutorial for Data Mining

GETTING STARTED WITH R

The R Project website describes, "*R is a free software environment for statistical computing and graphics. It compiles and runs on a wide variety of UNIX platforms, Windows and MacOS*".

INSTALLING R

Click on the official R programming site (http://www.r-project.org). Search for the Download section Click "download R" to get the proper mirror. This should take you to a page something like below.

Choose the link that you like.

Choose your operating system. In the tutorial case, it was selected Microsoft Windows.

Click "install R for the first time".

Click on "download" to download the installer (for Windows).

Click on "Save file" to save the installer to your computer.

Double click the .exe file for installation.

Click "Run" to start the installation. Follow the steps. Click next, accept the agreement, select your installation folder, and finish the installation.

WORKING ON R

Select the R application from your start menu. All coding styles should be the same as what you practiced in R code school. Get and set a working directory.

```
getwd()
setwd("/path/to/your/working/directory")
```

List of R Commands

Here are some commands that you can use in your R script.

Command/Word	Description	Example
#	The characters after are considered comment	#this is a comment
cat	Print a message to the console (like System.out. println in Java)	cat("Hello World!\n")
source	Execute an R script file previously created	source("myScript.r")
<-	Assign a value to a variable	one <- 1 Hello <- "Hello"
install.packages	Download and install a package	install.packages("rpart")
library	Load a installed library to your R script	load(rpart)

Note: R is case sensitive, so Variable is different from variable.

IMPORT A DATASET IN R

Before importing your dataset, you must convert your .xls or .xlsx file to .csv file and save it in the working directory. Otherwise, you will be required to specify its path when you are importing the data in R.

Load the data to a variable using `read.csv` command. For example, for the screen below we used the following command:

```
data <- read.csv("Ht-Wt+w+Dec15.csv") #Read data from the csv file and assign to variable "data"
View(data) #show all values from the "data" variable
head(data,5) #print in the console the first 5 rows from "data" variable
View(head(data,5)) #show the data loaded into "data" variable (5 first records)
```

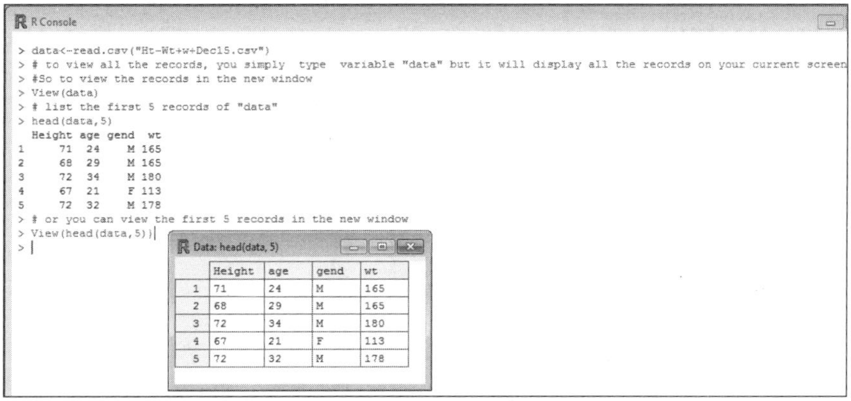

DATA VISUALIZATION

Plotting a Histogram

```
df <- read.csv("Ht-Wt+w+Dec15.csv") #Read data from the csv file and assign
to variable "df"

hist(df$Height,ylim(c(0,20)),xlim=c(55,80),main= "PEOPLE'S HEIGHTS",
breaks=32,xlab="Height", col="#FFFF0F",border="#000000") #plot the histogram
height
```

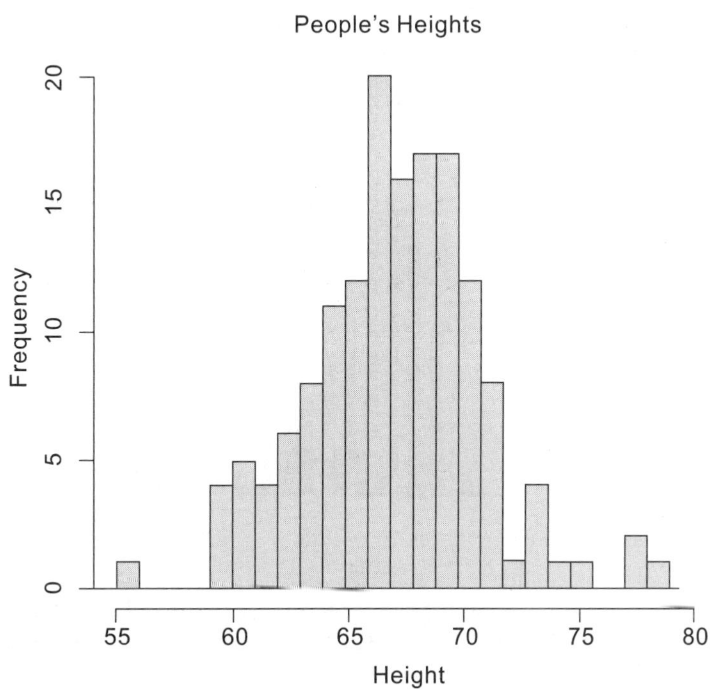

```
hist(df$wt,ylim(c(0,20)),xlim=c(99,240),main= "PEOPLE'S WEIGHTS",
breaks=32,xlab="Weight", col="#999999",border="#ffffff") #plot the histogram
for weight
```

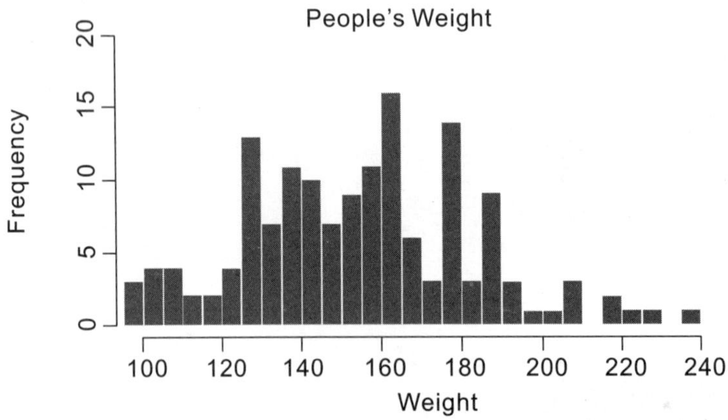


```
install.packages("ggplot2")
library(ggplot2) #load the library ggplot2, needed for ggplot command.
ggplot(df,aes(x=Height,fill=gend))+geom_bar(position="stack",binwidth=0.5,c
ol="black")+scale_x_continuous("Height")+scale_y_continuous("Frequency")+gg
title("Histogram of Height")
```

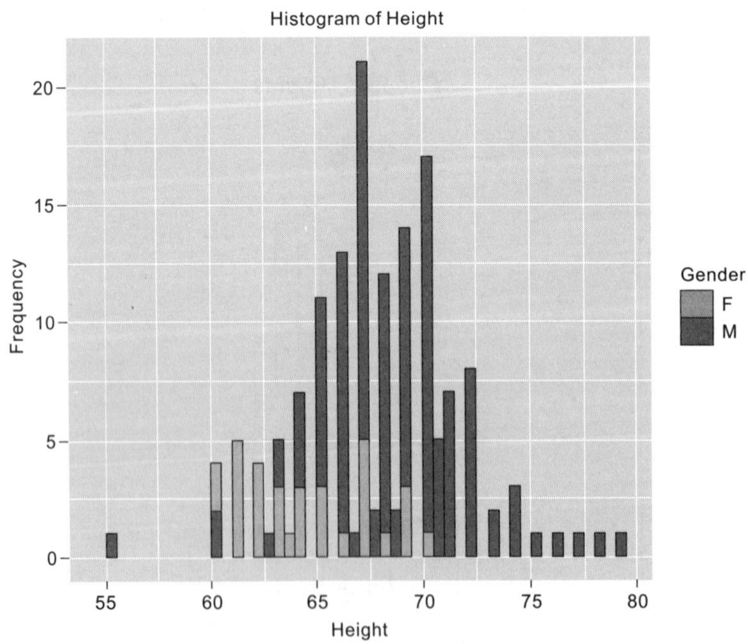


```
ggplot(df,aes(x=age,fill=gend))+geom_bar(position="stack",binwidth=0.5,col=
"black")+scale_x_continuous("Age")+scale_y_continuous("Frequency")+ggtitle(
"Histogram of Age")
```

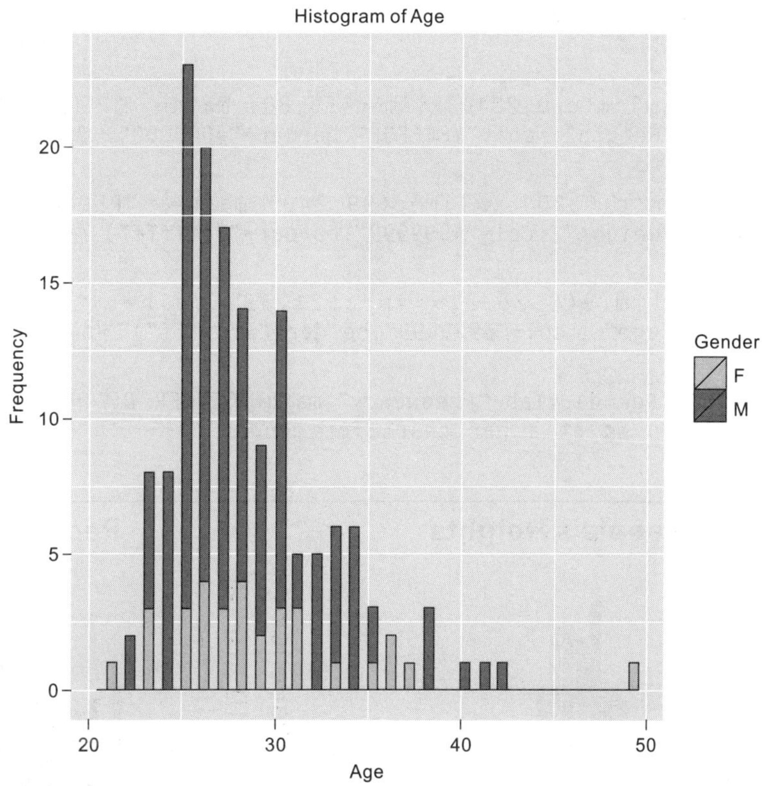

Ploting a Bar Chart

```
barplot(table(df$gend),ylab="Frequency",main="GENDER OF PEOPLE",xlab="Gende
r",ylim(c(0,120)) #plot a bar chart for gender
```

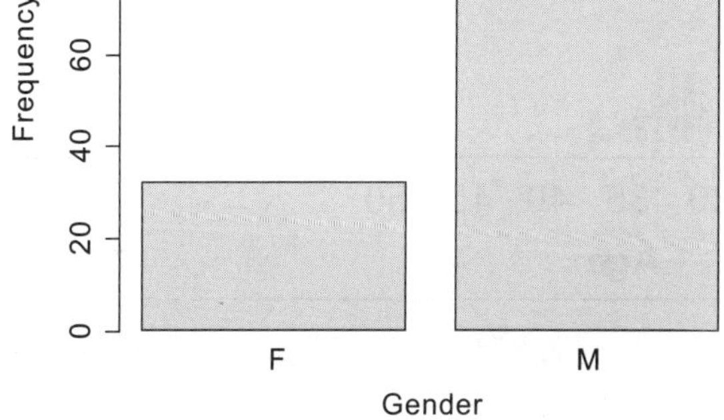

Ploting Charts Side by Side

```
Par(mfrow=c(2,2))
hist(df$Height,ylim(c(0,20)),xlim=c(55,80),main= "PEOPLE'S HEIGHTS", breaks=32,xlab="Heigth", col="#FFFF0F",border="#000000") #plot the histogram height
hist(df$wt,ylim(c(0,20)),xlim=c(99,240),main= "PEOPLE'S WEIGHTS", breaks=32,xlab="weight", col="#999999",border="#ffffff") #plot the histogram for weight
hist(df$age,ylim(c(0,25)),xlim=c(21,49),main= "PEOPLE'S AGE", breaks=32,xlab="age", col="#999999",border="#ffffff") #plot the histogram for age
barplot(table(df$gend),ylab="Frequency",main="GENDER OF PEOPLE",xlab="Gender",ylim(c(0,120)) #plot a bar chart for gender
```

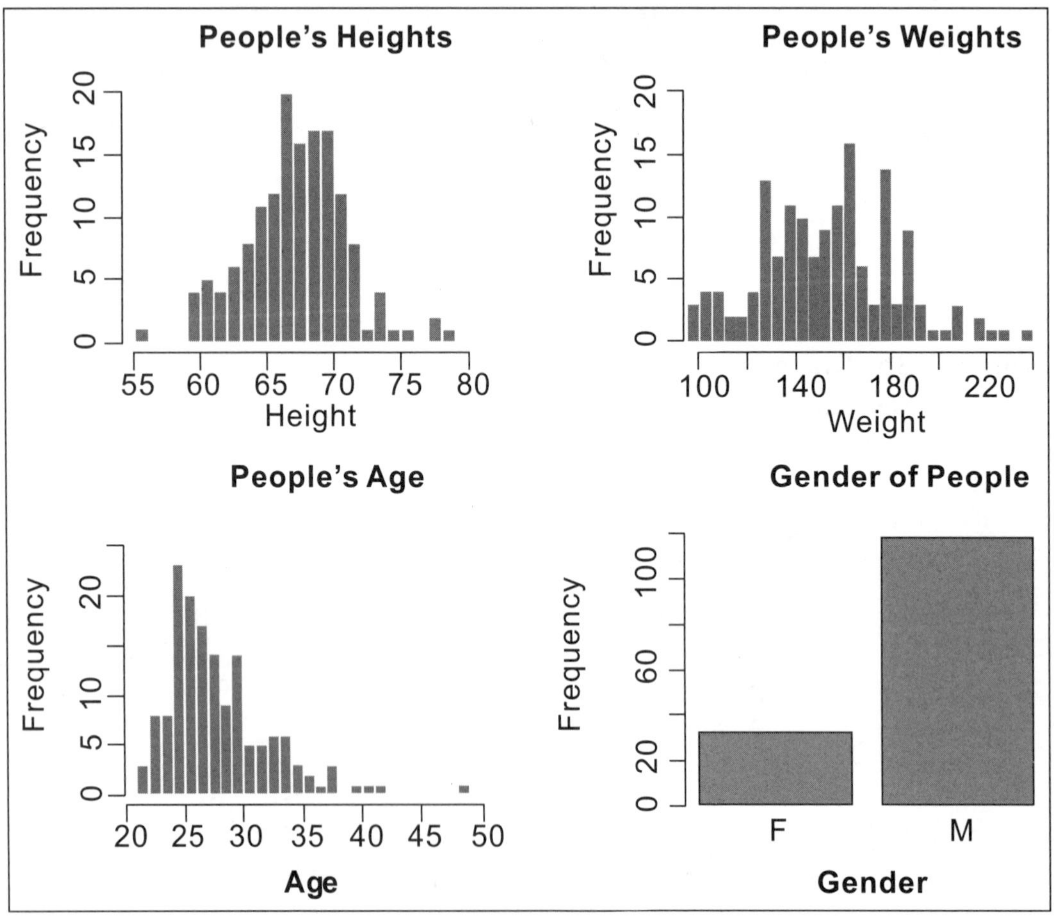

DATA MINING TECHNIQUES

Decision Tree

Use the LoanApproved Dataset at the end of Chapter 6 on Decision Trees.

```
library("rpart") #load the library for decision tree
# Draw the tree and assign to any variable (in our case, "myTree")
# Here Age, Job, House and Credit are column names and we are using decision tree to predict "LoanApproved" based on those columns, loanData is the variable name and
# method=class stands for classification.
loanData <- read.csv("Loan-Approval.csv") # read dataset
loan_tree = rpart(formula = LoanApproved ~ Age + Job + House + Credit, data = loanData, method = "class", control = rpart.control(minsplit = 5))
plot(loan_tree) # plot the tree
text(loan_tree) # Insert labels on tree
```

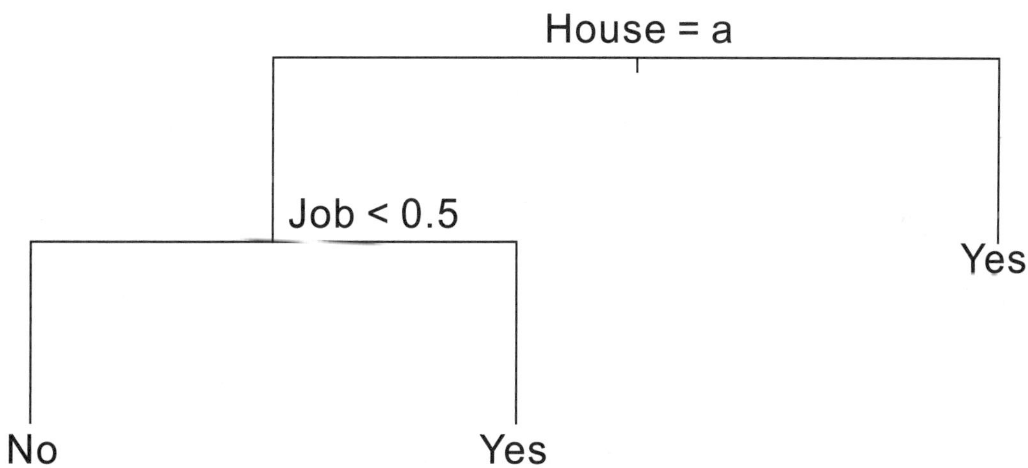


```
# To make the tree little bit fancy, install some extra packages
install.packages("rattle")
install.packages("RColorBrewer") # Don't forget that R is case sensitive
install.packages("rpart.plot")
library(rattle) # Load rattle library
library(RColorBrewer)
library(rpart.plot)
fancyRpartPlot(loan_tree) # We are using the same "loan_tree" variable previously assigned
```

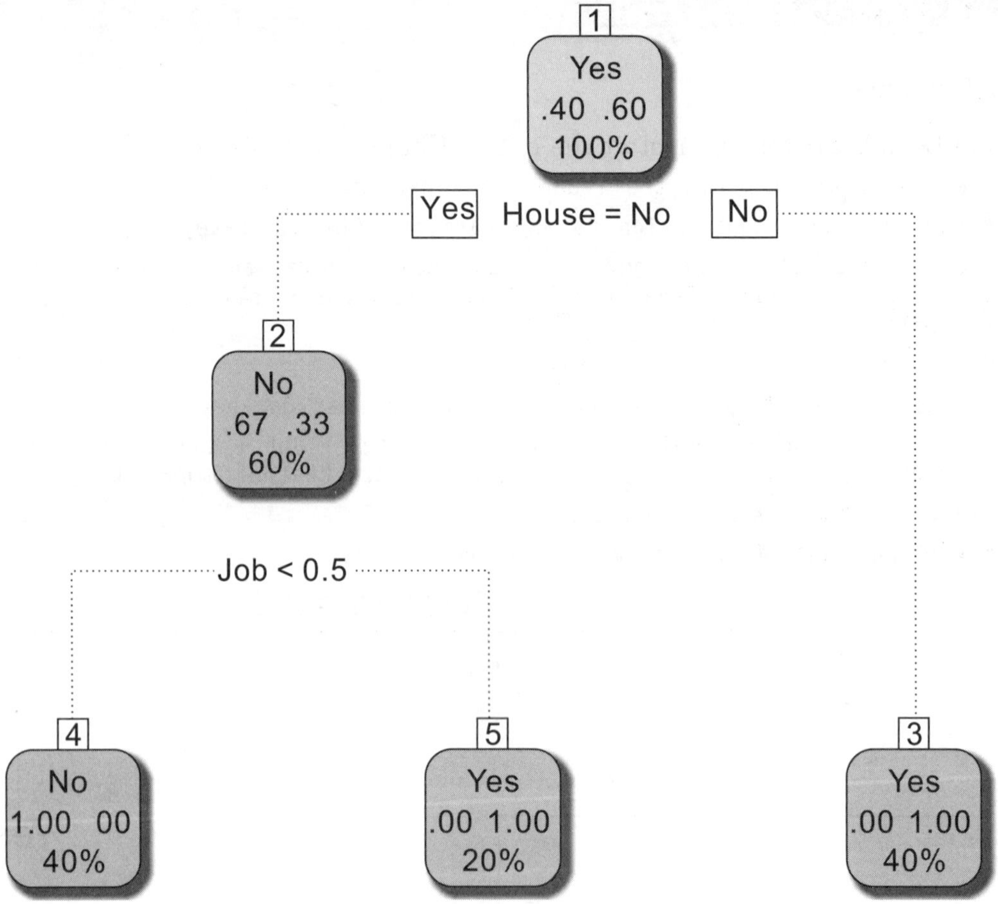

Correlation

In the same way described in decision tree, you can install the necessary library and load the data.

Using cov(data) you can see the relation.

Using pairs(data) you can see the regression.

```
library(rattle) # If not loaded previously
library(rpart.plot)
library(RColorBrewer)
data <- read.csv("height.csv")
cov(data)
pairs(data)
```

```
> data<–read.csv ("height.csv")
> cov (data)
            Height        age           wt
Height   14.750943  -1.892988    79.413229
age      -1.892988  21.559608     5.685839
wt       79.413229   5.685839  1028.802734
```

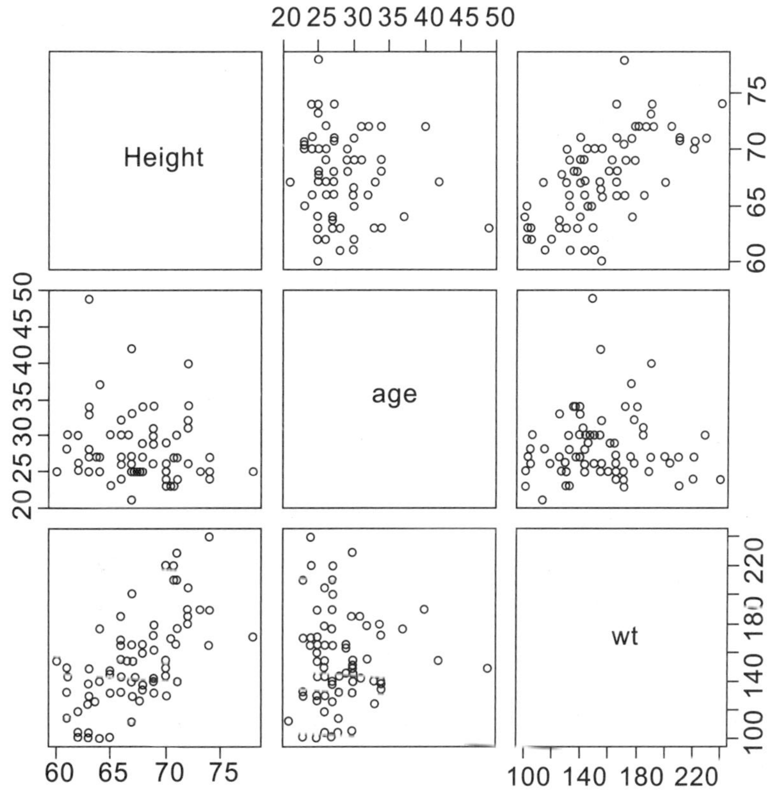

Regression

With R, it is possible to work with multiple linear regression.

```
myData <- read.csv("HtWt.csv")
head(myData,5)
Height age gend  wt
1 71   24   M 165
2 68   29   M 165
3 72   34   M 180
4 67   21   F 113
5 72   32   M 178
```

```
x <- lm(myData$wt ~ myData$Height + myData$age + myData$gend) #Runs the
correlation
summary(x)

lm(formula = myData$wt ~ myData$Height + myData$age + myData$gend)

Residuals:
   Min   1Q   Median   3Q  Max
-46.405 -19.329  -1.992  16.141  65.594

Coefficients:
   Estimate Std. Error t value Pr(>|t|)
(Intercept) -59.7711  37.7863  -1.582 0.115678
myData$Height 2.7103 0.5571 4.865 2.73e-06 ***
myData$age  0.5700 0.4251 1.341 0.181844
myData$gendM 19.9375 5.1898 3.842 0.000176 ***
---
Signif. codes:  0 '***' 0.001 '**' 0.01 '*' 0.05 '.' 0.1 ' ' 1

Residual standard error: 23.61 on 159 degrees of freedom
Multiple R-squared:  0.3024,Adjusted R-squared:  0.2893
F-statistic: 22.98 on 3 and 159 DF,  p-value: 2.068e-12

coefficients(x)
(Intercept) myData$Height  myData$age  myData$gendM
-59.7710660 2.7102542 0.5700159  19.9374996
```

Clustering – Kmeans (Unsupervised Learning)

There are different ways of plotting k-means clustering results.

Method 1

```
km <- kmeans(myData,3)
km$size
km$cluster
```

Method 2

BIG DATA MINING

WordCloud

Using file contents

```
# Install the packages TM, wordcloud, RColorBrewer
install.packages(c("tm", "wordcloud", "RColorBrewer"))
# Import the libraries
library(tm)
library(wordcloud)
library(RColorBrewer)

# select your file name below
#In my case I used obama speech from this link #http://www.cnn.com/2015/12/06/
politics/transcript-obama-san-bernardino-isis-address/
articleCorpus <- readLines("obamaSpeech.txt")
# Read text as a vector
# Create corpus
mycorpus = Corpus(VectorSource(articleCorpus))
# Transformation
mycorpus1 = tm_map(mycorpus, removePunctuation)
mycorpus2 = tm_map(mycorpus1, removeWords, stopwords("english"))
mycorpus3 = tm_map(mycorpus2, tolower)
mycorpus4 = tm_map(mycorpus3, stripWhitespace)
mycorpus5 = tm_map(mycorpus4, PlainTextDocument)
# Create Term document matrix. A document-term matrix or
# term-document matrix is a mathematical matrix that describes
# the frequency of terms that occur in a collection of documents.
tdm <- TermDocumentMatrix(mycorpus5)
m1 <- as.matrix(tdm)
# Sort data by freqency
v1<- sort(rowSums(m1), decreasing=TRUE)
# create dataframe with data and count/frequency
d1 <- data.frame(word=names(v1), freq=v1)
d1 <- head(d1,100)
# Create word cloud
wordcloud(d1$word,d1$freq,col=brewer.pal(8,"Set2"),
min.freq="5",random.order=FALSE)
```

OBS: type ?wordcloud in the R Console to get documentation about worldcloud

PAGERANK FOR SOCIAL NETWORK ANALYSIS

```
install.packages("igraph")
library(igraph)
myGraph <- graph(c( "A", "B", "A", "D", "B", "A", "B", "B", "B", "C", "C",
"A", "D", "C", "D", "D"), directed = TRUE)
plot(myGraph)
```

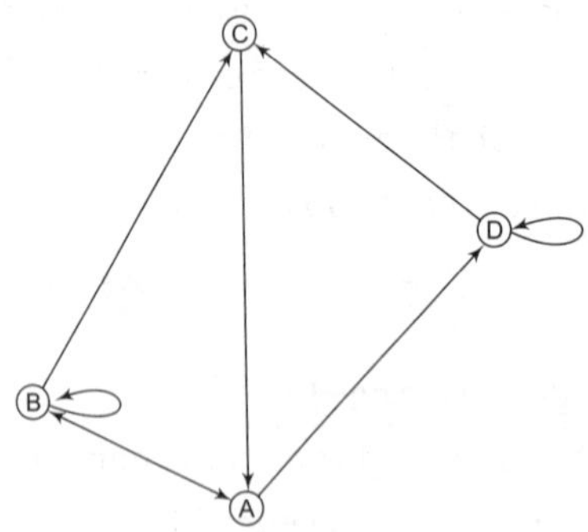


```
page.rank(myGraph)$vector
```

```
> page.rank(myGraph)$vector
        A         B         D         C
0.2851196 0.2214081 0.2759579 0.2175144
>
```

APPENDIX W

Weka Tutorial for Data Mining

This tutorial for Weka software platform is designed for use by a student studying Data Analytics. This tutorial will provide examples of solving certain data mining problems using Weka tool and the sample datasets provided with it.

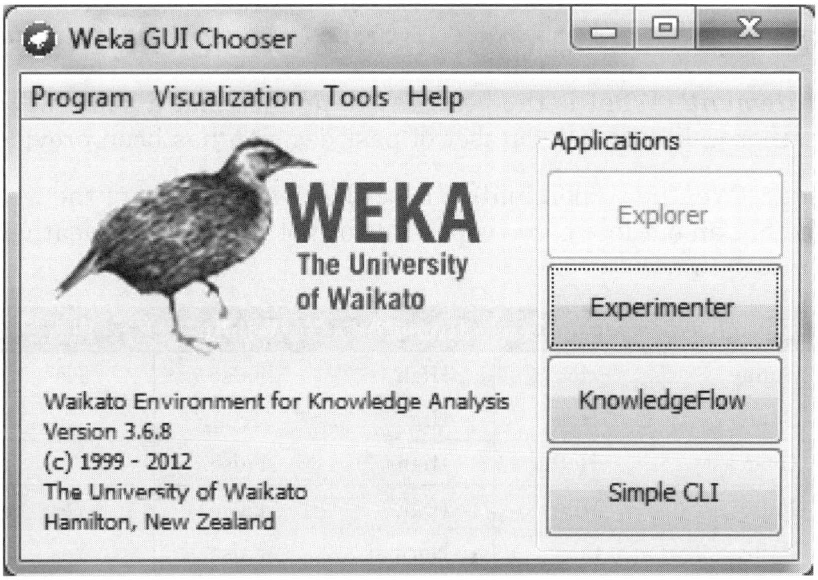

Following steps are to be followed to begin with Weka

Step 1 Download the free Weka software

http://www.cs.waikato.ac.nz/ml/weka/downloading.html

Step 2 Download the free Weka datasets

http://www.cs.waikato.ac.nz/ml/weka/datasets.html

Step 3 Access the associated textbook to learn about data mining

http://www.cs.waikato.ac.nz/~ml/weka/book.html

The data in this tutorial has been taken from the free Weka datasets. The following sample problems have been addressed in this tutorial

Classification Models These are the most important application of data mining. Decision trees and Regression methods have been used in this tutorial.

Clustering Using the *K*-means algorithm

Association Rule Mining Using Apriori algorithm

EXERCISE 1 CLASSIFICATION USING DECISION TREES

Problem Statement What is the best way to predict that a game will be on or off based on weather indicators? A dataset of past decision has been provided.

Dataset Used (Weather – nominal) It describes 14 instances of the weather conditions and whether an outdoor game is possible or not under these weather conditions. Here is the raw data.

Outlook	Temp	Humidity	Windy	Play
Sunny	Hot	High	False	No
Sunny	Hot	High	True	No
Overcast	Hot	High	False	Yes
Rainy	Mild	High	False	Yes
Rainy	Cool	Normal	False	Yes
Rainy	Cool	Normal	True	No
Overcast	Cool	Normal	True	Yes
Sunny	Mild	High	False	No
Sunny	Cool	Normal	False	Yes
Rainy	Mild	Normal	False	Yes
Sunny	Mild	Normal	True	Yes
Overcast	Mild	High	True	Yes
Overcast	Hot	Normal	False	Yes
Rainy	Mild	High	True	No

Load the Dataset It is nominal; however, there is no need for this insignificance of data for classification.

Analysis Used J48 decision tree algorithm which is an implementation of C4.5 algorithm. It is a top-down approach.

Results

Instances: 14

Attributes: 5

outlook

temperature

humidity

windy

play

Test mode: evaluate on training data

=== Classifier model (full training set) ===

J48 pruned tree

```
------------------
outlook = sunny
|   humidity = high: no (3.0)
|   humidity = normal: yes (2.0)
outlook = overcast: yes (4.0)
outlook = rainy
|   windy = TRUE: no (2.0)
|   windy = FALSE: yes (3.0)
```

Number of Leaves: 5

Size of the tree: 8

=== Summary ===

Correctly Classified Instances	14	100%
Incorrectly Classified Instances	0	0%
Kappa statistic	1	
Mean absolute error	0	
Root mean squared error	0	
Relative absolute error	0%	

Root relative squared error 0%

Total Number of Instances 14

=== Detailed Accuracy By Class ===

	TP Rate	FP Rate	Precision	Recall	F-Measure	ROC Area	Class
	1	0	1	1	1	1	yes
	1	0	1	1	1	1	no
Wtd Avg.	1	0	1	1	1	1	

=== Confusion Matrix ===

a b <-- classified as

9 0 | a = yes

0 5 | b = no

Note The model explains 100 percent of the instances correctly. The pruned tree shows the rules for making the decision in a text form.

Interpreting the Tree The first split variable is "Outlook". If outlook is overcast, then check for humidity. If outlook is sunny, the answer is yes. If the outlook is rainy, then check for windy.

Visualizing the Output Weka can create a visual version of the tree.

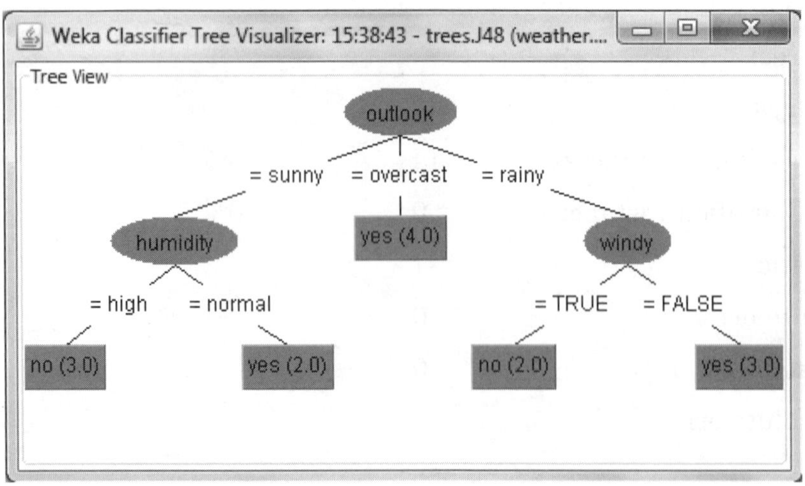

Interpreting the Visual Tree The visual decision tree is simple and self-explanatory.

Exercise

1. Try different decision tree algorithms in Weka for this simple dataset.
2. Compare the time taken, accuracy, and interpretability of the output.

Exercise 2 Classification Using Decision Trees

Problem Statement What is the best model to diagnose whether a breast lump is benign or malignant?

Dataset Used (breast-w) This is a much larger dataset. It shows many more variables and instances. It describes 699 instances of biopsy analyses of breast cancer suspects. There are 15 variables, some of which are nominal while others are numeric. The class variable shows if the instance was judged to be benign or malignant.

Load the Dataset There is no need for this insignificance of data for decision trees. For simplicity of analysis, however, only the nominal variables are kept, while others have been removed from the dataset before analysis.

Analysis Used J48 decision tree algorithm

Results

Scheme:weka.classifiers.trees.J48 -C 0.25 -M 2

Relation: wisconsin-breast-cancer

Instances: 699

Attributes: 10

Clump_Thickness

Cell_Size_Uniformity

Cell_Shape_Uniformity

Marginal_Adhesion

Single_Epi_Cell_Size

Bare_Nuclei

```
Bland_Chromatin
Normal_Nucleoli
        Mitoses
        Class – (Benign/Malignant)

Test mode:evaluate on training data
=== Classifier model (full training set) ===

J48 pruned tree
------------------
Cell_Size_Uniformity<= 2
|   Bare_Nuclei<= 3: benign (405.39/2.0)
|   Bare_Nuclei> 3
|   |   Clump_Thickness<= 3: benign (11.55)
|   |   Clump_Thickness> 3
|   |   |   Bland_Chromatin<= 2
|   |   |   |   Marginal_Adhesion<= 3: malignant (2.0)
|   |   |   |   Marginal_Adhesion> 3: benign (2.0)
|   |   |   Bland_Chromatin> 2: malignant (8.06/0.06)
Cell_Size_Uniformity> 2
|   Cell_Shape_Uniformity<= 2
|   |   Clump_Thickness<= 5: benign (19.0/1.0)
|   |   Clump_Thickness> 5: malignant (4.0)
|   Cell_Shape_Uniformity> 2
|   |   Cell_Size_Uniformity<= 4
|   |   |   Bare_Nuclei<= 2
|   |   |   |   Marginal_Adhesion<= 3: benign (11.41/1.21)
```

```
|   |   |   |   Marginal_Adhesion> 3: malignant (3.0)
|   |   |   Bare_Nuclei> 2
|   |   |   |   Clump_Thickness<= 6
|   |   |   |   |   Cell_Size_Uniformity<= 3: malignant (13.0/2.0)
|   |   |   |   |   Cell_Size_Uniformity> 3
|   |   |   |   |   |   Marginal_Adhesion<= 5: benign (5.79/1.0)
|   |   |   |   |   |   Marginal_Adhesion> 5: malignant (5.0)
|   |   |   |   Clump_Thickness> 6: malignant (31.79/1.0)
|   |   Cell_Size_Uniformity> 4: malignant (177.0/5.0)
```

Number of Leaves: 14

Size of the tree: 27

Time taken to build model: 0.07 seconds

=== Evaluation on training set ===

=== Summary ===

Correctly Classified Instances	686	98.1402%	*(i.e., 98 percent cases are classified correctly)*
Incorrectly Classified Instances	13	1.8598%	
Kappa statistic	0.959		
Mean absolute error	0.0355		
Root mean squared error	0.1324		
Relative absolute error	7.8614%		
Root relative squared error	27.8462%		
Total Number of Instances	699		

=== Detailed Accuracy by Class ===

TP Rate	FP Rate	Precision	Recall	F-Measure	ROC Area	Class
0.983	0.021	0.989	0.983	0.986	0.989	benign
0.979	0.017	0.967	0.979	0.973	0.989	malignant

Weighted
Avg. 0.981 0.02 0.981 0.981 0.981 0.989

=== Confusion Matrix ===

a b <-- classified as

450 8 | a = benign *(450 benign cases are correctly classified as benign, 8 are false positives)*

5 236 | b = malignant *(236 malignant cases are correctly classified as malignant, 5 are false negatives)*

Visualizing the Output The pruned tree looks very complex and unreadable and is therefore removed from this document. The visual decision tree makes it easier to grasp.

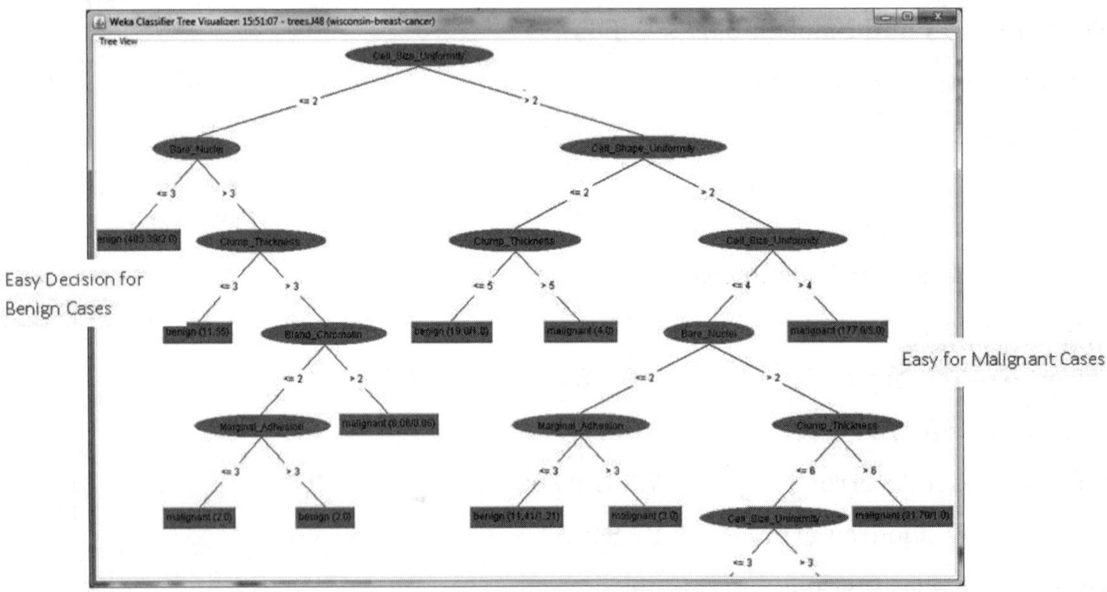

Interpreting the Decision Tree Output

- The numbers on the leaf nodes show the correctly and incorrectly classified instances for that node. The decision rule/node on the right, incorrectly classifies 5 instances; while it accurately classifies 177 of the instances correctly.

- Not all nodes are equally important. Some nodes explain many more instances than other nodes.
  (a) For example, a single node on the left of the tree represents a very simple rule (cell_size_uniformity<2 and bare_nuclei<3) which easily explains 90 percent (405 out of 450) of the benign cases, and more than 55 percent of the total cases (405 out of 699).
  (b) Similarly, the node on the right explains over 73 percent of the malignant cases (177 out of 241), and thus provides a clear rule or heuristic.
- The tree shows a clear path for diagnosing each case; and so on.

Exercise 3 Cluster Analysis Using *K*-Means Algorithm

Nature of Problem/Opportunity Understand the underlying cluster instances of breast cancer evaluations.

Dataset Used (breast-w) It describes 699 instances of biopsy analyses of breast cancer suspects. There are 15 variables, some of which are nominal while others are numeric. The class variable shows if the instance was judged to be benign or malignant.

Data Preparation Load the dataset.

Analysis Used *K*-means algorithm; choices include number of clusters to begin with.

Output of the Analysis

Instances: 699

Attributes: 10

=== Model and evaluation on training set ===

kMeans

======

Number of iterations: 5

Within cluster sum of squared errors: 259.92291180466714

Missing values globally replaced with mean/mode

Cluster Centroids

		Cluster#	
Attribute	Full Data	0	1
	(699)	(246)	(453)
Clump_Thickness	4.4177	7.1748	2.9205
Cell_Size_Uniformity	3.1345	6.5976	1.2539
Cell_Shape_Uniformity	3.2074	6.5732	1.3797
Marginal_Adhesion	2.8069	5.5325	1.3267
Single_Epi_Cell_Size	3.216	5.3089	2.0795
Bare_Nuclei	3.5447	7.5576	1.3654
Bland_Chromatin	3.4378	5.9634	2.0662
Normal_Nucleoli	2.867	5.8943	1.223
Mitoses	1.5894	2.561	1.0618
Class	benign	malignant	benign

=== Model and evaluation on training set ===

Clustered Instances

0 246 (35%)

1 453 (65%)

Interpretation There are two classes only – malignant and benign.

Sensitivity Analysis of Clustering The two classes above could be unduly influenced by the bipolar class variable (benign, malignant). So remove that variable and run the same analysis again.

K-means

======

Number of iterations: 6

Within cluster sum of squared errors: 243.1478671867869

Missing values globally replaced with mean/mode

Cluster centroids

		Cluster#	
Attribute	Full Data	0	1
	(699)	(233)	(466)
Clump_Thickness	4.4177	7.1588	3.0472
Cell_Size_Uniformity	3.1345	6.7983	1.3026
Cell_Shape_Uniformity	3.2074	6.7296	1.4464
Marginal_Adhesion	2.8069	5.7339	1.3433
Single_Epi_Cell_Size	3.216	5.4721	2.088
Bare_Nuclei	3.5447	7.874	1.38
Bland_Chromatin	3.4378	6.103	2.1052
Normal_Nucleoli	2.867	6.0773	1.2618
Mitoses	1.5894	2.5494	1.1094

=== Model and evaluation on training set ===

Clustered Instances

0 233 (33%)

1 466 (67%)

Interpretation

- The cluster structure is not changed.
- However, the strength of instances in each cluster is slightly changed from 35-65 percent to 33-67 percent. So there is more error of Type-2, i.e., more cases are marked in the 'benign' category than is actually the case.

Sensitivity Analysis of Clustering There are cases that are neither fully malignant nor truly benign. So, change the number of clusters to 3 instead of 2 and run the analysis again.

Results

Within cluster sum of squared errors: 227.7071391007967

Missing values globally replaced with mean/mode

Cluster centroids

		Cluster#		
Attribute	Full Data	0	1	2
	(699)	(222)	(178)	(299)
Clump_Thickness	4.4177	7.1982	5.0337	1.9866
Cell_Size_Uniformity	3.1345	6.964	1.7584	1.1104
Cell_Shape_Uniformity	3.2074	6.8829	2.0169	1.1873
Marginal_Adhesion	2.8069	5.9144	1.7191	1.1472
Single_Epi_Cell_Size	3.216	5.5045	2.4494	1.9732
Bare_Nuclei	3.5447	7.9578	1.8381	1.284
Bland_Chromatin	3.4378	6.2027	2.5225	1.9298
Normal_Nucleoli	2.867	6.1937	1.7303	1.0736
Mitoses	1.5894	2.6126	1.191	1.0669

Interpretation of Results

- The cluster structure has been obviously changed due to the change in number of clusters. It is clear that the real split has been in the benign group.
- A significant number of benign instances seems to have fallen into an intermediate/borderline category. Some marginally malignant cases have also fallen into the same category. These cases may need to be put under extra scrutiny.

Exercise 4 Association Rules Using Apriori Algorithm

Association Rules

Nature of Problem/Opportunity Understand the underlying associations among commercial aspects of life of foreign workers in Germany.

Dataset Used (Credit-g.arff) This shows data about demographics, job type, assets, and credit class of workers in Germany. It shows 17 variables for 1000 German workers.

Data Preparation Load the dataset; ensure all non-nominal variables are removed from analysis as association rules work only on nominal data.

Analysis Used Apriori algorithm; choices include changing the minimum level of confidence in a rule (say 90 percent) and minimal support level (10 percent).

Output of the Analysis

Instances: 1000

Attributes: 11

checking_status

credit_history

purpose

savings_status

employment

personal_status

property_magnitude

housing

job

own_telephone

class

=== Associator model (full training set) ===

Apriori

=======

Minimum support: 0.1 (100 instances)

Minimum metric <confidence>: 0.9

Number of cycles performed: 18

……

Ten Best Rules Found

1. housing=for free 108 ==>property_magnitude=no known property 104 conf:(0.96)
2. checking_status=no checking credit_history=critical/other existing credit housing=own 126 ==> class=good 120 conf:(0.95)
3. checking_status=no checking purpose=radio/tv 127 ==> class=good 120 conf:(0.94)
4. checking_status=no checking purpose=radio/tv housing=own 108 ==> class=good 102 conf:(0.94)
5. personal_status=male single property_magnitude=car job=skilled 124 ==> housing=own 117 conf:(0.94)
6. checking_status=no checking personal_status=male single housing=own job=skilled 121 ==> class=good 114 conf:(0.94)
7. checking_status=no checking credit_history=critical/other existing credit 153 ==> class=good 143 conf:(0.93)
8. checking_status=no checking employment=>=7 115 ==> class=good 107 conf:(0.93)
9. personal_status=male single property_magnitude=car class=good 129 ==> housing=own 120 conf:(0.93)
10. checking_status=no checking job=skilled own_telephone=yes 117 ==> class=good 108 conf:(0.92)

Interpreting the Output

- Rule 1 implies that 96 percent of those who live in free housing do not own any property.
- Rule 5 implies that single males that hold skilled jobs and own a car are also likely to own a house (94 percent chance).
- Rule 9 implies single males that have good credit history and own a car are also likely to own a house (93 percent chance).
- Rules 5 and 9 are highly overlapping. These are two candidates for potentially combining; and so on.

Additional Resources

Here are some other books, papers, and other resources, for a deeper dive into the topics covered in this book.

1. Ayres, I. (2007) **SuperCrunchers: Why Thinking-by-Numbers Is the New Way to be Smart.** Random House Publishing.
2. Davenport, T. & J. Harris (2007). **Competing on Analytics: The New Science of Winning.** HBS Press.
3. Gartner (2012). Business Implications of big data.
4. Gartner (2012). Technology Implications of big data.
5. Gordon Linoff & Michael Berry (2011). **Data Mining Techniques**. 3rd edition. Wiley.
6. Groebner, David F,P.W. Shannon, P.C. Fry. (2013). Business Statistics (9th edition). Pearson.
7. Jain, Anil K. (2008). "Data Clustering: 50 years beyond K-Means." 19th International Conference on Pattern Recognition.
8. Lewis, Michael (2004). **Moneyball: The Art of Winning an Unfair Game.** Norton & Co.
9. Andrew D Martin et al (2004). *"Competing Approaches to Predicting Supreme Court Decision making", Perspective in Politics.*
10. Mayer-Schonberger, Viktor; Cukier, Kenneth (2013). **Big data: A Revolution That Will Transform How We Live, Work, and Think**. Houghton Mifflin Harcourt.
11. McKinsey Global Institute Report (2011). **Big data: The next frontier for innovation, competition, and productivity.** Mckinsey.com
12. Sathi, Arvind (2011). **Customer Experience Analytics: The Key to Real-Time, Adaptive Customer Relationships.** Independent Publishers Group.
13. Sharda, R., D. Dusen, and E. Turban. (2014). **Business Intelligence and Data Analytics**. 10th edition. Pearson.
14. Shmueli, G, N. Patel, & P. Bruce (2010). **Data Mining for Business Intelligence**. Wiley.
15. Siegel, Eric, (2013). **Predictive Analytics.** Wiley.

16. Silver, N. (2012). **The Signal and the Noise: Why So Many Predictions Fail but Some Don't.** Penguin Press.

17. Statsoft. www.statsoft/textbook

18. Taylor, James (2011). **Decision Management Systems: A Practical Guide to Using Business Rules and Predictive Analytics** (IBM Press). Pearson Education.

19. Weka system. http://www.cs.waikato.ac.nz/ml/weka/downloading.html

20. Witten, I., E. Frank, M. Hall (2009). **Data Mining.** 3rd edition. Morgan Kauffman.

Index